DAVID HAMMONS

I0795339

OCTOBER Files

Rosalind Krauss (founding editor), Annette Michelson (founding editor, 1922–2018), George Baker, Yve-Alain Bois, Benjamin H. D. Buchloh, Huey Copeland, Leah Dickerman, Devin Fore, Hal Foster, Denis Hollier, David Joselit, Carrie Lambert-Beatty, Pamela M. Lee, Mignon Nixon, and Malcolm Turvey, editors

Richard Serra, edited by Hal Foster with Gordon Hughes
Andy Warhol, edited by Annette Michelson
Eva Hesse, edited by Mignon Nixon
Robert Rauschenberg, edited by Branden W. Joseph
James Coleman, edited by George Baker
Cindy Sherman, edited by Johanna Burton
Roy Lichtenstein, edited by Graham Bader
Gabriel Orozco, edited by Yve-Alain Bois
Gerhard Richter, edited by Benjamin H. D. Buchloh
Richard Hamilton, edited by Hal Foster with Alex Bacon
Dan Graham, edited by Alex Kitnick
John Cage, edited by Julia Robinson
Claes Oldenburg, edited by Nadja Rottner
Louise Lawler, edited by Helen Molesworth with Taylor Walsh
Robert Morris, edited by Julia Bryan-Wilson
John Knight, edited by André Rottmann
Isa Genzken, edited by Lisa Lee
Hans Haacke, edited by Rachel Churner
Michael Asher, edited by Jennifer King
Mary Kelly, edited by Mignon Nixon
William Kentridge, edited by Rosalind Krauss
Bruce Nauman, edited by Taylor Walsh
Sherrie Levine, edited by Howard Singerman
Michael Snow, edited by Annette Michelson and Kenneth White
Carrie Mae Weems, edited by Sarah Elizabeth Lewis with Christine Garnier
Donald Judd, edited by Annie Ochmanek and Alex Kitnick
Hollis Frampton, edited by Michael Zryd
Kara Walker, edited by Vanina Géré
David Hammons, edited by Kellie Jones

DAVID HAMMONS

EDITED BY KELLIE JONES

essays and interviews by Ben Okri, Gylbert Coker, Guy Trebay,
Kellie Jones, Steve Cannon et al., Robert Farris Thompson, Coco Fusco,
Glenn Ligon, Claire Tancons, Manthia Diawara, Alexander Alberro,
Greg Tate, Tobias Wofford, Abbe Schriber, Sampada Aranke,
Linda Goode Bryant, and Senga Nengudi

OCTOBER Files 29

The MIT Press
Cambridge, Massachusetts
London, England

The MIT Press
Massachusetts Institute of Technology
77 Massachusetts Avenue, Cambridge, MA 02139
mitpress.mit.edu

© 2024 Massachusetts Institute of Technology

All rights reserved. No part of this book may be used to train artificial intelligence systems or reproduced in any form by any electronic or mechanical means (including photocopying, recording, or information storage and retrieval) without permission in writing from the publisher.

This book was set in Bembo MT Pro and Bebas Neue Pro by New Best-set Typesetters Ltd. Printed and bound in the United States of America.

Library of Congress Cataloging-in-Publication Data

Names: Jones, Kellie, editor. | Okri, Ben, contributor.
Title: David Hammons / edited by Kellie Jones ; essays and interviews by Ben Okri [and 16 others].
Other titles: David Hammons (MIT Press)
Description: Cambridge, Massachusetts : The MIT Press, [2024] | Series: October files ; 29 | Includes bibliographical references and index.
Identifiers: LCCN 2024019130 (print) | LCCN 2024019131 (ebook) | ISBN 9780262549363 (paperback) | ISBN 9780262380249 (epub) | ISBN 9780262380256 (pdf)
Subjects: LCSH: Hammons, David, 1943—Criticism and interpretation.
Classification: LCC N6537.H3455 D38 2024 (print) | LCC N6537.H3455 (ebook) | DDC 709.2—dc23/eng/20240815
LC record available at https://lccn.loc.gov/2024019130
LC ebook record available at https://lccn.loc.gov/2024019131

10 9 8 7 6 5 4 3

EU product safety and compliance information contact is: mitp-eu-gpsr@mit.edu

Contents

Series Preface

OCTOBER Files addresses individual bodies of work of the postwar period that meet two criteria: they have altered our understanding of art in significant ways, and they have prompted a critical literature that is serious, sophisticated, and sustained. Each book thus traces not only the development of an important oeuvre but also the construction of the critical discourse inspired by it. This discourse is theoretical by its very nature, which is not to say that it imposes theory abstractly or arbitrarily. Rather, it draws out specific ways in which significant art is theoretical in its own right, on its own terms, and with its own implications. To this end, we feature essays, many first published in *OCTOBER* magazine, that elaborate different methods of criticism in order to elucidate different aspects of the art in question. The essays are often in dialogue with one another as they do so, but they are also as sensitive as the art to political context and historical change. These "files," then, are intended as primers in signal practices of art and criticism alike, and they are offered in resistance to the amnesiac and antitheoretical tendencies of our time.

The Editors of *OCTOBER*

Acknowledgments

Many people have supported this volume—first and foremost David Hammons, whose brilliance has been a guiding light for so many over the years and around the world. I am thankful to the wonderful writers, artists, and conversation partners whose words appear here: Alexander Alberro, Sampada Aranke, Linda Goode Bryant, Gylbert Coker, Manthia Diawara, Coco Fusco, Glenn Ligon, Senga Nengudi, Ben Okri, Abbe Schriber, Claire Tancons, Guy Trebay, and Tobias Wofford. Special recognition goes to those representing the writers who are no longer with us: the Estate of Steve Cannon, Mary Chen, Chavisa Woods, and *A Gathering of the Tribes* magazine; the Estate of Greg Tate and Brian Tate, along with Kerin Ogg at Duke University Press; and the Estate of Robert Farris Thompson, with thanks to Alicia Thompson Churchill. Thanks also to those who helped me pull together these pieces: Adrienne Edwards, Whitney Museum of American Art; Chie Hammons; Mary Miller, Getty Research Institute; Lois Plehn; and Ellyn Toscano, Hawthornden Foundation. I was particularly excited to include amazing photographs by Sylvia Plachy and Coreen Simpson. Thanks to all for the generosity and collaboration. Institutions and collectors have been equally supportive, including The Drawing Center; Glenstone; Hauser & Wirth; the Hudgins Family Collection; Lilia Taboada and T. Jean Lax at the Museum of Modern Art and the Museum of Modern Art Archives, Library, and Research Collections; the Mnuchin Gallery; the Fales Library and Special Collections at New York University; Connie Tilton of the Tilton Gallery; the Walker Art Center; and the Walther Collection.

I was thrilled when David Joselit reached out to me about participating in the OCTOBER Files series. Adam Lehner at *October* was helpful at all points in the process. A conversation with Abbe Schriber helped me begin thinking about this project, and my fantastic research assistants, Heather Nickels and Isabel Mendoza, were integral in getting it to the finish line. I am thankful to Columbia University and my colleagues in the Department of Art History and Archaeology and the Department of African American and African Diaspora Studies for the support of my research.

The care of family and friends is forever important. During 2020, my college crew got back together virtually: much appreciation to Wendy Blair, Inės Curbelo, and Victoria Kassa. My great friend C. Ian White always listens. Thanks to Cheryl Finley for gifting me the poster from David Hammons's *Sheep Raffle* performance many years ago. Deborah Willis has been there for this and a multitude of projects over the years. My mother, Hettie Jones, and my mother-in-love, Celia Ramsey Wynn, continue to be inspirations. Encouragement from the Browns of Harlem, the Ramseys of Philadelphia and Chicago, the Harvests of New Jersey, and the Archies nationwide is always right on time. The unconditional love and endless creativity of Guthrie Ramsey are things I am thankful to marvel at daily.

Ben Okri, "A History of New Forms," in *David Hammons: Give Me a Moment,* edited by George Economou and Skarlet Smatana (Athens: The George Economou Collection, 2016).

Gylbert Coker, "Human Pegs, Pole Dreams," *The Village Voice*, September 28, 1982, 75–79.

Guy Trebay, "Pole Vault," *The Village Voice*, May 13, 1986, 73.

Kellie Jones, "Interview with David Hammons," *REALLIFE*, Autumn 1986, 2–9.

Steve Cannon, Keith Gilyard, David Henderson, Jemeel Moondoc, and Gail Schilke, "David Hammons Interview," *A Gathering of the Tribes*, Fall 1991.

Robert Farris Thompson, "David Hammons: 'Knowing Their Past,'" (1992), *Aesthetic of the Cool: Afro-Atlantic Art and Music*, 92–105 (Periscope Publishing, 2011).

Coco Fusco, "Wreaking Havoc on the Signified," *Frieze*, May 7, 1995.

Kellie Jones, "In the Thick of It: David Hammons and Hair Culture in the 1970s," *Third Text* 44 (Autumn 1998): 17–24.

Glenn Ligon, "Black Light: David Hammons and the Poetics of Emptiness," *Artforum* 43, no. 1 (2004): 243–249.

Claire Tancons, "An Elective Affinity: David Hammons's *Hidden from View* and *Made in the People's Republic of Harlem*," *Third Text* 19, no. 2 (March 2005): 169–175.

Manthia Diawara, "David Hammons's *Sheep Raffle* at Dak'Art 2004: Reading Black Art through Léopold Sédar Senghor's Négritude," in *Recharting the Black Atlantic*, edited by Annalisa Oboe and Anna Scacchi, 11–19 (Routledge, 2008).

Alexander Alberro, "The Joke of Painting: On David Hammons at L&M Arts, New York," *Texte zur Kunst* 82 (June 2011): 232–236.

Greg Tate, "Dark Angels of Dust: David Hammons and the Art of Streetwise Transcendentalism" (2011), *Flyboy 2: The Greg Tate Reader*, 2016, 73–78. Copyright 2016, Greg Tate. All rights reserved. Republished by permission of the copyright holder and the publisher. Originally published in Jeffrey Deitch, Roger Gastman, and Aaron Rose, *Art in the Streets: The Official Catalog to the MoCA Exhibition*, 111–114 (Skira Rizzoli, 2011).

Tobias Wofford, "Can You Dig It? Signifying Race in David Hammons's *Spade* Series," in *L.A. Object and David Hammons Body Prints*, edited by Connie Rogers Tilton and Lindsay Charlwood, 86–134 (Tilton Gallery, 2011).

Kellie Jones, "Good Mirrors Ain't Cheap," in *David Hammons: Five Decades*, edited by Robert Mnuchin and Sukanya Rajaratnam, 15–28 (Mnuchin Gallery, 2016).

Abbe Schriber, "'Those Who Know Don't Tell': David Hammons c. 1981." This is a revised version of the essay that originally appeared in *Women & Performance: A Journal of Feminist Theory* 29, no. 1 (2019): 41–61, https://doi.org/10.1080/0740770X.2019.1571866.

Sampada Aranke, "How to See Like Hammons," *liquid blackness* 5, no. 2 (October 2021: 39–47.

Linda Goode Bryant and Senga Nengudi, "In Conversation." Originally published in *David Hammons: Body Prints, 1968–1979*, edited by Laura Hoptman, 16–31 (The Drawing Center, 2021).

This volume is dedicated to my always stylish and faithful great-aunt, Elise Jones Martin (1915–2023)—business owner, voter advocate, inspiration.

Contributors

Alexander Alberro is the Virginia Bloedel Wright Professor of Art History at Barnard College and Columbia University, New York.

Sampada Aranke is an associate professor of Art History and Comparative Studies at The Ohio State University, Columbus.

Linda Goode Bryant is a filmmaker, farmer, and entrepreneur. She founded New York's iconic Just Above Midtown Gallery in 1974.

Steve Cannon (1935–2019) was a poet, playwright, novelist and founder of the magazine *A Gathering of the Tribes* and the eponymous gallery.

Gylbert Coker is an art historian, curator, lecturer, and writer.

Manthia Diawara is a writer, cultural theorist, film director, and scholar. He is a professor of comparative literature and cinema at New York University.

Coco Fusco is an interdisciplinary artist and writer based in New York.

Kellie Jones is Hans Hofmann Professor of Modern Art in the Department of Art History and Archaeology and a professor in the Department of African American and African Diaspora Studies at Columbia University, New York.

Glenn Ligon is an artist living and working in New York.

Senga Nengudi is an interdisciplinary artist whose practice involves visual arts, dance, body mechanics, and matters of the spirit.

Ben Okri is a poet, novelist, essayist, short story writer, anthologist, aphorist, and playwright.

Abbe Schriber is an assistant professor in Art History and African American Studies in the School of Visual Art and Design at the University of South Carolina, Columbia.

Claire Tancons is a curator and scholar invested in the discourse and practice of the postcolonial politics of art production and exhibition.

Greg Tate (1957–2021) was a cultural critic, journalist, and band leader based in New York City.

Robert Farris Thompson (1932–2021) was an art historian who specialized in Africa and the Afro-Atlantic world. For over five decades, he was a member of the faculty at Yale University, New Haven, Connecticut.

Guy Trebay reports on culture for the *New York Times*.

Tobias Wofford is an associate professor in the Department of Art History at Virginia Commonwealth University, Richmond

A History of New Forms

Ben Okri

A hairy stone
On a white stool
On a metal stand.
Brooding about
The lost air and
The incandescent paint;

Those thoughts
of tarpaulin
Concealment,
Of mirrors dripping
With dark celestial matter.
Or the fan in which
The wind is still.

The yellow table
Where Caravaggio
Is beheaded
And the old testament
Of Duchamp
Made into the history
Of Harlem
And beyond the masks
Floating on the sea
A new dream
Broken through
The hands of the silent
Enchanter.

Here is where
A new African
Genius is made,
Changing the dream-
Less lids of Duchamp
Into the spring
Of Hammons.

Blue time is passing.
The smaller the form,
The bigger
The conversation.
Keep moving it
Away from what
It was. From the old
Field, the old time,
To the *novum organum*.
Music in the stone.
Alchemy in the transcended
American air.

The art is that book
In which the history
Of new forms
Is written
By the firedreams
Of Harlem.
The throwing
Of the stone
Into the open sea
Into the sunrise
Over Brooklyn.

Human Pegs, Pole Dreams

Gylbert Coker

Rushing through the streets has become a bad habit with me and here I am rushing up Broadway to meet David Hammons, who I can see in the near distance leaning against a railing looking like a rather out-of-place Mexican dressed all in white and green leaves climbing up the front of his shirt, brown sandals on his feet, a white painter's cap on his head and a black sweater that hints ever so slightly of the orient. Inside Happy Burger we find a booth, settle in, and place our orders. We make the usual light chatter that goes well with clattering dishes and greasy smells. I have learned over the years not to rush David when he has something to say, that given his own time his point will be made. I politely listen to his conversation as I eat the traditional sunny-side ups with English muffin, french fries, and orange juice. David has chili, crackers, and a soda.

Halfway through the meal the conversation shifts to the new project he is working on. Hammons has just received a rather large NEA grant and the art piece he wishes to construct will cost him more than $2000 to realize. David explains that the project involves 10-story-high basketball poles. In order to hold them in place, seven-foot holes have to be dug. He begins to chuckle. Each hole will cost $2000. I start to laugh too. The irony is ludicrous. Before me sits an artist whose philosophy for almost 15 years has been to encourage the creation of art without the need to spend money. Here he is at the threshold of national and international acclaim. Requests for larger works continually come his way and he finds himself having to shell out money in order to execute the works. And we're not just talking money here, we're talking MONEY. We both shake our heads.

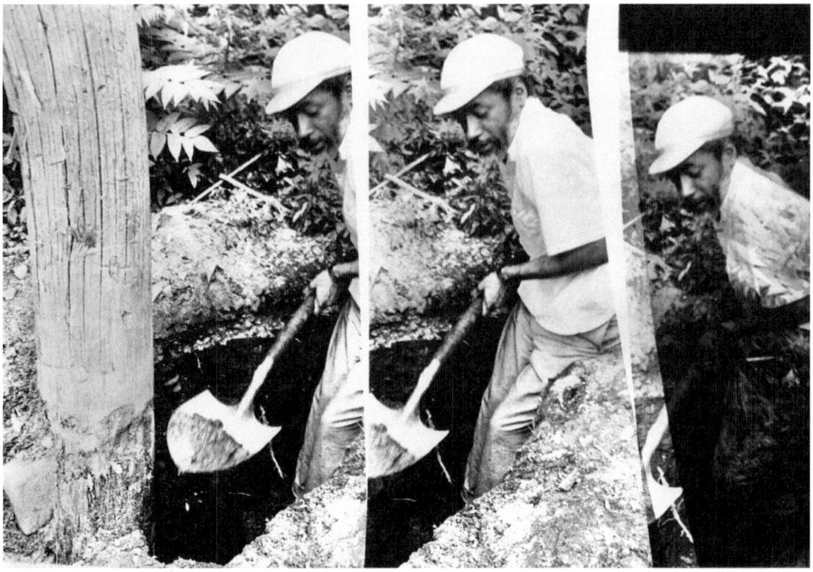

David Hammons, *Human Pegs / Poles Dreams*, 1982, photo collage. © Coreen Simpson.

The project *Pole Dreams* grew from Hammons's wanderings through Harlem. One day he happened to notice a basket made with two U-clamps and a two-by-four on a pole in the middle of his block. It was a set-up for a basketball game. From that point on Hammons began to notice basketball set-ups hooked to something everywhere. They were made out of paper bags, cardboard boxes, wooden crates, and more.

Basketball is the dream machine for the city kid. For some it is a way out of the ghetto, for others it is the cheapest sport in town—all you really need is a ball (when times are really bad, rolled paper will do). It is certainly the most flexible of sports, you can play it alone, you can play for points with one other person, or you can have a game with teams. Basketball is a city game, it has city aggression and city rhythms. The Jackson Five play basketball, Smokey Robinson and Bill Cosby each have their own basketball court, and Hammons can still muster up a "serious" game. *Pole Dreams* was to be Hammons's monumental tribute to basketball. But the large project would come later. For the moment he was in the process of preparing a performance, *Human Pegs / Pole Dreams*. which would be the prelude to *Pole*

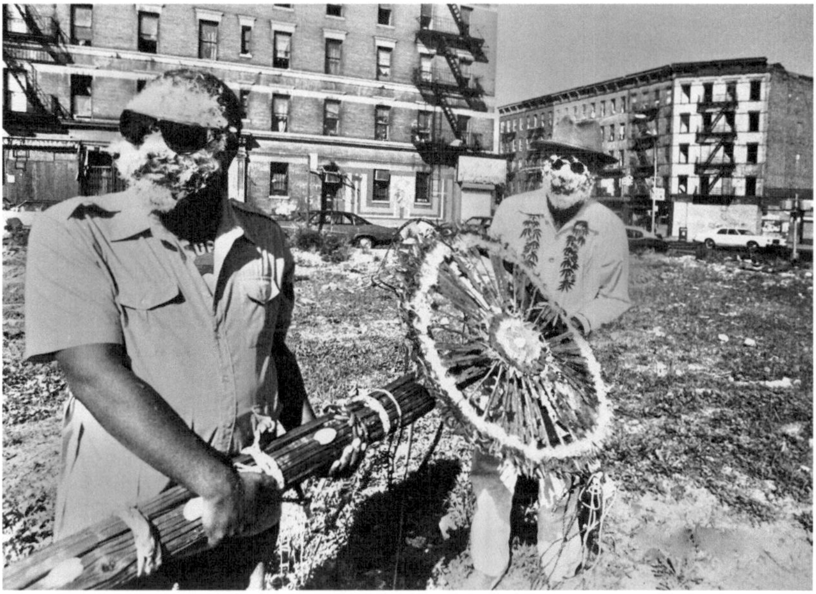

David Hammons, *Human Pegs / Pole Dreams*, 1982, performance.
Photograph © Coreen Simpson.

Dreams. I realize that we have arrived at the point of this meeting. When will this performance take place? David avoids a direct answer and continues his presentation, letting me know that I have been rude in interrupting his rhythm and also that there is more involved here than just the performance. It seems that *The Village Voice* is working up a special supplement in which three artists will explore the process of their art. David is to be one of the three, and this performance is the work to be discussed. The editor wants to know if I would write the article.

"Fine," I answer. "But when is it taking place, David?"

"This afternoon."

My mouth drops. "David!" I squeal. "How can you do this to me?!! Why didn't you tell me this before? When did you know you were going to do the piece?"

Hammons sheepishly replies, "A few weeks ago."

This was Hammons at his finest. Regaining my composure, I ask in my most professional tone where the performance will take place and how long will it be. *Human Pegs / Pole Dreams* would be performed at 3 this afternoon on 121st Street. It would begin in the firehouse where David lives, move to the backyard behind several abandoned buildings up the street, and then back to an empty lot on the avenue. I agreed to join David and his people but I absolutely had to leave by 4 because I had promised to play the part of Moonshine in a small play. "Sure, sure, plenty of time," encouraged Hammons. Yeah, I'd heard that before. Famous last words, "plenty of time." I knew I wouldn't leave there at 4, I knew it. Thanking David for the brunch, I rushed back down Broadway.

Harlem on a Sunday afternoon. Eighth Avenue and 121st Street is Stevie Wonder, Duke Ellington and Aretha Franklin all playing at the same time, with a funky side order of Millie Jackson on the main drag. All things are possible in Harlem, all forms of coexistence go on here—the church, the police station, the artist, the people—all kinds of people doing all kinds of things.

Now, 121st Street, David's street, is the hippest street in New York if you know how to move with it. It's the most abstract art piece I've ever seen that never intended to be art. Seriously, this block is somethin' else. On the avenue from 120th to 121st Street is a very large lot where buildings once stood. Halfway down the block a row of battered but still-functioning brownstones leans in position. Facing this lot and these buildings stands the old firehouse that now houses a church and David's loft. Out in front of the building the good people of the church have gathered. The women and little girls are dressed in their pastel blues, purples, pinks, and whites. The men and boys are all in their synthetic suits of brown, blue, and gray. All very respectable, all very friendly. Sitting on the stoops across the way rest the other neighbors, well into their 10th beer, wine, or whatever. Everyone is into his or her own rhythm, and me, I am into mine as I climb the stairs, pausing briefly to whiff the succulent smells coming from the church's kitchen. Man, those ladies could almost make me join the heavenly choir.

Entering David Hammons's studio I am struck by the contrast in mood. The church just below and the action outside are filled with conversation, smells, and bright colors. Up here the light is low, the music subdued, and the tone is spiritually respectful. People speak to one another quietly, moving softly through the rooms looking at the various artifacts hanging or lying about the space. Willie Birch, his son Freedom, Coreen Simpson, David Henderson, Marina Gutierrez, and Juan Sanchez. Hello, how are you, glad to see you, what's happenin'. On the floor lies the 13-foot pole that David hoisted up to his studio. It is now covered with feathers, beads, shells, and colored cord. An old Japanese umbrella makes the head of the pole and a series of nails run up and down its side. This was the first time I had been formally invited to attend one of Hammons's performances (although I have always maintained that all my experience with David Hammons have been performances, if only minor ones). Further, I was invited to be a member, musician within the piece. This was quite an honor, one I did not take lightly.

As a creator and conductor Hammons gives out the final instructions. This one will carry the bag with the feathers, someone else will carry Freedom. Birch and Hammons will bring the pole down into the street over their shoulders and Coreen will go downstairs first in order to catch on film both the expressions of the people below and the movement of the pole as it is eased from the upstairs studio into the street. I am given money and told to run across to the grocery store and buy two sacks of flour. The group will be waiting in the backyard. As the last person down I watch the pole go into the shadowy stairwell then out into the bright street. Crossing Eighth Avenue we stop traffic. Off to the store I go, confident that I will have no problem finding them. After all, who wouldn't recall a small group of people carrying a 13-foot pole?

I couldn't believe it. I lost them. I ask people in the street, no one saw them pass by. What did they mean they weren't paying attention? How could anyone miss all of that wildness, even here? Harlemites, you've failed me. Realizing that I must have come down the street too far, I turn in time to see David appear from a corner building. He beckons and I follow.

Behind these empty buildings lives a secret green world forgotten by the outside. It almost doesn't feel like New York. David has opened the sacks and is shaking flour all around. The whiteness flies upon the foliage. Next he lays out two jars of Vaseline, puts a scoop of the jelly into each of his hands, rubs them all over his face, and places his head into the bag of feathers. When he pulls free we see Hammons's face transformed into a mask.

Each of us is asked to follow his lead (with the exception of Coreen Simpson, who is shooting the entire process). The effect is startling. Squinting or standing away from the group, the feather-covered faces look like clouds resting upon individual bodies, while up close there is this eerie sensation, a fuzzy out-of-focus quality to the whole of the head. Feathers all in place, we are directed to take hold of long cords attached to the pole. Slowly we begin to raise it to its full height. How curious is this score of

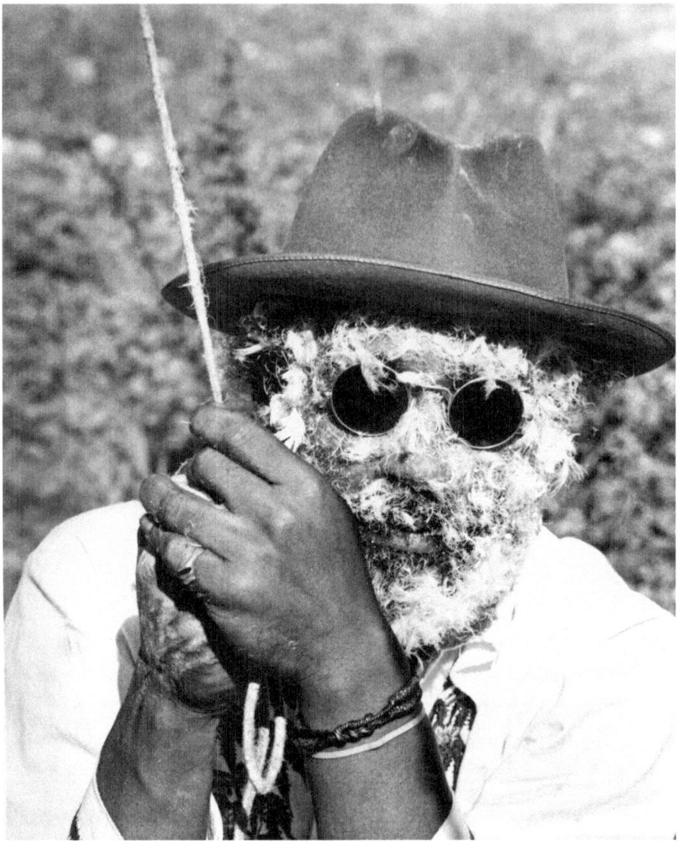

David Hammons, *Human Pegs / Pole Dreams*, 1982, performance. Photograph © Coreen Simpson.

David's. The energy within the group is concentrated and united while the energy that circles us is disjointed and aggressive. A guard dog left in one of the abandoned buildings hasn't stopped barking since we entered the area, and the windows from another abandoned building across the way begin to crash to the ground, wooden frames and all. David Henderson calmly remarks, "Someone's moving out."

The performance completed, the pole is lowered to the ground and we prepare to return to the lot. This time we are masked, and as we emerge onto the street the people who earlier couldn't remember a group with a

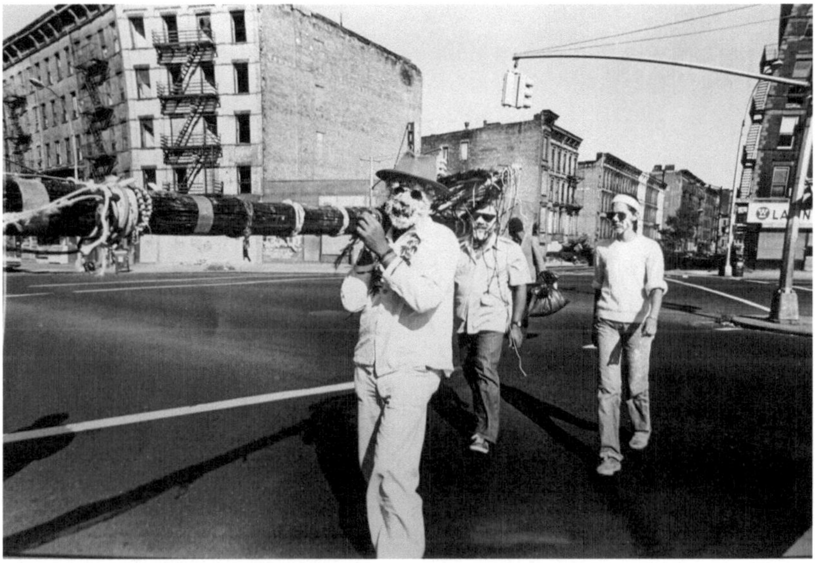

David Hammons, *Human Pegs / Pole Dreams*, 1982, performance.
Photograph © Coreen Simpson.

long pole now notice us. Back we go across the avenue to the lot. A large hole David had previously dug becomes the resting spot for the pole, and in minutes we are lifting the pole again. This time people move around us and some come over for a better look.

"Hey, baby, what you doin'?"

"Man, that's far out—now that *is* far out."

One woman calls to me, "Say, sista', what are you doin'?"

"Art. That's artist David Hammons and he made this pole and we're placing it into this hole. Our faces are covered with feathers and Vaseline like masks. It could be African but it's definitely American."

"Yeah," she said. "I gotchya."

David Hammons has always concerned himself with the total space he chooses to work with, and I suppose for this reason he could be called an environmentalist. But I would suggest that to use this term, even in its broadest sense, would be both misleading and limiting, for Hammons is a musician and each work he creates is a musical composition. For him it doesn't matter if the space is indoors or outdoors, a wall, ceiling, ground, small, large. The point or objective is to make visual images from musical sound; that is, he concerns himself with the relationship of colors, the variation in movement, and the spontaneity of the total piece—a quality very hard to maintain in a visual work.

This is not an unusual direction for a visual artist to take. Back in 1980 I reviewed a photographic exhibition and noted that artists who strive to imitate visually the cries, swoops, squawks, and slurs of musicians do so in their desire to utilize sound as their expressive root. This desire seems to be particularly an American cultural trait. It is Hammons's belief that the greatest compliment anyone can pay a visual artist is to compare his or her work to that of a musician. He has often drawn inspiration from the compositions of Thelonius Monk, the humor of Charles Mingus and Dizzy Gillespie, the elegance of Duke Ellington, the eccentricities of Sun Ra and the arrogance of Miles Davis.

In the late 1960s into the 1970s, Hammons did a miniseries of spades: *Spade Run Over by a Volkswagen*, *Spade Covered with Sand*. These sight gags reflect another important aspect or the Hammons oeuvre—the ability to create abstract forms through the use of identifiable Afro-American images. The spade, of course, is a play on the slang expression for black folks—Spades. Body prints—of full bodies, parts of bodies, bodies in clothes—followed this series. Much more subtle in their identifiable element, the prints nonetheless grew from a black object—grease. How many times has your momma told you to go get yourself some grease 'cause your legs were ashy? Next came greasy bags and bar-b-que bones with glitter, then hair pieces using nappy hair—hair designs on the greasy bags, then hair on wire, hair on wire with eggs, feathers, and broken pieces or records.

Many of Hammons's works are solo flights, but like any good solo musician Hammons will gather a group to create a large combo or orchestral piece. In last year's huge installation at the Studio Museum in Harlem, the lead instrumentalist and composers were Hammons and Charles Abramson, with such sidemen as Jorge Rodriquez, George Mingo, and the people of Harlem. The energy was unbelievably high. What example can I give to describe it? If you have ever heard a 10-minute recording of Ella Fitzgerald scatting "Take the A Train," you'd know what it was like.

Of the many quantities I know and admire in the artist and person David Hammons, the one I appreciate most is his ability to use fear as a source. Years ago he told me that one always had to jump cliffs. Most people know this to be so but also need the guarantees—who went before,

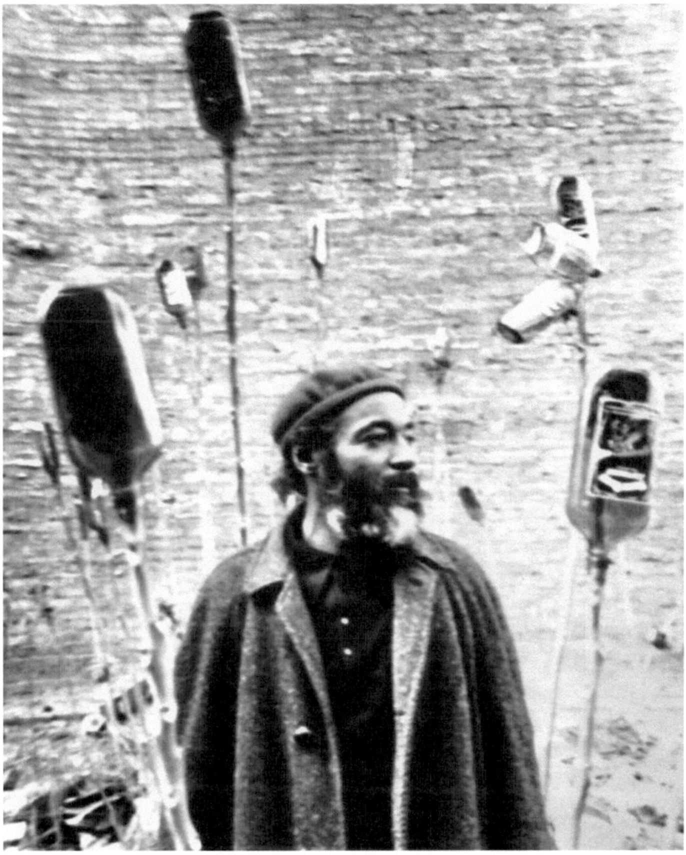

Coreen Simpson, *David Hammons*, ca. 1982.
Photograph © Coreen Simpson.

is there water to break the fall, how high is the cliff, how will the story end? For Hammons, chances must be taken. It is this attitude that gives him the freedom to float easily from solo to group works. It is, I might add, this same perspective that allows Hammons to accept the possibility that all art need not be permanent to have a lasting effect. To be valid, if you will.

Grabbing the local CC train (no I didn't leave at 4, but 4:30—well, that isn't bad for David), I take a seat and head downtown to the theater. I think about David and how he conducted us this way and that, and I knew he was pleased. It was, like all of David's pieces, a work in itself, and I knew he felt comfortable with this small production that cost all of $2.05. I wonder if he will go on to the larger project with its outrageous price tag. I wonder too what would win him over: the understanding that there was no longer a need to do the larger piece, because it had already been designed and discussed and therefore existed? Or was the idea of actually constructing the piece, thus contradicting his own principles or not spending large sums of money to create art, a greater challenge?

Pole Vault

Guy Trebay

From an island in Cadman Plaza, David Hammons gets his daily fill of courthouse drama. Down the steps of State Supreme Court of Brooklyn it flows, in a stream of legalese and tears. Whether the Mafia capos and workaday miscreants ever notice the artist in their midst is hard to say. But he keeps an ear out for their troubles—which tend to presage trips up the river—as he hammers away on the lawn. "It's kind of entertaining," Hammons says.

The artwork is lying on the grass between the courthouse and a bronze of Henry Ward Beecher, near a hot red crabapple and some clumped yellow tulips. From a distance its diamond shapes look like snakeskin, or mosaic, the surface compressed in dense interlocking patterns. Up close, the grid expands, and you can see that the diamonds covering the telephone pole are made of bottle caps: red and silver Buds, gold Lites, pale blue Hamms, silver foil Becks.

There are three telephone poles, bought from Active Pole in Queens for $1000. "I asked for crooked ones," says Hammons. "I wanted to get some kind of movement going." Each will eventually have a basketball backboard anchored atop it, also covered with bottle caps, as well as a hoop and net, and pentatonic wind chimes, "for a nice ring." The poles will stand upright, glistening and slightly skewed.

"I'm calling the piece *Higher Goals*," says Hammons, who received the commission from the Public Art Fund. "The issue," he says, "is, I was deprived of a basketball career by being too short."

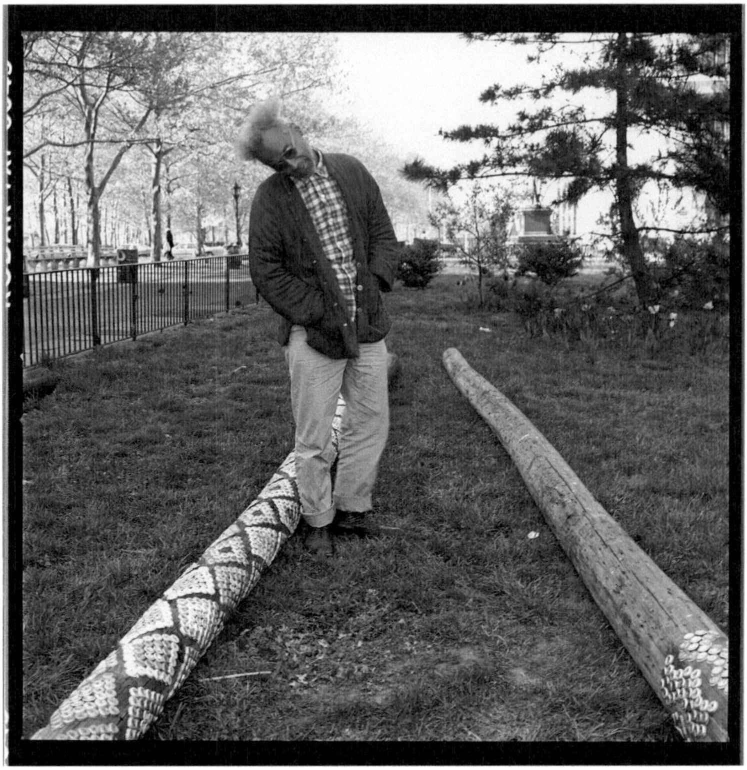

David Hammons standing between two poles, 1986.
Photograph © Sylvia Plachy.

In fact, Hammons is about Spud Webb's height, although any resemblance ends there. With his gold stitch earring, graying beard, and blue Chinese worker's jacket, Hammons looks less like a point guard than a sage.

For weeks Hammons has spent eight-hour days in the park nailing bottle caps to poles. Sliding along on a piece of foam rubber, he takes a half-inch nail and affixes each cap by hand. He estimates it takes 20,000 to complete a design. The deadline is the end of May. "That rubber is the most important part of this sculpture," Hammons says. "It saves my butt."

Despite the deadline, Hammons's approach is unhurried. He takes time to answer questions from passersby and responds to people's "wacky comments."

"They ask me all kinds of crazy things," he says. "'Is that art?' 'Are you a gardener?' A cop came up to me one day and said, 'Do you have a permit?' I looked at him. What would I be doing over here with 40,000 bottle caps and three telephone poles without a permit?"

Hammons shrugs. The public is almost always involved with his work, intentionally or not. He has created a mysterious "garden" in a Harlem lot by upending bottles on weed trees. He has created unlikely reliquaries of found objects on traffic islands. He once considered setting up a Night Train redemption center, during a period when wine bottles were the centerpiece of his work. He let that idea lapse. "They changed the colors of the bottles. They're not that beautiful green anymore. They're blue."

The primitive, slightly fugitive quality of Hammons's art is cultivated. He is a sophisticate and a respected art world presence. His inspirations are the Dadaists, Antoni Gaudí, and Simon Rodia, the naive genius of Watts Towers. The tramp art quality, and the unmistakable Africanness of his work sneak in unawares, he says. "Someone mentioned to me that in Africa when people visit they leave their staffs outside the house, so you know who's visiting. It occurred to me that these poles I'm making are like those staffs."

Hammons is not one of the 15 most successful black artists named in a current issue of a national magazine, and he says he never hopes to see himself on such a list. "I always admired the renegades, Duchamp and those cats," he says. "I've always thought the outside was the place to be."

A measure of his accomplishment is how determinedly he has remained outside, while still making his presence felt. Like many outsiders he has patience and a somewhat magisterial sense of his fate. You wouldn't call him aloof from the scene, but his encounters with it aren't frenetic or desperate. Museums own his work. He is the recipient of numerous residencies and grants. Still, he hardly ever makes an object that sells.

This is not because David Hammons's artworks lack beauty. Hammons is an accumulator and organizer and pattern maker and has a sharp eye for material affinities. "I'm attracted to anything that's available and free," he recently told *The New York Times*. Debris, soil, and elephant dung are among his media. During one period he collected hair clippings from barber shops in Harlem, the strands later to be woven onto bristles dismembered from streetsweepers. He added colored string and glass to his fetish objects.

"Whatever comes along, I jump on it," says Hammons. "If you're open to that, your ideas don't get locked in a room."

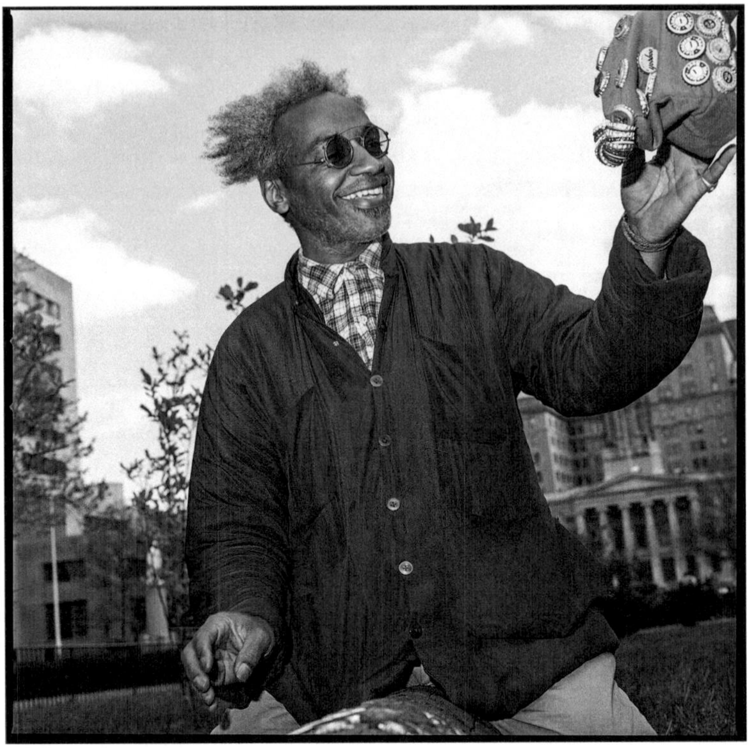

David Hammons holding a cloth covered with bottle caps, 1986.
Photograph © Sylvia Plachy.

And work that's done inside that room is, as a friend would say, "Cry-able." It says, "Buy me, consumer me, take me home. Outside work is free."

David Hammons says half-jokingly that *Higher Goals* is driving him to drink. "I used to have the fantasy of going to a bar and the bartender would set the drink up before I sat down. I thought that was hip." He pauses. "Actually, I used to drink about a six-pack a year." Now he finds himself consuming extraordinary quantities of Guinness stout in order to get the caps.

"They're my favorites," he says. "That nice caramel color." The ugliest caps are also the most plentiful. "Rolling Rock is all anyone's drinking nowadays."

Hammons harvests caps in the early hours of the morning from Manhattan bars. Starting in the 30s, he works his way to Tribeca, acquiring bottle caps and social information along the way.

"Up around Madison Square Garden, they like their Millers," he says. "Down at Puffy's, where the college kids drink it's mostly Heineken and Rolling Rock."

From Tribeca he walks across town to the East Village. "I usually wind up at an old hangout, where I got most of my caps for *Art on the Beach* there."

Last summer Hammons erected a shanty at the Battery Park landfill made entirely of found objects: flattened cans, scrap metal, cardboard, plywood, and bottle caps. Sun Ra and his Arquestra staged a concert there that concluded with fireworks. At summer's end, vandals set the house on fire. "I probably might have burned it down myself," Hammons says.

Over the fall and winter Hammons made artworks from elephant dung. "It's huge and very heavy," he says, "but when it dries, it turns feather light. I collected it, mainly from one elephant named Nancy at the Prospect Park Zoo."

He painted some of the dung pink and adorned it with ivory miniatures from Chinatown. He decorated some with peanut shells. One piece had a huge chain wrapped around it to symbolize strength, and another he covered with gold leaf. "I noticed at the zoo that people looked at her droppings as much as at the animal," he says. "You can really feel the enormous presence of things in what's left behind." Some day he wants to exhibit his art in front of Nancy's cage.

During the 1983 blizzard, Hammons had the whimsical notion of selling snowballs. "They were going for $1," he says, adding that there were several takers. Hammons saved one of the snowballs and stored it in his freezer. Last week a midtown gallery put the three-year-old snow-ball on display. "It's a five-inch snowball," he says, "and it cost $300 to display."

Hammons's drollery has a chiding edge. He's impatient with the art world and makes no effort to hide his impatience with its conventions. This doesn't affect his work in any particular way, since the art remains discursive, meandering, and pure, leavened by the benison of humor.

"A friend gave me 10,000 pairs of tiny rubber shoes," he says, "and I've been selling them in Cooper Square. Fifty cents a foot. I tell the ladies, 'If you buy these shoes, he'll never walk out of your life.' People ask me if they're Imelda Marcos's shoes and I say, 'No, they're Nancy Reagan's. You just haven't looked in her closet lately.' I arrange them in intricate patterns. It takes me about 20 minutes. People's idea of time is so warped in the work world that they say, 'That must have taken you all day.' If I see a member of the art crowd coming, I jump behind a door. I like the kind of things people will say to me when I'm nailing my bottle caps or when I'm selling the shoes. Sometimes one of them sees the little rubber shoes all in patterns and says, 'You should make art.' And I say, 'Oh, I never thought of that.'"

Interview with David Hammons

Kellie Jones

DAVID HAMMONS: I can't stand art actually. I've never, ever liked art, ever. I never took it in school.

KELLIE JONES: Then how come you do it if you can't stand it?

DH: I was born into it. That's why I didn't even take it in school because I was born into it. All of these liberal arts schools kicked me out, they told me I had to go to a trade school. One day I said, "Well, I'm getting too old to run away from this gift," so I decided to go on and deal with it. But I've always been enraged with art because it was never that important to me. When I was in California, artists would work for years and never have a show. So showing has never been that important to me. We used to cuss people out: people who bought our work, dealers, etc., because that part of being an artist was always a joke to us.

But like someone told me: "Art is an old man's game, it's not a young man's profession." He said it was a very lonely, lonely, lonely profession. Most people can't deal with all the loneliness of it. That's what I loved about California though. These cats would be in their sixties, hadn't had a show in twenty years, didn't want a show, paint everyday, outrageous stamina. They were like poets, you know, hated everything walking, mad, evil; wouldn't talk to people because they didn't like the way they looked. Outrageously rude to anybody, they didn't care how much money that person had. Those are the kind of people I was influenced by as a young artist. Cats like Noah Purifoy and Roland Welton. When I came to New

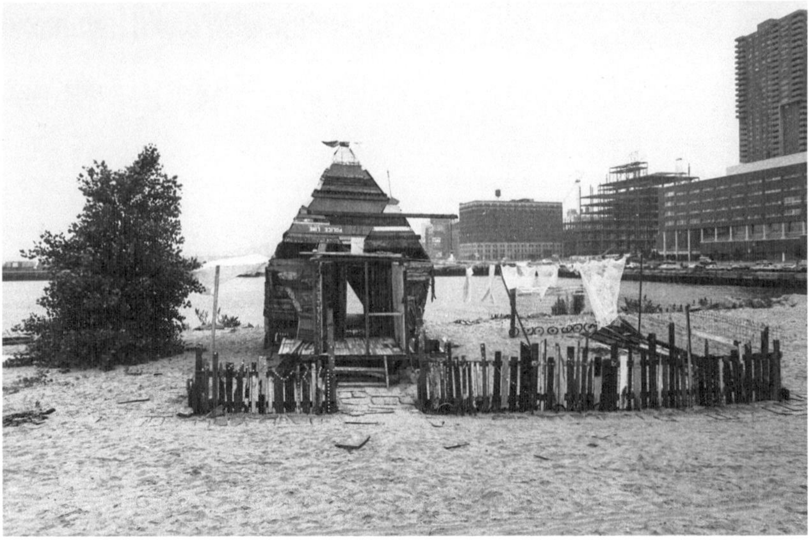

Installation view of *Spirit House*, collaborative work by David Hammons, Angela Valeria, and Jerry Barr, 1985, resin-coated print, 8 × 10 in. (20.3 × 25.4 cm), from *Art on the Beach*, exhibition, New York, organized by Creative Time. MoMA PS1 Archives, II.A.795. The Museum of Modern Art Archives, New York.
Photograph © Dawoud Bey.

York, I didn't see any of that. Everybody was just groveling and tomming, anything, to be in the room with somebody with some money. There were no bad guys here, so I said, "Let me be a bad guy," or attempt to be a bad guy, or play with the bad areas and see what happens.

In Los Angeles, Senga Nengudi and I shared a studio. Her work was so conceptual and I was working in frames then. So by us sharing a studio, she got more figurative and I got more conceptual. That's when she started doing the pantyhose; those pieces are all anatomy. Before, she used to put colored water in plastic bags and sit them on pedestals. This was the Sixties. No one would even speak to her because we were all doing political art. She couldn't relate. She wouldn't even show around other Black artists her work was so "outrageously" abstract. Senga came to New York and still no one would deal with her because she wasn't doing "Black Art." She was living in Harlem. So she had to leave here and go back to L.A. and regroup. Then I came in after her; I said, "I'll try it, I'll try it with my shit."

It was a totally different thing when I came here in 1974. It was a painter's town exclusively. If you weren't painting you could forget it. And I was doing body prints then and was moving into conceptual art. I had to get out of the body prints because they were doing so well. I was making money hand over fist. But I had run out of ideas, and the pieces were just becoming very ordinary, and getting very boring. I tried my best to hold on to it. It took me about two years to find something else to do.

I came here with my art in a tube. I had a whole exhibition in two tubes. I laid that on the people here and they couldn't handle it, nothing in it was for sale. This was after the body prints. This was after I had taken off for a couple of years and come up with an abstract art that wasn't salable. These things were brown paper bags with hair, barbecue bones, and grease thrown on them. But nothing was for sale. Other Black artists here couldn't understand why you would do it if you couldn't sell it.

I was influenced in a way by Mel Edwards's work. He had a show at the Whitney in 1970 where he used a lot of chains and wires. That was the first abstract piece of art that I saw that had cultural value in it for Black people. I couldn't believe that piece when I saw it because I didn't think you could make abstract art with a message. I saw the symbols in Mel's work. Then I met Mel's brother and we talked all day about symbols, Egypt and stuff. How a symbol, a shape has a meaning. After that, I started using the symbol of the spade; that was before I did the greasy bags. I was trying to figure out why Black people were called spades, as opposed to clubs. Because I remember being called a spade once, and I didn't know what it meant; nigger I knew but spade I still don't. So I just took the shape, and started painting it. I started dealing with the spade the way Jim Dine was using the heart. I sold some of them. Stevie Wonder bought one in fact. Then I started getting shovels (spades); I got all of these shovels and made masks out of them. It was just like a chain reaction. A lot of magical things happen in art. Outrageously magical things happen when you mess around with a symbol. I was running my car over these spades and then photographing them. I was hanging them from trees. Some were made out of leather (they were skins). I would take that symbol and just do dumb stuff with it, tons of dumb ignorant corny things. But you do them, and after you do all the corny things, and all the ignorant things, then a little bit of brilliance starts happening. There's a process to get to brilliancy: you do all the corny things, and you might have to go through five hundred ideas. Any corny thought that comes into your head, do a sketch of it. You're constantly emptying the brain of the ignorant and the dumb and the silly things and there's nothing left but the brilliant ideas. The brilliant ideas are hatched through this process. Pretty soon you get ideas that no one else could have thought of because you didn't think of them, you went through this process to get them. These thoughts are the ones that are used, the last of the hundred or five hundred, however many it takes. Those last thoughts are the ones that are used to make the image and the rest of them are thrown away. Hopefully you ride on that last good thought and you start thinking like that and you don't have to go through all these silly things.

It was just like a chain reaction. I started doing body prints in the shape of spades. So when I moved into using just the spade image it flowed. Then I started painting watercolors of spades. After that, I stopped using the framed format entirely; I had chains hanging off the spades. I went to Chicago to a museum and saw this piece of African art with hair on it. I couldn't believe it. Then I started using hair.

KJ: So where did you get the hair from, barber shops? People didn't want to give it up, did they? They thought you were going to do some serious magic on them using that hair.

DH: No they didn't mind it. Except there was a place in Harlem that said no they wouldn't give it to us, this Haitian place.

In L.A. I had one place that I got hair from, this one shop, because it was so hard to ask people. I'd wait until everyone left the shop. I'd sit out front until the shop closed. I would always ask this one guy. Eventually, I got used to him and he got used to me. In New York, I wouldn't get the hair. I had this friend get it for me. He was very outgoing, you know, sold you insurance and all that kind of stuff, a gallery dealer, he'd talk to anybody. He'd talk to the barber and I'd just pick up the hair.

There's so much stuff that I want to do with the hair that I didn't get a chance to do, because I just can't stay with any one thing. Plus I got really bad lice. Everyone kept telling me I was going to get lice. I shrugged it off as just a possible occupational hazard. But I did get a really bad case of head lice. Hair's like the filthiest material. It's a filter. When the wind blows through it the dirt stays on the hair. You could wash your hair every single hour and it would still be dirty. But I have information on Black people's hair that no one else in the world has. It's the most unbelievable filter that I've ever run across.

I was actually going insane working with that hair so I had to stop. That's just how potent it is. You've got tons of peoples' spirits in your hands when you work with that stuff. The same with the wine bottles. A Black person's lips have touched each one of those bottles, so you have to be very, very careful. I've been working with bottles for three years and I've only exhibited them a couple of times. Most of my things I can't exhibit because the situation isn't right. The reason for that is that no one is taking the shit seriously anymore. And the rooms are almost always wrong, too much plasterboard, overlit, too shiny and too neat. Painting these rooms doesn't really help, that takes the sheen off but there's no spirit, they're still gallery spaces.

I think the worst thing about galleries is, for instance, that there's an exhibition opening from 8–10 p.m. The worst thing in the world is to say, "Well I'm going to see this exhibition." The work should instead be somewhere in between your house and where you're going to see it, shouldn't be at the gallery. Because when you get there you're already prepared, your eyes are ready, your glands, your whole body is ready to receive this art. By that time, you've probably seen more art getting to the spot than you do when you get there. That's why I like doing stuff better on the street, because the art becomes just one of the objects that's in the path of your everyday existence. It's what you move through, and it doesn't have any seniority over anything else.

Everybody knows about *Higher Goals*—the telephone pole piece—up there in Harlem. If I'm on the street up there I say, "I'm the guy who put that pole up there." I'll be on 116th or 110th and Amsterdam and talk to anybody and they'll say, "You're the one who did that. Yeah, I know where that is, I know you. Brother, come here; this is the cat who did the pole, yeah." So sometimes I'll just say that to talk to somebody on the street, at three or four in the morning or something, it's like a calling card. I've been trying to put it in the *Guinness Book of Records* as the highest basketball pole in the world but I don't know who to call.

I like playing with any material and testing it out. After about a year, I understand the principles of the material. I try to be one step ahead of my audience. Some artists are predictable. You've seen their patterns over the last ten years. They're staying within these frameworks because it's financially successful. I look at these cats and this is what I never ever want to be or never ever want to do. Why should I stay safe? It takes a long time to analyze a form—whether it be metal, oil paint, whatever—it may take them their whole lifetime to analyze this material. But who gives a fuck? There are so many things to play with. And I question if what these artists are doing is art or not. I don't think it is. An artist should always be searching and searching for things. Never liking anything he finds, in a total rage with everything, never settling or sacrificing for anything. That's what I enjoy anyway.

I always try to use materials that are not easy to obtain. Like now I have all this elephant dung that I'm working with.

KJ: How did you get that?

DH: It was for a garden. Angela (Valeria) was getting some for her plants. I was there with her and saw some of this elephant manure. It was interesting. It's about the size of a coconut. So I'm painting on it now. I've been working with it since about April 1985.

KJ: You did pieces for a while that had dowels with hair and pieces of records on them. Like the piece you did for the Atlanta Airport.

DH: Those pieces were all about making sure that the Black viewer had a reflection of himself in the work. White viewers have to look at someone else's culture in those pieces and see very little of themselves in it. Like looking at American Indian art or Egyptian art, you can try to fit yourself in it but it really doesn't work. And that's the beauty of looking at art from other cultures, that they're not mirror reflections of your art. But in this country, if your art doesn't reflect the status quo, well then you can forget it, financially and otherwise. I've always thought artists should concentrate on going against any kind of order, never accepting any order not even their own, but here in New York, more than anywhere else, I don't see any of that gut. Because it's so hard to live in this city. The rent is so high, your shelter and eating, those necessities are so difficult, that's what keeps the artist from being that maverick.

KJ: It's funny, though, because people always think that the starving artist is the most important one. That all that angst and starvation is what makes your art good.

DH: It does make the work good if you understand the starvation. Like Van Gogh said, he who lives in poverty and loves that poverty that he lives on will always be in the heartbeat of the universe. But you have to love the poverty, and there are very few people who love poverty; they want to get out of it. So if you are in poverty and dislike it, well then you have a real problem and it's going to reflect in the work. But if you're in poverty and enjoy it and can laugh at it, then you have no allegiance to anything and you're pretty much free.

Anyone who decides to be an artist should realize that it's a poverty trip. To go into this profession is like going into the monastery or something; it's a vow of poverty, I always thought. To be an artist and not even to deal with that poverty thing, that's a waste of time; or to be around people complaining about that. Money is going to come, you can't keep money away in a city like this. It comes but it just doesn't come as often as we want.

My key is to take as much money home as possible. Abandon any art form that costs too much. Insist that it's as cheap as possible is number one and also that it's aesthetically correct. After that anything goes. And that keeps everything interesting for me.

KJ: Would you say that your work has any political element in it? Because of not running after the status quo or being more free to do what you want and not really worrying about the money thing like so many people are doing? In other words, by abandoning running after the money, does the work become more political in a certain sense?

DH: I don't know. I don't know what my work is. I have to wait to hear that from someone.

KJ: Like who, regular people on the street?

DH: They call my art what it is. A lot of times I don't know what it is because I'm so close to it. I'm just in the process of trying to complete it. I think someone said all work is political the moment that last brushstroke is put on it. Then it's political, but before that it's alive and its being made. You don't know what it is until it's arrived, then you can make all these political decisions about it.

Sometimes I do say, "This is going to be a political piece." Like *Soweto Marketplace* that was at Kenkeleba House (*Dimensions in Dissent*, December 1985). Then trying to make it is so difficult, because I want it political and I want it conceptual and I want it visually interesting. I want it gloomy, I want it hidden away from the crowd. All of these kinds of things come into play. So I'm dealing with about five different levels.

I'm learning a lot from Fellini, watching his movies over and over again. I think the movie people are much more advanced than other visual artists. They can make you cry, they can make you laugh, they can scare you. Paintings don't do that, they used to but not anymore because the audience knows the game too well. But it's the artist's fault because the artist isn't researching and making the game more real. We've let filmmakers take the game from us because of our nonchalance.

If you know who you are then it's easy to make art. Most people are really concerned about their image. Artists have allowed themselves to be boxed in by saying yes all the time because they want to be seen, and they should be saying no. I do my street art mainly to keep rooted in that, "who I am." Because the only thing that's really going on is in the street; that's where something is really happening. It isn't happening in these galleries. Lately I've been trying to meet a new kind people in this city and not the art scene. Otherwise you end up with, "Man, you shit's baaad, your shit's happening, you're the man," all this absurd praise. You start flying and thinking that your shit don't stink. I've invented a rule book for myself that's gotten me over all of this stuff. If an artist doesn't have his own rules then he's playing with those of the art world, and you know those are stacked against you.

I have all these safety valves that I use. Like if it's on the ground, I pick it up and put it on a branch. It's still outside of me, I just found it. One artist accused me of "showing a bad image of Harlem." And I said, "I'm not showing anything. I'm just putting stuff that's on the ground onto a tree. I'm not responsible for that wine bottle getting there. All I'm doing is playing with it, activating it in some form."

Selling the shoes and other things on the street I think is my personal best; those little shoes, that's my best shot. I do it whenever I need a fix, I guess; when I know I need attention and want to make someone laugh. It's like having an opening, for me when I do that piece because I interact with the people. And I don't have to wait for these galleries. It's a way for me to show people how I see the world. I get a chance to watch people interact. It's interesting . . . if you have an item between you and other people, then they can relate to you. If you don't have an item you're enemy number one. But if you have an item between you then it cools them out and they can deal with you. It's amazing how something like a little shoe can just turn someone's head around.

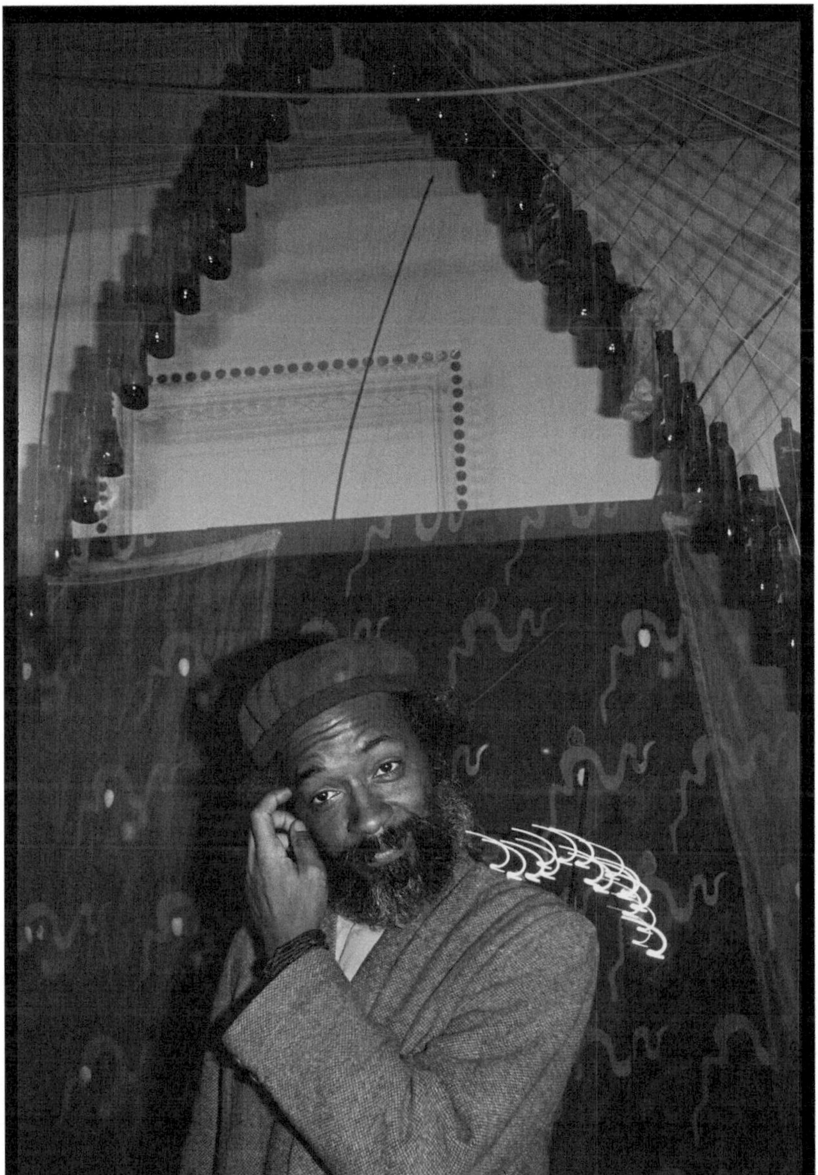

David Hammons standing under an arch of bottles, 1981.
Photograph © Sylvia Plachy.

KJ: Have you ever talked to people on the street—like when you had that bottle tree piece in the vacant lot next door to Studio Museum, did you ever stand around there and listen to what ordinary people said about it?

DH: I was in there one time and some people asked me what I was doing and somebody said, "He ain't got nothing better to do." And I thought, I didn't have anything else to do, that was the reason I was doing that. So they ask the questions and answer them themselves. If you're quiet or don't have anything to say, they say it all for you.

KJ: Do you think everyday people have a greater grasp of what you're doing than—

DH: Than I do.

KJ: —than you do or than other people who are politically astute or versed in art?

DH: They're the number one, because they're already at that place that I'm trying to get to. Sometimes I carry a whole arch of wine bottles around in the neighborhood. I walk from 125th up to 145th Street and people follow me, ask me questions, give me answers, tell me what I can do. They just give me tons of information and I don't give them any. I'm just carrying this piece around like it's a log or something. Once a woman said to me, "Mr., excuse me, but could you please tell me what that is?" I said, "What are you speaking of?" Then I said, "Oh, it's just some wine bottles." I play off it. I do this every once in a while to cleanse myself. It's putting myself out there on the street to be made fun of. I think it's important to be laughed at.

Black people, we have more problems with being made fun of than any people I've ever met. That's why it's so important for us to be cool, cool, cool. If you're not cool then you're something else and no one wants to be that other thing. But that other thing is what I'm interested in, because you have to really work at getting to that other space. Black artists, we are so conservative that it's hard to get there, you have to work at it, really, really work to be non-conservative. We've come up under this Christian, puritanical, European form of thinking and it's there, deep-rooted.

It can be worked at, loosened up some, but it's very difficult. What happens with my work is like I'll be working on piece (A) but I'll do some little aside things on my way across the studio to get to piece (A) and these aside things will be more important because they are coming out of my subconscious. These aside pieces will become more interesting and haphazardly loose and piece (A), that I've been working on for months, will be real tight.

Doing the things in the street is more powerful than art I think. Because art has gotten so . . . I don't know what the fuck art is about now. It doesn't do anything. Like Malcolm X said, it's like novocaine. It used to wake you up but now it puts you to sleep. I think that art now is putting people to sleep. There's so much of it around in this town that it doesn't mean anything. That's why the artist has to be very careful what he shows and when he shows now. Because the people aren't really looking at art, they're looking at each other and each other's clothes and each other's haircuts. In other sections of the country I think they're into seriously looking at art. This is the garbage can of it all. Maybe people shouldn't look at art seriously here because there's so much.

The art audience is the worst audience in the world. It's overly educated, it's conservative, it's out to criticize not to understand, and it never has any fun. Why should I spend my time playing to that audience? That's like going into a lion's den. So I refuse to deal with that audience and I'll play with the street audience. That audience is much more human and their opinion is from the heart. They don't have any reason to play games, there's nothing gained or lost.

KJ: The piece that was at *Art on the Beach*, does it have a name?

DH: I called it *Delta Spirit* because it was about that kind of spirit that's in the South. I just love the houses in the South, the way they built them. That Negritude architecture. I really love to watch the way Black people make things, houses, or magazine stands in Harlem, for instance. Just the way we use carpentry. Nothing fits, but everything works. The door closes, it keeps things from coming through. But it doesn't have that neatness about it, the way white people put things together; everything is a thirty-secondth of an inch off.

So working with the architect was fun because our shit was outrageous. You had to have an architect on this project. So I hired Jerry Barr;

we did *Higher Goals* together in 1983. He came up with the structure of *Delta Spirit*; he designed it. It was very puritanical. You know he's a big time architect, all over the world. He's designed houses in Paris, Cuba, and Africa and places. So this was one of his concepts. What I had to do was take that concept and put Negritude in it, which was a porch. He wanted to buy brand new wood; he wanted to spend about one thousand dollars on wood. But I had found all this lumber in Harlem and had stacked it up in these piles on various corners. So we just went around with a truck and picked up all the lumber, took it downtown and started making the house. It was built in the shape of a hexagon, a six-sided figure, using six foot poles, everything is six feet long.

KJ: Was that your idea?

DH: No, that was all Jerry's. I don't know how to stack wood, to keep wood from falling down. That's why he was important to the project. He knew how to stack wood and he knew how to get the best out of a piece of wood. I was just going to build a lean-to, a little shed, and take all the money and go home.

KJ: Do you think by doing a piece as cheaply as possible, that puts you on the same footing with a lot of people who are just trying to survive? Like you said, these newspaper stands in Harlem, I mean obviously these people don't have—they're not going to spend three thousand dollars on wood. . . .

DH: Exactly. But these stands serve the same functions and they do the same things. They're just aesthetically different.

KJ: When you were doing *Delta Spirit* did you go down South and look at houses, or did you make the piece from memory?

DH: It's based on memories of the South. It also had a lot to do with Simon Rhodia's *Watts Towers*. I love his work, it's one of the best. When I was in L.A., these towers just really influenced me. I would like to work on one piece for the rest of my life; just one piece, like him. As opposed to toying around with all these other little things. Just make one piece. Most artists want at least one piece to be immortalized. So one piece would do it. Because we're making one piece anyway, I guess, fragments of it.

KJ: So what ever happened to *Delta Spirit*?

DH: It's still there. Yeah, I go out there all the time.

KJ: Really, I thought it was taken down. I thought it was going to be moved to Harlem.

DH: All of that got too boring to deal with. I got tired of thinking about it. So it might be there for a couple of years. But I didn't get the five hundred dollars that they paid the artists to dismantle their work. I'm waiting for the snow because I wanted to photograph it in the winter and document it under all seasons. I just see it as a piece of public sculpture. That's the other reason why I haven't taken it down.

I would like to burn the piece. I think that would be nice visually. Videotape the burning of it. And shoot some slides. The slides would then be a piece in itself. I'm getting into that now: the slides are the art pieces and the art pieces don't exist.[1] I have video of *Delta Spirit* now, taken in the summer (1985). It's also on this Fat Boys video; they showed it for about 60 sixty seconds. Their managers thought it would be good to have as a stage prop.

I have no idea if there was any real connection between the Fat Boys and *Delta Spirit*. My position is that it's just irrelevant to me. I was working on the house, if someone wanted to use it, I stay away from that thing because it doesn't relate to what I was doing. But if anybody can relate to it, good. Let them weave themselves in it and through it.

The Fat Boys were like big, heifer cows who waddled out of a limousine, who are going to die within three years if they don't take care of their physical situation. These young boys, three hundred pounds each, waddling down to the house and out of breath before they get there. And everyone else making all the money around them. So their whole thing is out to lunch.

KJ: But I wonder if a lot of people see the Fat Boys video and see that house and are affected by that image.

DH: It's not on long enough. There's a close-up and they're on the porch and they come off. You'd only know about it if you knew about the house. I told my kids in California to watch for it.

KJ: To me, that house, *Delta Spirit*, was a conglomerate of Black people's living. The way they put things together. It's not exactly the way a white or European person would do it.

DH: But it transcended that and went on into another level. Its significance changed as it got more ornamented; as it got more detailed, it went universal. People started seeing it who were from places like Tibet and Viet Nam, for instance, and told us about houses they've seen like that in all corners of the world. Getting this type of feedback also affected the piece.

KJ: That's why I thought the connection with the Fat Boys might be kind of interesting. Kind of bringing it back to city kids, and maybe giving them a chance to identify with it.

DH: It was really funny working on *Delta Spirit* because the other artists were so embarrassed by us or for us. They didn't know what we were going to do. They just saw this huge junk pile and everybody wanted to get rid of the wood, they thought it was an eyesore. We were the last ones to get the structure up, and we had a ball. We never got it finished, even though we worked on it every day.

KJ: It's still not finished, and it might not ever be finished. Like you said, it's that same piece that you work on and work on, and even when you die it's not finished.

DH: The way I see it, I have two pieces of public sculpture up on the island of Manhattan now. And looking for a third.

KJ: The pieces that you are doing now with bottles, your standard wine bottle with things like crosses and the Georgia clay inside of them. Are they related at all to the Thunderbird bottle pieces that you were doing before?

DH: With these bottles I'm using now, I got the inspiration from the book *Flash of the Spirit* (by Robert Farris Thompson). On one page I saw this little juju man sitting up there with a cross in a bottle. The thing about these bottles I love is that people have to ask how you got those things in there. It's like a trick. It's like they're saying, "How'd you do that trick?" Or I get this from people, "Oh, I know how you did it, you took the bottom off the bottle and glued it back on." And I say, "Yeah, that's how I did the trick." But visually it's hard now to mess with people because everybody is so hip on what's happening. I like when people ask how I do these things because that means they don't know. Whereas in a painting everybody knows, or everybody thinks they know "it's an extension of such and such that's coming out of Picasso, or that's a collage from the such and such school," that kind of stuff. So I'm trying to find these holes or these gaps to play in.

I just finished a piece with a voodoo doll in the bottle. That was fun. And then there's the bottle caps. I love bottle caps. Because I can get trillions and billions and zillions of those things. Whatever you see a lot of, you can use, you can build something off of. So I want to work with them forever. I also want to come back to the hair. All of these things I want to come back to at another time. Now I'm just laying down some kind of foundation; these pieces are like visual notes, like how you put notes in your notebook. These are all notes to come back to at another time, elements to reconnect in the future. The hair, the bottle caps, the bottles they'll all represent themselves in another salad on up the road somewhere.

—*January 20, 1986.*[2]

Notes

1. *Delta Spirit* was vandalized before Hammons could realize his concept of burning and videotaping the piece.

2. During the summer of 1986 Hammons completed another work entitled *Higher Goals* with a grant from the Public Art Fund. Situated in Brooklyn at Cadman Plaza in front of the Supreme Court building, it consisted of five telephone poles embellished with bottle caps and topped by basketball hoops. *Higher Goals* was on view in Brooklyn until October 1986.

David Hammons Interview

Steve Cannon, Keith Gilyard, David Henderson,
Jemeel Moondoc, and Gail Schilke

As loose as a cooked goose, as gumbo before it turns into soup, as jazz before it turns into sazz, the six of us sat in the living room and tossed it all around. Among those present were poet and visual artist Gail Schilke, jazz musician and composer Jemeel Moondoc, poet and radio producer David Henderson, poet and essayist Keith Gilyard, and yours truly, Steve Cannon. We tossed the questions around; David Hammons gave the answers.

STEVE: The first question is, why Europe?

DAVID: I've been here long enough, I guess. I mean, it's a taxicab ride to me, going to Europe. It's like going across town. When you get off the plane, it's not really that different.

STEVE: Why Italy?

DAVID: Italians are Black folks, really. They're so much like us, it's like . . .

STEVE: . . . talk loud, make a lot of noise . . .

DAVID: Yeah . . . eat, dress, hang out all the time. That's not Europe though. Italy is the bridge between Europe and Africa. Especially anything below Rome is Africa, anything above Rome is . . . Switzerland, Sweden, some shit. Plus Italy is very romantic, like a Duke Ellington kind of place.

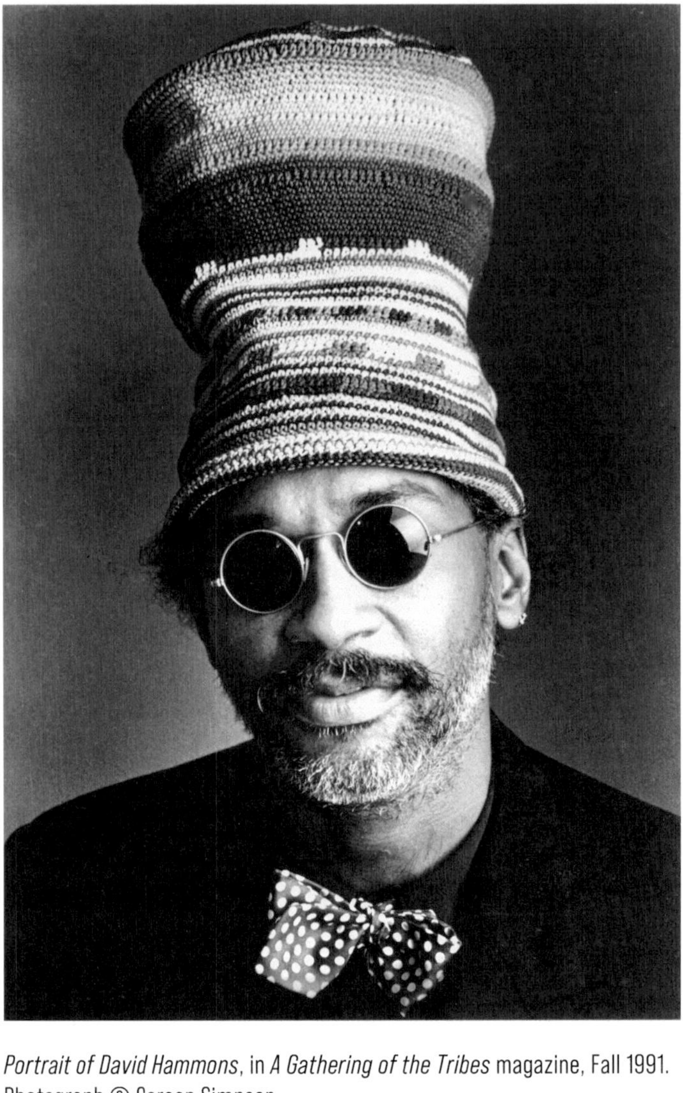

Portrait of David Hammons, in *A Gathering of the Tribes* magazine, Fall 1991. Photograph © Coreen Simpson.

Visually, you can see the music Ellington plays. And there's all that water in the streets, and the chandeliers! I want to hang this huge chandelier in the middle of 125th St. and 8th Avenue. Then it'll be like Naples, chandeliers on every block in Harlem! They're really so much alike, Naples and Harlem. 'Cause don't nobody else in the world wear gold chains, 'cept Italians and Black folks. It's that simple. It ain't even complex. You know, shirt open all the way down to the belly button, you know, white loafers, you know, beer bellies and slick hair. Incredible. Wearing their suits with their sleeves rolled up . . . everybody on a motor scooter, the whole family buzzing through town in Naples . . . throwing garbage out the window . . .

STEVE: All that shit! Oh, goddam.

DAVID: Just feels right, sounds right . . . the right thing to do.

STEVE: Well, where do you see the audience for your art? Do you see it over there, over here, and in terms of your inspiration, do you get it from both places, or what?

DAVID: Yeah, it's coming from all over.

STEVE: But there's gotta be a difference between that environment and this one.

DAVID: I don't really see it that much. Except that they're much more treacherous towards Black people. Like, I was standing on this corner and this cat backed all the way up two blocks just to call me some names. I mean, a fast cat! I couldn't believe how fast he was backing up. I didn't even understand it, so it didn't pay me no mind. That's the great thing about modern language, you can't get your feelings hurt, because that shit just goes on by.

STEVE: Where was this at?

DAVID: In Rome.

STEVE: But you don't feel alienated over there, like you're missing something and shit?

DAVID: Yeah, of course, that's why I come back. After 3 to 6 months, you miss the rhythm and you gotta come back and get recharged. You start missing Junior, and y'all [Junior, a.k.a. The Mayor of Tompkins Square Park, a homeless sculptor who has lived in the park for seven years].

STEVE: Have you been to any galleries here lately, find any artists here interesting?

DAVID: I don't go to any, don't even go to galleries.

STEVE: And the galleries in Europe?

DAVID: Don't go to them either.

JEMEEL: Same shit.

DAVID: I feel safe around musicians and poets. I'm serious, if an artist is coming down the street, I'll duck behind a car. I can't deal with them . . . it's like talking to a dentist, a lawyer, they got all them degrees and shit. And they lost it all at the university. They lost the pureness of themselves, gave it up for the academic, the resumes. You know, I won't even allow people to write my resume. I say, did you ever see Elvis Presley's resume? Or John Lennon's resume? I mean, fuck that resume shit!

STEVE: Well, how about the art scene over there?

DAVID: It's pretty bad. The young art scene is just totally like the American art scene. The best artists are the older ones, those cats are incredible, working with found objects. But it's the way they put it together. It has an opera quality to it that's what I like.

STEVE: All grand and shit.

DAVID: You know, operas, and carpets on the wall. Tapestries, you know, chandeliers and crosses. They make fun of all that stuff. They don't take the Jesus thing seriously.

STEVE: Uh-huh. That's just for fun. It's only over here where they take that shit seriously. So, tell us about that experience in Berlin, you said that was wild as a motherfucker. What's all this anti-East German stuff?

DAVID: Oh yeah, they talk about, "They lazy." All the westerners say, "They lazy, they won't show up on time. I said, oh shit, this sounds familiar. You know, it sound like the first time they've had a ghetto. You know, they go like, "East Germany's the bad side of town."

GAIL: Ever since the Jews left town, they've been looking for someone to blame.

DAVID: I know, and everywhere you go, they say, "This is where Hitler started the Nazi movement, in the basement of this place." Everybody's got a story!

GAIL: Do you see a resurgence of fascism in Europe, not just in Germany, but in Italy also?

DAVID: Well, when I got to Berlin, the whole place, every plate glass window, was broken in every store. They had a peace demonstration! (laughs) And at the peace demonstration in Rome, same thing happened. They turned violent!

GAIL: What do you think that means?

DAVID: There's this one young group, this one party, they're just against everything. Some anarchist group. They just come and start chasing people and creating violence.

STEVE: Well, go further into the art thing. You said you don't see the difference in making art over here and making art over there, but do you find the source of your art over there to be as rich as the source of your art over here?

DAVID: No, it's different. It's about different material. Like the Jesuses. There's no way I can find fifty, a hundred glowing Jesuses. (laughs) You ain't gonna find that here in America! So you bring them back over here and use them here. It's like the musicians going to North Africa and being influenced by the music there. You know, same kind of thing. Ornette, Don Cherry, you hear the travel in their music.

GAIL: Worldbeat . . .

DAVID: Yeah. So, I'm into water fountains now. They got twelve, fifteen hundred water fountains in Rome alone. This friend of mine came to Harlem from Florence. He said, "This looks like Rome to me." All the fire hydrants were open! (laughs)

JEMEEL: Fire hydrants and chandeliers!

STEVE: That'd be hip, right? Now, how about your experiences in France, and in Germany, England, or the Scandinavian countries. I mean, do you feel as special an affinity with that part of Europe as you do in Italy?

DAVID: No, it's like being in, uh, Queens. (laughs) All that shit I mean, you don't come over there to be in that . . . that's disgusting, you know, cause there's nothing, no spirit.

STEVE: Uh-huh. There ain't nothing shaking, no fire and shit.

GAIL: Cold.

DAVID: Cold. In Germany, it was like clean, too. (laughs)

STEVE: OK, but for you as an artist, how is it different for you being an artist there than it is here?

DAVID: It isn't. I mean, when I go into the studio, it's all manipulation of materials that I collect in the street.

GAIL: But don't you think that artists get treated with more respect and dignity in Europe than here?

DAVID: Oh, it's incredible. I don't know, I've been wondering what it is, but the Indians follow the buffaloes, right? That's all I'm doing. (laughter) I'm just going where they treat me good, that's all. You know, ticket, "We need you over here," boom, I'm gone. Ain't no big feelings about it, get up and go. Don't fight, don't scratch where it don't itch. I'm not moving, I'm being moved.

JEMEEL: Did you have a show in Italy?

DAVID: Not in Italy, no. But I had an exhibition in a bar, in the middle of town, that was run by an Italian. And I have four pieces of sculpture up now. One of them is an oil can chained to a parking meter. And we took a book and drilled a hole through it and chained it to a parking meter, and watched people walk by and read this book. And my lady and I, we're sitting in a sidewalk cafe with two glasses of wine . . . I said, "We're gonna have an opening here. We sat and watched people look at this book that was chained to a parking meter.

DAVID HENDERSON: Did you choose the book? Any book?

DAVID: Well, my lady friend, she wanted a Russian/English translation book. But I said, there's no time for it, time's a wasting. That's how you don't get things done. Stop the thought patterns, and let's just act! 'Cause otherwise, you know, like you could be late!

STEVE: And the shit never happens!

DAVID: Yeah, it gets all thought out! There was this piece I did in Germany, that I thought of when I was in Tunisia with my lady. She was sleeping in our hotel room and snoring like hell. So I dropped a microphone in front of her nose, right, and recorded her snoring for like an hour. So the next day I said, "Listen at you snoring!" She said, "Damn!" She said, "Why don't we take the tape recorder and put it in the bed." So in the hotel, we put the recorder in the bed and the snoring was coming out of it. So then, we go back to Rome and she's throwing out an old mattress and it's rolled up. So I stuck the tape recorder in this mattress for the show in Germany, and you know, the room is very dark and the door is barely open, so when

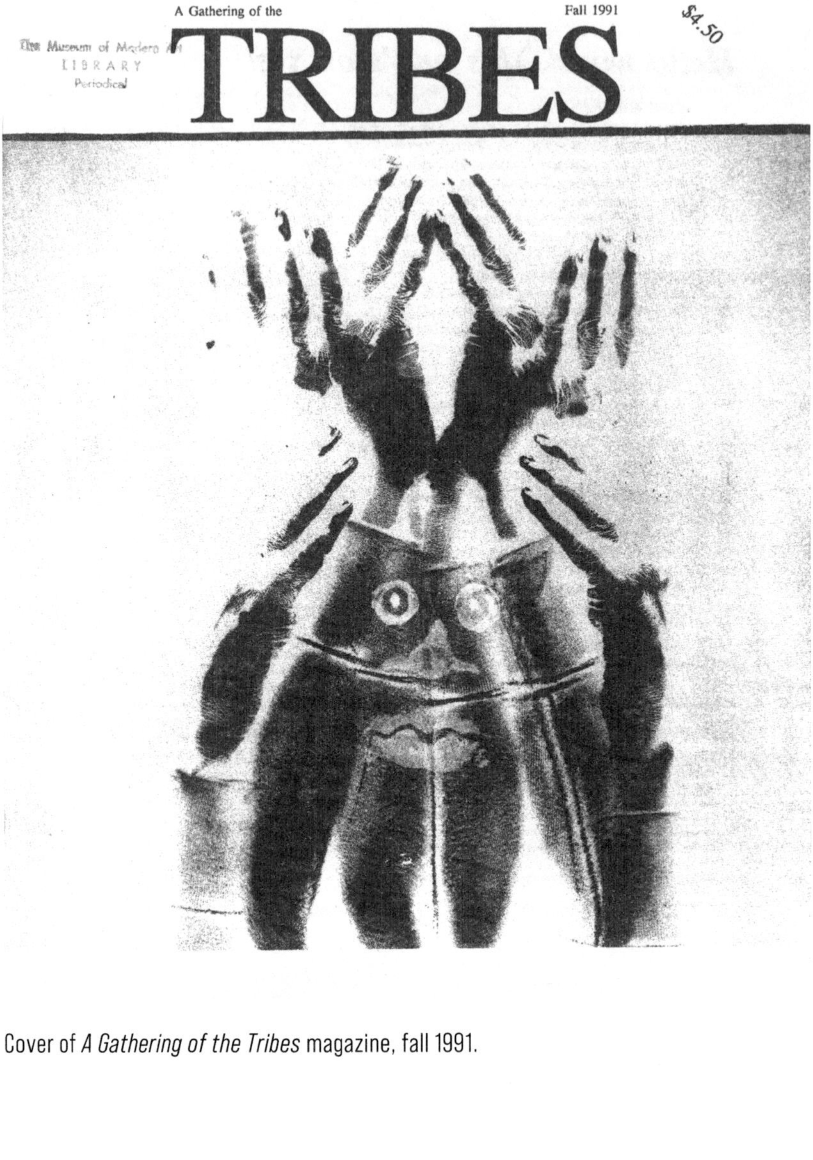

Cover of *A Gathering of the Tribes* magazine, fall 1991.

you come in the room you hear this noise coming out of the mattress. And they dug it! You know, "Oh yeah, I've been to New York, lots of homeless there."

JEMEEL: Opened that shit up!

DAVID: And I had this show in Amsterdam where I took 300 Amsterdam newspapers and threw them on the table. And these white folks came in and saw that paper; man, it freaked them out.

GAIL: *Amsterdam News* [a weekly Harlem paper]!

DAVID: I called it *The Newsroom* . . . big table, chairs all around. I threw the papers all over the table, you know, like a long business table. If they were neatly stacked, people would never touch them. I had to say, you know, "Please experience the art." You know, "Please! This thing is information."

STEVE: Now tell us about when you came back and had the *Rousin' the Rubble* show in Philadelphia. What provoked you to have that yellow ribbon, how did that come about?

DAVID: Well, I was shocked when I came back and this shit was going on! It was like America got invaded.

GAIL: Yeah, invasion of the body snatchers!

DAVID: Yeah, it was unbelievable. Going down there to Philadelphia, all you saw were yellow ribbons, all the way down. So it was there. And when I got to Berlin, everyone had white sheets hanging on their fire escapes, you know, for peace. So we hung one, asked the chick if we could hang one at the gallery. She said, "What? What are you talking about?" She didn't even see it! I was only there an hour, and I saw the shit, you know, driving around, looking for a clue. When you come to town and don't bring anything . . . like everybody else be bringing in their crates and you sitting around, waiting for their crates, smoking and shit, crating and uncrating . . . I just come and try to play off . . .

STEVE: What's there in town already!

DAVID: Walk the streets a couple of nights . . .

STEVE: Uh-huh, case the joint . . .

DAVID: And then react to it. You know, "Goddam, that's just like Miles Davis and shit." Then they look at it and say, "Damn! We ain't never seen no shit like this!"

JEMEEL: What about the piece in Philadelphia with the elephant shit?

DAVID:That came out of the snowballs, after the snowballs.

JEMEEL: But how did you, uh . . . obtain . . . ?

DAVID: I was watching that Big Apple Circus that travels around Brooklyn and I saw this cat taking some elephant shit for his garden, for fertilizer. And I had just done the snowball piece, so it was an easy move. (laughs) And like in the zoo at Prospect Park, I would see all these people looking at the elephants, and you would hear them say, "Damn! Look at that elephant shit!" They wouldn't even talk about the elephant. It'd just be, "Look at that elephant shit!" So, I looked too. I said, that's it! Then I started to add the peanuts, because it looked like it needed peanuts on it, and putting the elephant shit on pedestals and sticking peanuts on it.

STEVE: How did you come up with *Higher Goals*?

DAVID: That came from playing basketball, you know, eight hours a day for twenty years, and I got pissed with the shit, because it was always these 6′ 8″ cats coming around knocking down my shit. So I said, fuck it! You know, you put all that time in, and you're enraged! So, you act against it. Plus, I like political cartoons. You see these symbols, like bullets with faces on them. So I wanted to work it that way, like a political cartoon, visually.

STEVE: So, what possessed you to hook it up with the music, and the dance?

DAVID: I don't know, I don't know, it just came. Like, I used to stand on 6th Street and watch them play and think, "Ornette!" I was like, Ornette should be right here now, blowing with this. And then Jemeel came along. See, you have to get rid of these thoughts and make them happen, otherwise they'll never get out of your system. Now that it's activated, I can think new thoughts.

JEMEEL: But you know what happens is you're starting to incorporate styles, not just music, but like the piece with the tape recorder and the mattress, using sound. Isn't that something that is really new to the art world?

DAVID: No, it's not new. What I'm doing, these are old tools that white boys have been using, but I'm using it to bring my culture through theirs, like we bring our culture through the European ancestors. White boys still have more freedom in the art world, with materials and experimentation. And most of them listen to Black classical music when they make art. But they put their name on the painting and take the shit to the gallery, and they don't bring the music with it. They just use Miles.

STEVE: Use Miles, use 'Trane . . .

DAVID: Right, just turn on Monk or Mingus when they go into the studio to get them in the spirit, drink a few beers, go off and paint their abstract painting . . . sign their name, the shit's gone, so that's it with them. (laughs) I had a piece in Venice where I had a boom-box sitting on this wagon, and I had a timer fixed so this drill went on for about 5 minutes. When it went off and the fan went on, and the fan was playing these cards stuck in there with clothes pins. Meanwhile, Ornette's blowing on "Virgin Beauty," and the drill is going, then the fan goes on with the cards. Meanwhile, Ornette's concentrating . . . and this room is so beautiful that it's in, 200 years old, red carpet wallpaper, and these 3 objects are sitting on this beautiful carpet . . . and the people couldn't . . . leave the room! 'Cause it provided music for the exhibition. Everybody else's shit was quiet. Music, beautiful music, that never gets in art galleries! Like the glowing plastic Jesus piece with Aretha Franklin singing gospel music. But this is all about humor too, humor in the art world. See, when someone laughs at a piece, you don't have to ask if they like it. You can see they got it. It's like a dog wagging its tail. Visually, you can see the pleasure!

JEMEEL: What about the street pieces, like the snowballs and the little shoes?

DAVID: That snowball piece came out of hanging out on 2nd Avenue all those years, studying all those cats. The stuff they'd come up with to sell! One time I saw this cat selling thirty pairs of false teeth! You know, I said, goddam! I said, shit, I got to do that. I couldn't believe it, two in the morning, he'd be out there with 30 pairs of false teeth. I said, shit, I got to do something like this. So I said, I'm going for the snowballs!

STEVE: Right, now did the shoes . . .

DAVID: Oh, the shoes! It came after the snowballs, yeah. You know what it is?

STEVE: Go ahead.

DAVID: Like, when you have an object between you and them, people will talk to you. They'll say, "What is that? Is that for sale?" But if you're just standing on a street corner, everyone's an enemy of each other. But one object . . . it becomes a conduit for conversation with someone you've never met before.

GAIL: The marketplace.

DAVID: Yeah. See, I can't go two days without talking to somebody, so I would have to do this sometimes. And especially talking to someone I don't know. It's redundant talking to everyone you know all the time. So you figure out ways to talk to new people. In Harlem, I'll carry my wine bottles like I'm carrying a shopping bag, you know. And some woman will say, "Mister, excuse me, I been following you." (laughs) She'll say, "What are you doing with these?" I say, "'Pardon me, what?" "You know," she'll say, "with these?" I say, "Nothing. I'm just taking them for a walk." (laughs) Everybody thinks . . . they'll say, "Is that Krazy Glue?" It's weighing like sixty, eighty pounds . . . Krazy Glue is that glue that comes on late night television, and they think that's the glue to use for everything! And I'm using silicone. That shit has to dry for a week before you can move one of these pieces! But I take it for a walk. To get the feedback.

JEMEEL: But what about someone who might just call you a garbage collector with a talent for assembling things?

DAVID: Well, usually when you see a lot of something thrown around, it means you can create something out of it, you can tell a story. Like popcorn, you pop a lot of popcorn and you can take that popcorn and I could make a sculpture that looks like Michelangelo's baby if I wanted. Or take a hundred thousand peanuts and make a sculpture of George Washington Carver. You know. But if you only find one or two of something, it's not enough to really make a sculpture with.

DAVID HENDERSON: What about those doll shoes? Where did you find them?

DAVID: This cat just gave them to me. He was living in Brooklyn in an old doll factory. So there were all these heads . . . I took like, 50 little heads from Black dolls and thousands and thousands of shoes. For three years, I was selling these shoes on St. Mark's, every summer, all summer long.

DAVID HENDERSON: Yeah, and it's a chance to get out there and bullshit!

JEMEEL: OK, so here's a person who had the opportunity to give somebody this stuff, but he gave them to you.

DAVID: Well, he wanted to get rid of them, too! But he saw me collecting the shit. I already had like a hundred thousand bottle caps out there, so he said to himself, well, I might as well give him these shoes too! (laughs) My place looks like Fred Sanford's [*Sanford & Son*]. My grandfather always had a thrift shop, and there was always all these shoes on the ground, and I would look up and see the bottoms of racks and racks of suits. And I'd take a pair of shoes, wear them a couple of days, and take them back to his thrift shop. What I'm doing now might just come out of that thrift shop he had!

JEMEEL: Yeah, but you can collect things and put them in a shop and sell them, right? But you collect things and assemble them into works of art.

DAVID: To tell a story. A lot of people didn't like those wine bottles in the trees, 'cause they interpreted it as making fun of the culture. I mean, why just let them lay there? These incredible bottles! Just pick them up and raise them a little higher, into one of those ginkgo trees.

JEMEEL: What about that taxicab piece you're planning for the Modern? [The Museum of Modern Art.]

DAVID: Yeah, I'm trying to get a taxicab now on the third floor of the Modern.

JEMEEL: A gypsy?

DAVID: No, it's gotta be a yellow cab. From the line, "yellow cabs don't haul coal." So there's gonna be a ton of coal, about ten feet past where the cab has already gone by, and the ton of coal will be sitting there . . . with a yo-yo on top of it.

JEMEEL: But another point to your work is these things on words . . .

STEVE: Puns, visual puns.

JEMEEL: Like the Night Train–Coltrane show you did over there on Broadway.

DAVID: That's coming out of Farris [writer John Farris], Junior, watching them for the last five or six years, Darius [writer Darius James] and Steve [Cannon] . . . that whole word play. You sit in the park and get that word play all the time. It's funny as a motherfucker, too.

JEMEEL: It's poetry.

DAVID: I'm hearing you. 'Cause you're sitting there and talking some shit and someone talks about this cat from Chicago who had some gold pockets. So I go out and get a pair of pants and tell the tailors, "Put some gold pockets in these." They say, "What?" I said, "'Just put them in, you know, all the way down to the ankles." When I got them back they weren't nearly as exaggerated as I wanted. You know, I was talking Deep Pockets. The cat, he got LONG money and shit. So it was like that, you hear the words, and a visual light comes on.

JEMEEL: Remember that time, David, we were in that abandoned building in Harlem . . .

DAVID: Yeah. And I had them feathers. I had Vaseline on my face and dipped my face in feathers and a pillowcase, and a sack of flower . . .

STEVE: You know, just like . . .

DAVID: I don't know what it is. You just do these things. No rhyme or reason, just to go through the thing. Visual artists are afraid to be laughed at. Black folks are afraid to be laughed at. But you must be willing to be laughed at, 'cause it's that feeling that hurts.

DAVID HENDERSON: That's a post-modern thing, though, Black folks being afraid to be laughed at.

DAVID: No, I mean being laughed at in terms of . . . like if you fall, that's the only time everybody gets to see you uncool. One leg's going somewhere and another leg's going somewhere, and you're not in control of your whole style of carrying yourself, right? So you get laughed at when you get caught outside your aura of presenting yourself. So to go out and put yourself in the position to be laughed at, you cleanse yourself when you interact with that deep feeling that we're all afraid of. So nothing they say or do can upset you, 'cause you're way ahead of them. You know, I used to go to these Black art colonies, and they used to like, destroy me! You know all those cats saying, "My shit's about Madonna and child, the solar system, another sun coming up, the universe is the Black man" . . . and I'm talking about making art out of ice cubes! (laughs) Man, I'm talking about Black folks buying $200 worth of paper to make art on. And then they're uptight because the paper's so expensive, they're afraid to be loose on it when they already put the investment up. And they're like, "I got to make a good piece of art!" (laughs) Ain't nothing gonna happen with that kind of consciousness.

GAIL: Well, you lose the "play" . . .

DAVID: I know. And it ain't got nothing to do with . . .

STEVE: . . . the real deal.

DAVID: . . . the real shit. You know, I looked at these cats and I said, I cannot do it this way. I mean, the art object is just the result of the thought . . . the pure outrageous thought.

JEMEEL: Yeah, but there was a period of time when Black artists painted on canvas, but what they did was cut the canvas, ripped it and made alterations to the canvas. But they still felt they had to paint on canvas . . . and they still do.

DAVID: 'Cause that's the European way. Canvas is the sacred cloth. I tried it, but I couldn't get it . . . you end up with a geometric shape that has come out of the architecture of the room that it's in, a geometric canvas on a geometric wall in a geometric house on a geometric block . . .

GAIL: All boxed in!

DAVID: Yeah and you know, it becomes a window. And plus all artists, all painters, they want to create magic on a flat surface. Why don't they just go ahead and create magic?

STEVE: That's all!

JEMEEL: Period.

DAVID: And forget about the depth on a flat surface, and just be magic men.

JEMEEL: And be true to their culture.

DAVID: And just be a magic person, make magic in front of people's eyes!

David Hammons: "Knowing Their Past"

Robert Farris Thompson

> In the long run men hit only what they aim at. Therefore, though they should fail immediately, they had better aim at something high.
>
> —Thoreau, *Walden,* 1854

Introduction

"I live in Harlem to protect myself from getting too European." He mentioned Ellington and Robeson. "You know they stood at this very corner. You feel their presence, because you know their past." "I am," he said, echoing the words to a certain spiritual, "a soldier in the army of that history."

Harlem cuisine—grease, bone, and greens; Harlem parlance—puns, rhymes, and put-downs; Harlem ecstasies and spirit possession; Harlem beauty and continuity amounting to the same thing; Harlem fusings of matter to memory—all this, and more, much more, keeps Hammons moving, cool, serene, across the staggered grids of black Manhattan.

"You can't live in Harlem and produce a downtown art." Living close to elemental things, like dreadlocks and wine bottles, basketballs and bone, ice and air and rubber, he protects himself from "white cube spaces" and money mindset.

Hammons secures this freedom with cultural openness. He sometimes aligns scattered objects by the sidewalk and waits for people on the street to voice impressions. He once piled shoes on a corner; it was not a

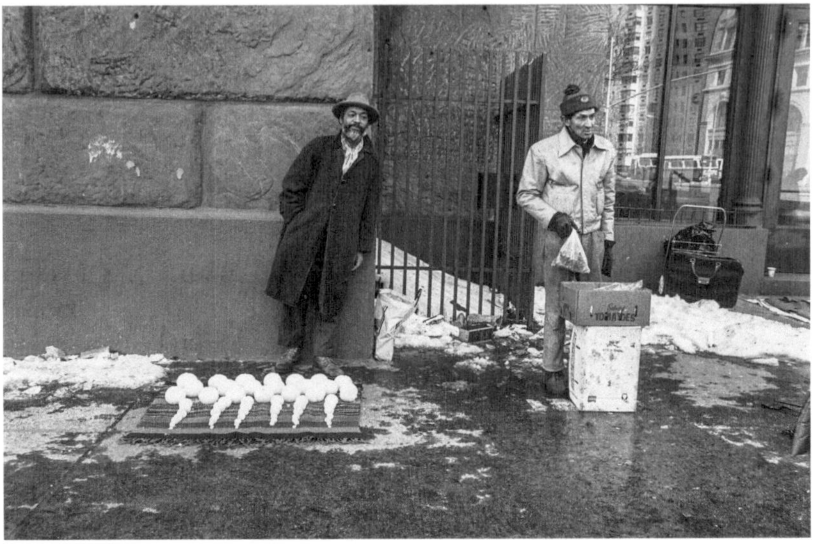

Dawoud Bey, View of the performance of David Hammons's *Bliz-aard Ball Sale*, Cooper Square, New York, 1983, resin-coated print, 8 × 10 in. (20.3 × 25.4 cm). MoMA PS1 Archives, II.A.794. The Museum of Modern Art Archives, New York. © Dawoud Bey 4/8.

"happening." It was materially coded, material banter, a search for counter wit. "Imelda Marcos!" "Check out Nancy Reagan's closet," his response. Watching all this, we discover the artist, smashing the atoms of the black stereotype, releasing healing archetypes.

Artist's Studio, Harlem

> The Promethean bard of Lenox Avenue,
> Rabelaisian I's of the Boogie-Woogie
> dynasty in barrel houses, at rent parties,
> on riverboats, at wakes.
>
> —M. B. Tolson, "Harlem Gallery," 1965

I first visited Hammons's Harlem studio, July 4, 1991. He was seated on a low stool, spare ribs in his hands. He was not, however, eating. He was transforming flesh and bones, by pun and wire, into a xylophone.

Rap blared through open windows. Against a wall, a pair of crutches "walked" in a pair of sneakers, something Hammons had observed at Broadway and 72nd. A crucifix gleamed inside a bottle. Antelope horns adorned a metal fan. There were other compositions, some finished, others not. I stopped to gaze, fascinated, at a work fashioned from beer bottle caps and bits of African American hair and another work, materially complicated, centered on a basketball. In the middle of the floor arose an "altar for people who died from wine." By the street side window hung strips of flypaper, tiny human figures trapped on their sticky surface.

No wonder he told Kellie Jones, "I can't stand art actually. I've never, ever liked art, ever." A man of his convictions could not live in somebody else's language. Meanwhile, the slick and the studio-trained, especially since Hammons won the coveted MacArthur "Genius" Award and European recognition, circle around his work. They want into the secrets of his stature. But they are afraid to let their blood run in the wrong direction, afraid of black religious trance, afraid to turn their pockets inside-out, and step with confidence into a Harlem morning. Above all, they fear the humiliations they correctly sense lie behind his grandeur.

The World Became a Chandelier

> Make language stammer, or make it "wail," stretch tensors through all of language, even written language, and draw from it cries, shouts, pitches, durations, timbres, accents, intensities.
>
> —Gilles Deleuze and Félix Guattari, *A Thousand Plateaus*, 1980

To begin discussion of Hammons's art with his LA body prints of the late sixties implies the California city made him. In point of fact Hammons's vision was shaped by persons of African descent in Springfield, Illinois, where he was born July 24, 1943. Thanks to key members of his family, he grew up in contact with the roots of Harlem. This reflects a secret education, beyond the West, shaping and grounding his sensibility. Apropos of his pursuit of a career in art, he has said, "I was born into it. That's why I didn't even take it in school."

"Devastating" is his term for the Eurocentric education he received in Springfield schools. "I'm amazed that Black people can learn anything from an educational structure that systematically excludes them."

Even if there had been "black studies" in schools of that era, the teachers and the texts would have been patronizing, or worse. Remember what Malcolm X experienced in schools during the thirties in Lansing, Michigan. Fortunately, Hammons's cultural upbringing was secure. His confidence stems inviolate from a major source, Claude Champ, his foster grandfather.

In the forties the main black section of Springfield was where Union Street crossed Second Avenue. Right at that point, in a corner house, lived Hammons's foster grandfather. "His wife raised my mother," Hammons told me. "Mother and me and my brothers and sisters, we all used to eat Sunday dinner with the Champs and all the important meals, Thanksgiving, Christmas, Easter."

Claude Champ, who died in 1959, offered young Hammons access to a deeper sustenance. He "decorated out" his house and yard in an idiom which traces back, in part, to Kongo and Angola.

In ancient Kongo cities of Mbanza Kongo and Lwangu, people placed crystals (*ngengele*) or white stones (*matadi ma mpembe*) on the ground before their houses. These stones or crystals provided mystic barriers. Following the same logic, Bakongo also outlined yards with mystically protective plants and, again, crystals or, failing that, stones painted white, as a sign of danger, color of death, to frighten off negating presences.

Sometimes they built rock piles, like cairns marking graves, right in the front yard of the house; "that sign tells you this house is under protection, not simple, but very powerful, an ancestral power that if violated can lead to death." They also hung anti-thief guards in bottles or packets from trees before the house. Such gestures, in effect, transformed house and yard into a *nkisi*, a spatial charm, a "medicine of God." God's medicine blessed, with life and continuity, all those living within the enclosure (*luumbu*) of plants and stones. In addition, a person might hang an herb called *yemba* on the verandah to bring affection to the household. The word *yemba* puns on *mayembo*, ecstatic trembling of the shoulders at the coming of the spirit. The plant associated hearth and yard with the ecstasy of arriving spirit as well as love.

Bakongo also planted *saku-saku* herbs around the house. These plants called on qualities of blessing through wordplay with the verb of benison *sakumuna*. According to Fu-Kiau Bunseki, an authority on Kongo traditional culture, another herb called *ngwangwa* was grown by the house as a further sign of love, attracting caring persons to the yard.

Walls of Kongo houses facing the street were sometimes decorated with four-pointed stars, invoking the protection of *simbi*, the highest class of the dead. *Simbi* signs (pools, quartz, waterfalls) logically include the sparkle of the stars.

These themes reemerge in black North America with thundering redundancy. One reason for this is that about one-quarter of the slave population came from Angola. There are bottle trees, rock piles on lawns, and whitewashed rock boundaries galore in black America. Star and heart emblems decorate some black properties, lined with whitewashed stones, in association with other recurring elements, like pinwheels and rubber tires painted gleaming white.

The African American yard show appears across the South. It occurs wherever black women and men migrated, including Watts in California and Seattle on the northwest coast. In America, such emblems were apparently reinforced by contact with the star of the Masonic Lodges and the human desire, universally, carefully, to mark out property. The more spectacularly spiritualized yards belonged to visionaries, who worked with roots and stones and other objects, avatars of a parallel classical tradition. Their heritage of healing and philosophy came, in the main, from Kongo. To me, the outward European appearance of certain objects favored—like tires and pinwheels—recalls the chromolithographs of Roman Catholic saints on Cuban and Brazilian Yoruba and Kongo altars which became convenient pegs on which to hang an older, blacker mode of vision.

Claude Champ lived this tradition. He whitewashed the trees and a telephone pole around his house at the corner of Union and Second Avenue "with paint so thick you could peel it off with your fingers." And he whitewashed stones and put them all around the boundaries to his house. He used the same medium to outline his flowerbeds, which were raised up within the stones. These white-stone–marked beds were arranged in the shape of five-pointed stars and hearts. Command of luck and affection (the hearts) and a reference to heaven (the stars) lent not only beauty but an air of encrypted protection to this black property. The signs also symbolized the essential care and generosity of the owner.

As a child Hammons would eagerly await the sight of Claude, riding an old bike. "When the bags on the back were full, you knew that something had been brought for you—Christmas stockings on wheels in any time or season."

Had Claude Champ lived in an ideal world, devoid of danger, the stones, the stars, the hearts, the boundaries would have formed a superfluous protective art. But the adoptive grandfather had to pass through an all-white part of town each day en route to his railroad job where he cleaned out the insides of steam locomotives. Young whites threw tomatoes at him. It didn't stop him. He called on strengths they never knew.

Backed by such courage, young Hammons plunged into high school athletics. He played basketball, wrestled (soon dropped: "I didn't like getting that close, the guys were too sweaty"), and did a turn as halfback for his high school football team.

There are other memories. "I lived one block from the railroad. I heard the trains, the whole night long." He lived, in other words, beside a master icon of the blues, train whistles moaning in the night, "recurrent Negro symbol of yearning." This sound made the whole world wail, with "timbres, accents, and intensities" in the rise of blues and jazz. Visual echoes of which haunted the 1989 Hammons exhibition at Exit Art in New York. An electric train, painted azure to honor an early John Coltrane LP *Blue Train* (Blue Note 1577; 1958) snaked through a mound of coal and a field of upturned piano lids.

His foster grandfather's thrift shop fascinated Hammons. "Two hundred shoes, three hundred garments, all those suits, over my head." "This may relate to clothes in some of the work I do today." Two examples: *Death Fashion* of 1990 and *Central Park West* of 1991.

Claude Champ's transformation of property, telephone pole included, with gleaming lines of white, encoded intelligence in flash. This traces back, ultimately, to ancient Kongo belief that spirit itself is caught—and warded off—in the gleam of mirrors embedded in figurated charms and in the flash of crystals or stones painted white to guard important boundaries.

Perhaps this mode of cultural preparation explains, at least provisionally, why Hammons came to savor Illinois ice storms as works of art. Availing himself of an extraordinary image, he recalled, "The ice-covered trees in Illinois winters were extremely elegant. When it rained on trees and froze, the weather turned the world into a chandelier."

Body Prints

> Judo is the discovery by the human body of a spiritual space.
>
> —Yves Klein, *Les Fondements du Judo*, 1954

In 1963 Hammons left Illinois for subtropical Los Angeles. Some of his siblings were already there. Champ had been dead for several years. There was little to hold him back.

In Los Angeles two years later, summer 1965, the flames of Watts communicated inner city rage to the indifferent suburbs. Watts affected Hammons. "The riots had started. I had to find a medium to express them in."

His choices were wide. Los Angeles of the sixties seethed with modernist vitalities. Some looked to Paris and New York. Others, like Charles White, an African American who trained with the Mexican muralists, was advancing the challenging beauty of African American art and life. White surprised Hammons with his strong outlines and monumental faces, with his very existence, though Hammons was much too independent to imitate him. But White's take on Mexican murals plus the Black Power movement plus Pop Art provided a field of competing energies. The catalyst that brought them together was the California metamorphosis of a Parisian.

Yves Klein, as if anticipating Levi-Strauss structuralism, was then creating art out of the ultimate anthropology, the ultimate structure, the naked human body. For his *Anthropometries of the Blue Epoch*, performed on March 9, 1960, at the Galerie Internationale d'Art Contemporain in Paris, Klein directed three nude models, coated with blue pigment, to imprint their bodies against paper while an orchestra played his *Monotone Symphony*.

In ways that remain fully to be explored, this action reflected insights Klein, a 4th degree Black Belt, acquired in learning judo. It was at the home of a fellow judo enthusiast, Robert Godet, in the spring of 1958, that Klein conducted an experiment: "a naked model smeared with blue . . . creating a monochrome painting by crawling over a sheet of paper laid on the floor." His now famous technique of applying paint with "living brushes" paralleled his belief that judo is "the discovery by the human body of a spiritual space."

The Bakongo of Central Africa, before Klein, had translated athletic moves, like handstands and cartwheels, into passages of the spirit, what Fu-Kiau Bunseki called "walking in the other world." Klein's body-written spiritual spaces converged, therefore, on Central African beliefs. The "soul" that distinguishes twentieth-century black basketball stemmed from this heritage. Hence when Hammons, studying art in Los Angeles, continued to play basketball with fellow blacks, he maintained contact with a subtly spiritualized athleticism. Klein, the judoist, and Hammons, the ballplayer, were unwitting brothers in a search for bodily transcendence.

An instructor at the Chouinard Art Institute in Los Angeles, where Hammons was enrolled, knew of Klein's work with "living brushes." Impressed, the instructor had his students experiment. Enter Hammons:

"I was walking down a hall, looked in a classroom, and saw them doing body prints and went straight home and experimented." Hammons taught himself how to use his body, as Kellie Jones put it, as a "printing plate, smearing it, as well as his clothes and hair, with margarine or other grease. Then, he pressed himself against a board and, finally to set the impression, dusted the board with fine chalk or other pigment (i.e., graphite dust)."

Hammons took almost seven years to refine his mastery of the process. When the smoke cleared, the medium was his. "I was using a Klein technique to achieve a Charles White feel," Hammons recalled, planting a clue as to the nature of his achievement. He "creolized" the Parisian mode to the point where sources disappeared in a cluster of African American improvisations. First, he added a new ingredient—grease, prime element of black cuisine, "cooking" his imprint. Second, he balanced back home funk with another form of elegance—silkscreened patterns of play.

Klein made naked paint-covered women "body brush" blue pigment against sheets of paper, leaving lush, oddly Matisse-like traces of thighs and breasts, heads and buttocks. In contrast, Hammons left careful traces of himself, naked, bare chested, or fully clothed. "It was always a very accurate stamp, never like an Yves Klein, a very clear Renaissance image." "And by using my own body, it definitely became black art."

Bruce Talamon's photographs, ca.1972–73, show Hammons lowering greased head to paper, palms flat upon the floor, and, in another instance, balancing on toes of left sneakered foot and side of right foot, plotting "the logistics of a smudgeless departure." Body prints, in any event, matched the taste of a risk-taking, cocky athlete.

The Wine Leading the Wine is the masterpiece of the body prints. It confronts the fact of alcoholism. The rendering is tragic. One young lush leads a friend into his addiction. The shaping of their bodies, by means of a kind of holy Africanizing symmetry, implies wasted nobility of heritage.

Athletic youth (the baseball cap), ecstasy (drinker's head, tilted back, receiving pleasure), and lean vitality (Hammons's own basketball-disciplined frame) impart aliveness to the composition. As the figure on the left drinks his wine, sheathed in euphemistic paper, the figure on the right taps his buddy's shoulder, begging entrance into his vice. When Hammons made this body print, he executed the face of the drinker first. The look of that face set things in motion. "Something about the expression in that face suggested that a second person should come behind, following in procession."

Half-lights and half-darks eerily immortalize the figures as if caught in the ashes of Pompeii, or the permanent shadows of Hiroshima. The grease, the margarine, which Hammons applied to his own shirt, magically illumines the shirts on the men's dark bodies with the transparency of sweat, creating an intimacy that is disquieting.

The Wine Leading the Wine sold for one thousand dollars. The price signaled the end in this chapter of his career. Had he stayed with body prints, he would have risked predictability. Abandoning them at the height of success was difficult. But he was determined to avoid "slotting," i.e., "artists becoming time-bound to the moment of their greatest contribution and not allowed out of it." Nonetheless, Hammons would maintain his body art. Today, he still uses himself as medium but in miniaturized form and in an entirely different way. In the late eighties, Hammons deftly elaborated a type of black puppetry into what he called "bar-performance pieces" and performed for fellow artists in "the Lower East Side, the last creative haven in all America, Alphabet City."

In a bar near Avenue B and Second Avenue, Hammons dressed the fingers of his right hand with a mime's white glove, placed a doll's boots on the tips of his index and middle fingers, and cut away the cloth of the glove above them. Then he pasted on, immediately above, a Xerox of Joe Louis, glued to a piece of paper. He named the work *Saint Louis*.

The flesh between the two knuckles of his own hand restored black living flesh to the legs of Joe Louis. The motions of his hand reincarnated African American pugilist history. When Hammons again performed his Joe Louis puppet on the sidewalk near the Apollo Theater on 125th Street, he brought back one of Malcolm X's richest memories. "On June twenty-second, nineteen thirty-seven, Joe Louis knocked out James J. Braddock to become the heavyweight champion of the world. And all the Negroes in Lansing, like Negroes everywhere, went wildly happy with the greatest celebration of race pride our generation had ever known." Hammons keeps the celebration going.

Hammons sometimes works with inner tube rubber. His inspiration was the art of the extraordinary Senga Nengudi made from inner tubes as in *Inside/Outside* (1977), a fully realized example of her use of rubber as a "determinant for form." In his apprenticeship to the medium, Hammons uncovered its special logic: "Rubber shapes itself into curtains and folds. The material has its own attitude, like skin, giving and moving, with almost the same thickness."

For *Cobra* (1988), Hammons cut the rubber with a razor and allowed it to surge, in darks and lights, stopping when the image of a hooded cobra came suddenly into focus.

Hammons sewed the rubber to a hard surface, the seat of a chair, to stabilize the figure.

Intuitive linking of rubber's flexibility to blacks in motion enabled Hammons to develop yet another aspect of a distinct aesthetic. *Air Jordan* (1988) honors basketball superstar Michael Jordan whose nickname, Air Jordan, refers to his power to stay in the air, keeping his body flying. Hammons complements this pure felicity.

First, he sexes the composition; the air-stem represents the player's penis. The random folds of rubber equal the calculated nonchalance of Jordan in motion, cool masking imminence of motion. Part of the rubber suddenly surges to the right, like a play completed in the air. Hammons decks this line with cowrie-like bottle caps, honoring the pattern-making reputation of the athlete through allusion to sub-Saharan elegance. *Air Jordan* points to further series where Hammons reclaims the ritual bases of a favorite black sport.

Basketball

> [New York basketball] tradition is so rich that, in the parks, it is broken down into geographical categories. "The great Brooklyn backcourt men are usually outstanding jump shooters," explained Spivey. "The dudes from Harlem tend to drive to the hoop more."
>
> —Pete Axthelm, *The City Game*, 1970

> Basketball is jazz: improvisatory, free, individualistic, corporate, sweaty, fast, exulting, screeching, torrid, explosive, exquisitely designed for letting first the trumpet, then the sax, then the drummer, then the trombonist soar away in virtuoso excellence.
>
> —Michael Novak, *The Joy of Sports*, 1976

> Alone is white.
>
> —Jim Carroll, *The Basketball Diaries*, 1978

Unlike sports in the West, sports south of the Sahara take place in the presence of percussive music. Hammons divined this past and reunited it with United States basketball. He made, for example, an altar to basketball studded with candles and black-eyed peas, a food brought from Africa. The point about cultural transformation is delightfully concrete. Additional works from 1991 fuse the action of electric paint-shakers with basketballs and music. Set to a timer, the machine agitates a ball every five minutes while, simultaneously, playing James Brown soul. Basketball set to music. It recalls the Harlem Globetrotters who moved to the beat of their theme song "Sweet Georgia Brown."

Further back in black athletic tradition, we find ourselves in a ring of handclapping Bakongo in the midst of which drummers encourage wrestlers having at it in the ring. Hammons's 1991 "basketball mobiles" epitomize a transatlantic heritage of merged percussion and sports originating in sub-Sahara Africa. Fusions of athletic combat in the Black Atlantic world include Afro-Cuban *mani*, *ladja* on the island of Martinique, and Afro-Brazilian *capoeira*. The latter art is specially noted for *malicia*. *Malicia* refers to technical cunning, a thousand feints, the arts of deception.

Comparable feints and cunning made serious inroads in United States black athletic culture via Kongo and other sources. We know that on an antebellum plantation in South Carolina slaves born in Africa "did not join the dance with the others, but by themselves gave us a specimen of the sports with which [traditional Africans] divert themselves." This notice illustrates one of the roots of Afro-North American "knocking-and-kicking," an "ancient martial art practiced by slave clergy and their followers," according to John Langston Gwaltney. The fact that knocking and kicking was taught by deacons from the founding days of North American black religion is more than a hint that the linking of sports to spirit, sports to philosophy and religion, had not been broken in transmission from Kongo and elsewhere on the Guinea Coast.

In any event, from the moves and feints in knocking-and-kicking emerged the quintessence of body attack used by U.S. black athletes. With the same roots that sparked *ladja* in Martinique and *capoeira* in black Brazil, they inevitably transformed basketball into a "game of fake and feint and false intention; instantaneous reversal; catlike moves, cool accuracy, spring and jump."

This excursus into the cultural history underpinning the rise of Afro-Atlantic sports and martial arts is meant to deepen our understanding of the kinds of spiritual/athletic forces Hammons marshals and merges.

When he works with basketball, he transforms hoops and backdrops into soaring, beaded icons, lofty chandeliers, high-rise altars to the spirit.

Hammons unveiled his heroically tall "basketball sculptures" twice in Harlem in 1982 and once in 1986 in Cadman Plaza, Brooklyn. The editors of *Sports Illustrated* with their front-line perspective pronounced them "easily understood."

Hammons grew up in Springfield, Illinois, where, he says, he averaged 30 points a game as a junior high guard and made basketball rims out of just about anything he could get his hands on. His basketball pieces are all backboards and rims of some sort. They are partly celebrations of black improvisation and imagination. One of them, however, is also a powerful reminder that advancement through pro sport holds promise for only a lucky few. In 1982, on a rubble-strewn lot in the heart of Harlem, he set up three telephone poles, each with a backboard, 20 to 30 feet above the ground. Into both the backboards and the poles, he had nailed thousands of bottle caps arranged in African and Islamic mosaics. He hung wires from one piece and wind chimes from another and called the piece *Higher Goals*. He later placed a variation of *Higher Goals* in a second Harlem lot and another in a Brooklyn plaza.

"It's an antibasketball sculpture," Hammons has said of *Higher Goals*. "Basketball has become a problem in the black community because the kids aren't getting an education. They're pawns in someone else's game. That's why it's called *Higher Goals*. It means you should have higher goals in life than basketball."

Intricately nailing hundreds of bottle caps across the lengths of three telephone poles for the Cadman Plaza commission alone—clearly this communicates deep affection and cultural commitment as well as a touch of humor. "Basketball gave me the only discipline I ever had. I played twelve hours a day. It was beautiful."

Hammons's reaction to the contemporary fetish of player height generated even more creative sparks. For today's basketball is, one might say, "Nilotic," as in Tutsi and other Nilotes of the eastern Sudan, world famed for their slender, tall bodies. The Nilotes took the Bantu out of the game, Hammons included. In revenge, Hammons lifted his Cadman Plaza hoops twenty to thirty feet into the air, defying the aristocracy of height.

The Cadman Plaza hoops can themselves be interpreted as giant players. Each wears its own bottle-cap mosaic. Each displays strong breaks in pattern; they are icons of on-court unpredictability. One pole shimmers in a wrap of diamond patterning; each diamond sparkles with inner, shifting accents. Another is striped, but the direction of the spirals suddenly is suspended. Still another sports a clash of circular, then linear, then triangular designs, like a player dribbling in, confusing opponents with three breaks in style. A fourth starts with complex interlace. This ceases, without warning, leaving a section of undecorated wood. Hammons garlanded the remaining portion with bottle cap netting, a structure possibly inspired by Afro-Cuban beadwork (*mazos*) used to cover vessels containing sacred stones. Friendship with the late Charles Abramson gave Hammons easy access to this and other forms of Afro-Cuban art.

A fifth pole has shaggy, random clusters of bead-like strands, inspired by an ivy-encrusted tree in Cadman Plaza. "I looked around and the answer (for varying the shape of this particular sculpture) was right next to me. There was a tree that had ivy growing on it—I rode in on that." Wind chimes placed on one of the backdrops made use of wind blowing through Cadman Plaza.

Protean in size, shape, and patterning, these sculptures mirror the grammar of inner city basketball. They can be read as odes to spin-moves, "dribbling forward, planting the left foot, then spinning behind, switching the hand that carries the ball." Or odes to "faking with your eyes, looking one way, passing another." Or to stutter stepping, "blasting full speed down the court, kicking up, hesitating—then exploding." Finally, a handsome "beard" of bottle caps on one of the backdrops exhibited in Brooklyn in December 1990 suggests the antiquity of such feints.

For a 1990 exhibition, *Rousing the Rubble* (Institute for Art and Urban Resources, Queens), Hammons filled an entire exhibition area with handmade hoops, including the example with a "beard," and called the space *Ballroom*. The play on words served notice that Hammons intended to reunite basketball and jazz, recalling the days in the thirties when Harlem lindy hoppers used to warm up playing basketball before they danced to jazz and vice versa.

In another room, Hammons improvised a bandstand/altar to jazz and covered it with tinfoil. "I wanted a little funk." He set the bandstand before a backdrop made from crepe paper to bring back the elegance of Harlem ballrooms in the twenties. His immediate source was the richly pleated structure seen behind Fess Williams and his Royal Flush Orchestra in a photograph, ca.1928, reproduced in *Harlem on My Mind*.

Before this scenario, on opening afternoon, Jemeel Moondoc and the Jus Grew Orchestra played free jazz while A. C. Hudgins, Paul Bryant, Tom Korn, and other friends of Hammons played ball. They used the hoops he had made and fastened to the walls.

In Illinois, when Hammons came back home from church, dressed in shirt and tie, the guys would shout out to him from the courts. Dressed up or not, he would be unable to resist their invitation to play basketball. Hammons brushed in this memory as a stage-direction. "All the guys have to play in shirt and tie." And they did. The implications of the bottle cap mosaics on the wall—Harlem moves brought into simultaneity—dropped to the floor and took on flesh and blood.

Handblock after handblock happened, fingers wide apart, Kongo signs of ecstasy. There were dunk shots galore. Players sometimes held infants up to help them realize their own shots. Stimulated by the incessant jazz, the players filled the room with dribbling between legs, passing behind the back, side-tilted shots, and premier Nilotic leaping. Sweat pasted shirts to bodies.

Then Moondoc suddenly turned around. He faced the athletes. He studied A. C.'s dribbling beat and fit the band's metrics to that pattern. A woman ululated. Jazz was basketball and basketball was jazz. "It was all on time," said Hudgins one year later.

Hegel, had he been there, ghost purified by God of ethnocentrism, might have repeated, ecumenically, words which he wrote with ancient Greece in mind. "Sport presents the higher seriousness; for in it nature is wrought into spirit. In this exercise of physical powers, man shows his freedom, he shows that he has transformed his body into an organ of spirit."

ICE

> Greenland and Antarctica both retain continent-sized glaciers, giving us a sense of what the broader world was like when ice flowed widely.
>
> —Thomas Levinson, *Ice Time*, 1989

Basketball is not the only medium in which Hammons interweaves the ordinary with accents from another world. Master of visual commutation, he substitutes one spirit-laden element for another, continuously engaging chance and change. For instance, frozen water. "There's a metaphor in ice," Hammons says. "Ice always changes. The process is beautiful. You look at this ice, come back—it's changed its shape." Hammons locks memories of Illinois winters into this changing quality. He also refers to an abiding metaphor of discipline and beauty, inner city cool.

Yesterday's King Kool III or Breeze is today's Ice T, Ice Cube. In contemporary hip hop, or so it seems, all the kids have ice names. Hammons works with ice, then, in part to make his art vernacular, in part to attract attention, in part to drive 57th Street crazy, and in part because he never forgot, from his Illinois days, how frozen water transforms space.

In the winter of 1983, Hammons turned snow into objets d'art. He says he just made some snowballs. If so they were, in the words of an admirer, "the most perfect snowballs I've ever seen." They could be assessed and purchased at *Bliz-aard Ball Sale*, an operation Hammons staged the day after a blizzard blanketed New York. He repaired to Canal Street, purchased plastic butter-molds, and, within minutes, mass-produced spheres of ice in graduated sizes. He went north a few blocks to the Cooper Union Art School, chose a strip of sidewalk, spread a Moroccan rug, arranged his wares. Why? In quest of purity. "I felt the need to put myself in a bottom situation, to be ridiculous. It was scary, but I put myself out on the street, to be laughed at, to cleanse myself."

But the tantalizing beauty of the pristine spheres, glittering on the textile from North Africa, changed the situation. True, one joker passed by, remarking that he could make his own snowballs, fuck you very much, and didn't need to buy them. But most who did stop stared in fascination.

Enter a good-looking couple, the guy in dark tweed coat, the woman in Irish sweater. They kneel, they haggle, they buy. The wild look of the shopaholic enters the eyes of the young woman trying to pick out the best ball. Perhaps she knew, instinctively, she was buying from someone exceptional. Perhaps she raced home to her icebox to keep her frozen treasure forever as if in a private Antarctica.

Hammons was amazed to hear a person on television say that one merchant's ice was colder than the ice of a black competitor. "It became a metaphor for the madness of a whole attitude." *Whose Ice Is Colder?* (1990) took this ignorance to the level of deadpan art. He unfurled an African American flag, a Korean flag, and a Yemeni flag, each above a slab of ice. The ice impartially melted beneath the banners. He added a wooden club, stamped *HEAD WARMER*. He was not exhibiting a walking stick. He was illustrating paranoia, the tensions created as blacks, Asians, and Arabs competed for space on the streets of New York City.

Hammons has also used frozen water to comment on the exclusive and the rude. Draping coats over three slabs of ice, he made *Cold Shoulders* (1990).

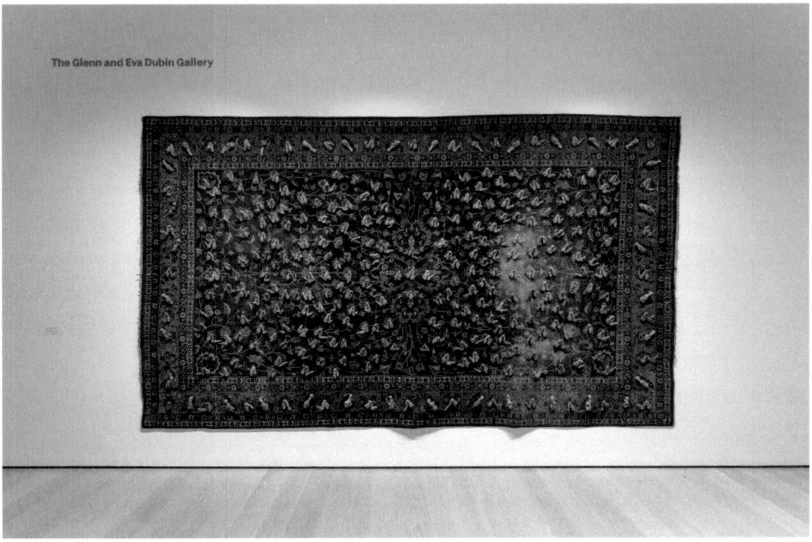

David Hammons, *Flying Carpet*, 1990, Persian rug, wire, and fried chicken, 9 ft. 5 in. × 15 ft. 5 in. × 4 in. (287 × 420 × 10.2 cm.). Installation view from *Just Above Midtown: Changing Spaces*, an exhibition at the Museum of Modern Art, New York, October 9, 2022–February 18, 2023. Photo: Emile Askey. Hudgins Family Collection.
Digital image © 2022 The Museum of Modern Art, New York.

Grease and Fat-Fried Chicken

> Sweet potato pies . . . taste like memory.
>
> —Amiri Baraka / LeRoi Jones, *Home*, 1970

Hammons's capture of African cuisine in America is remarkable. He is alive, like no one else in art I know, to "after-images of dynamism that can be reactivated." This he discovers in the African American culinary presentation of grease, chicken, and bones.

Lady with Bones (1990) recreates a work of 1983 now long gone and itself commemorative. It documented the spirit left in shopping bags, grease, hair, and barbecue bones. The grease that spilled on a black woman's shopping bags, the barbecue spare ribs she fed her children, add up to a calculus of love. Hammons discerned a hidden mathematical order in the number of creases folded into each shopping bag. Using these lines as guides, Hammons pieced several bags together. In the zigzag contours, wings of grease-stained paper centered on a vertical axis of hair suggesting a delicate ascension, as of a kite or butterfly. Hammons has been making kites in paper for more than twenty years.

There are other culinary works: a spare ribs xylophone, "a sculpture" of bone dusted with glitter, a wall installation of fried chicken and chains. All intuit deep fat sizzling, sound of survival, presence of a civilizing grace. Sub-Saharan cooking with fat in a container over fire explains the dominance of "southern fried chicken" in U.S. kitchens sharing this African heritage.

Flying Carpet (1990) takes note of this transatlantic passage in the most sardonic way. It is a "combine": Persian rug with fried chicken wings attached to the textile with fishhooks. The chicken wings add a third dimension to the floral patterns of the rug, turn textile into sculpture. But humor reigns: "Some people eat so many chicken wings they going to fly away." Most viewers at opening day at *Rousing the Rubble* took one look, checked the wall label, and smiled. "If they didn't, they were asleep at the switch," recalled A. C. Hudgins.

Nevertheless, the work exalts a classical cuisine. "Deep fat frying, the Dutch found out in seventeenth-century New Amsterdam, was an African specialty. There are probably more restaurants in Harlem whose staple is fried chicken than in any other place in the world." No wonder Charles Mingus composed a jazz tune called "Eat That Chicken." Dizzy Gillespie spotlit Chano Pozo's composition "Manteca" (grease), and Anthony Braxton confounded the critics of Paris by eating fried chicken as part of a 1969 performance. Hammons phrased it this way: "The roots were laid out. I simply brought them to the visual arts."

Hair

> So, Rome has finally been given back to herself . . .
> Ethiopians, with their hair all in knots
> The multiple sounds of the voices
> of your people.
>
> —Martial, *Epigrams*, ca. 100 CE

> *nsinga a mayembo*,
> telegraph line (lit. ecstasy on the wire)
>
> —Wyatt MacGaffey, *Art and Healing of the Bakongo Commented by Themselves: Minkisi from the Laman Collection* (Stockholm: Folkens Museum—Etnografiska, 1991)

> Roots natty congo I.
>
> —Bob Marley, "Natty Dread," 1974

Ancient Greece and Rome esteemed the hair of Africans. There was no color line. Blacks were simply different. They were, like blonde Scythians, emblems of the furthest reaches of the world. At the opening of the Colosseum, Martial celebrated "Ethiopians, with their hair all [done] in knots" as part of the voices of "Rome given back to herself."

Much later came the Atlantic slave trade. This generated a negative correlation in the mind of the West that linked blacks to slavery and menial labor. African languages were consequently downgraded to "dialects," nations to "tribes," richness of literature to "animal tales." It was all part of a pattern of what Anthony Braxton termed "suppressing African intellectual dynamics."

African hair was similarly "othered" in Roman antiquity. Pliny the Elder noted the distinctive nature of sub-Saharan hair with a striking phrase, *capillo vibrato*, as if African coiffure were a form of music. The associative values of slavery and racism changed all that. In the United States, black hair became "nappy" from an old English adjective for shaggy. Short, kinky African hair became "bad," straight European hair "good."

Malcolm X, whose life and example liberated millions from such self-effacement, revealed with characteristic frankness, how he himself, in the late thirties when he was a Roxbury, Massachusetts, homeboy, had been "conked":

> "Feel the jar," Shorty said. I cupped my hand against the outside and snatched it away. "Damn right, it's hot, that's the lye," he said. "So you know it's going to burn when I comb it in—it burns bad. But the longer you can stand it, the straighter the hair."

In the sixties in the wake of black African independence, African American coiffure emerged as a language of heritage and identity. Imagine the emotion Hammons and Betye Saar felt when, in 1972 at the Chicago Field Museum, they found themselves before an African shirt, studded with clumps of wiry hair. This hair was not hidden, nor straightened. It was worn as the very declaration of a person. Saar and Hammons interpreted what they were viewing as a cultural critique of a history of shame.

> [Betye Saar] took this photo at the Chicago Field Museum a couple of weeks ago. And I remember the day we discovered [in] a basement full of African/Oceanic art [this] coat covered with nappy hair [which] triggered a lot out of us.

Their response to this hair shield paralleled Bob Marley's 1974 reggae text, "Natty Dread," in which he exhorted black Jamaicans to "get their culture" by returning to their Kongo heritage, their roots, their knotty, nappy hair. "I couldn't believe it," Hammons recalled. He started using black hair in perfect enactment of the manifesto: "Our hair is positive, powerful . . . It all depends on who is seeing it, and we've been depending on someone else's sight."

His colleague in LA, Senga Nengudi, helped. "Why don't you," she suggested, "put hair in the end of your cornet," i.e., put the fiber in a shape that existed, let the object hold the hair. Which was exactly what he later did. He first mixed the medium experimentally with grease-stained shopping bags and bones. Hammons, with further work, let experience guide him into sequence. Much as he had adapted a tea strainer in making his body prints, he transformed a window screen into a sieve/filter for the hair.

Rubbing the material over the screen released contrasting essences. Fine dust passed through the sieve. Hammons glued the sediment to supporting surfaces, like stones. Or he shaped it into geometric forms, like pyramids. Using the screen as filter, Hammons plucked clumps of hair adhering to the upper surface and used them as inserts on long wires.

In the late seventies, he did a dreadlock series and created several other installations featuring hair. In these the hair was attached to found objects or placed behind glass in frames. In one instance he incorporated hair-threaded wires with a Yoruba mask suspended from the ceiling and provided with a gown of plastic. Hammons recaptured lost texts of sub-Saharan grace as he threaded minute gatherings of nappy hair on upright wire, then added eggshells to symbolize delicacy and rubber bands to symbolize the ordering of hair by African American mothers. Another gesture of recollection.

Hair-studded wires, each with its own rhythmic signature, left standing in the sand, breakers coming in on the beach at Venice, California.

In Jamaica, Rastafarians consider dreadlocks antennae to God. Traditionalist Bakongo in Central Africa interpret the hum of telegraph wires as an ecstasy of communication with the other world. Hammons's celebrations of black hair as pulsing wire touch upon these potent images. He found that sifted hair could be molded to assume stable forms. In a 1976 installation, he shaped such sediment into twenty-nine small, black pyramids. He organized their placement on the floor in syncopated patterns, open and closed. Nappy hair redistilled in ancient avatars of permanence and resurrection. This led, logically, to hair-embellished stones—building on further emblems of immortality.

On a Wednesday afternoon, fall 1991, Hammons took a stone, sifted hair glued on top, to a Harlem barbershop. The barber gave the stone a haircut. The triumph was double. The barber vindicated the magic reality of the work, adding elegance to a horizon of black indestructibility.

Bottles

Hammons's vision into abandoned wine bottles, into the mentality and experience they embody, is potent. With a clairvoyance equal to his reading of the nuances locked in nappy hair, he translates bottles left by winos on the streets of Harlem into altars to their spirit.

Kick the Bucket (1989) maps points along an alcoholic's life, contrasting pleasure to finality. The drinkers pass through coal, the color of their skin, the warmth of the liquor in their being, the sounds of Coltrane jazz they grooved to, getting high. And then they "kick the bucket" and die, from cirrhosis or other consequences of addiction.

Without prompting from readings in Kongo lore, Hammons is well aware of what it means to work with bottles once touched by human lips. Jamming such bottles on the branches of wild ginkgo trees, which defiantly push up in the debris-scattered vacant blocks of Harlem, Hammons makes the barrios face facts another way. He knows all the places where the winos hide their bottles under mailboxes, inside street lamps, between buildings. Displaying liquor bottles on high, Hammons at once exalts traces of the spirit and arrests the seal and substance of addiction. Great storms of being and despair laugh and cry in the glass suspended on these ginkgos in the lots of Harlem.

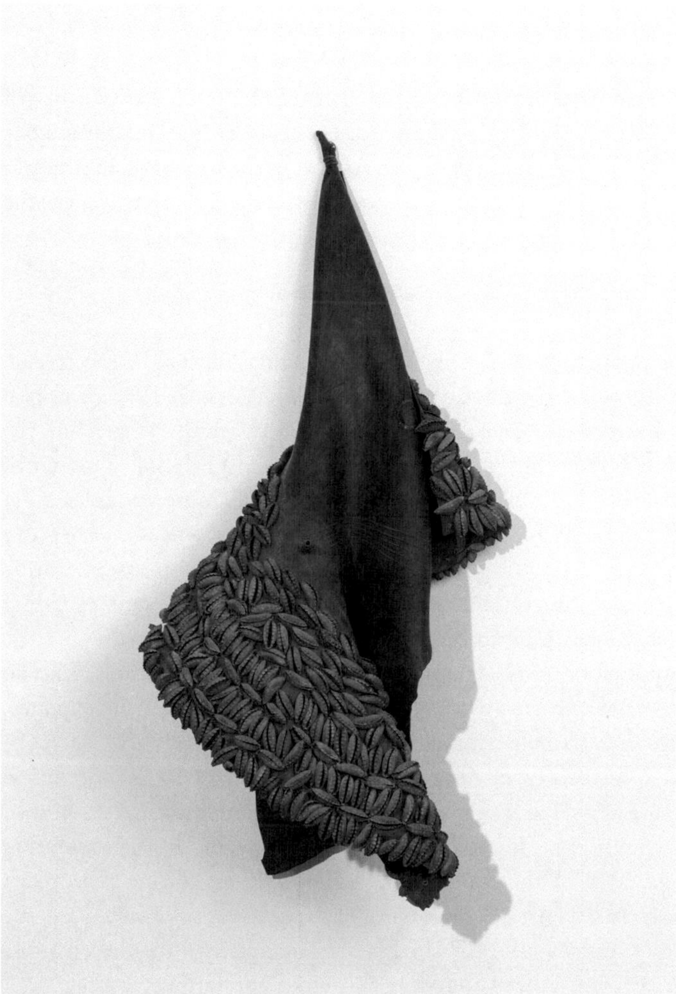

David Hammons, *Air Jordan*, 1988, found object with tire and beads, 34 × 16 × 8½ in. Hudgins Family Collection.

Envoi

> If it were expected of the anthropologist that he predict the future of humanity, he would undoubtedly not conceive of it as a continuation or a projection of present types, but rather on the model of an integration, progressively unifying the appropriate characteristics of the "cold" [traditional] societies and the "hot" [technocratic] ones.
>
> —Claude Lévi-Strauss, *The Scope of Anthropology*, 1967

Hammons spent time, 1989–91, in Rome, bringing Harlem to the eternal city. He funked up Italy as fluently as he did New York. A 1993 example: *Fear Not: La Mosca nella Zuccheriera*. This roughly translates as, I'm the fly in the sugar bowl—but don't worry about me, I'm cool. This work unites a sugar bowl and a black fly. Yes, the fly is Hammons, amused "at being virtually the only black in the American Academy in Rome." Read another way, however, you glimpse his ability to divine pleasure in difference, sweetness in uncertainty. "Over here," Hammons said, meaning New York, "there are many more flies than there are sugar bowls."

In the summer of 1991, Hammons constructed a gutbucket fountain with trickling water and tape deck bells. A "portrait of Rome," he explains, "fountains and church bells ringing every fifteen minutes." He has constructed other fountains from African masks, a parody of Roman love and skill at street theater. Hammons plays with European culture. The humor is relentless, always "on." In August 1990 he participated in the exhibition *Casino Fantasma*, one of the few alternative exhibitions during that year's Venice Biennale. In the entrance courtyard of the casino, he decorated a statue of Venus with armfuls of fake Gucci bags and gold chains—the merchandise hawked by Senegalese street vendors in Italy's art and fashion capitals.

The affection hidden in these installations shows us Hammons transplanted to Europe, alive to possibility and love as well as to hurt and accident. "I like Rome," he says. "I don't know what it is, it's fun." It's typical of him to have noticed the baroque paper hats of Roman construction workers and to have brought one back to Harlem. Only Hammons could answer the elegance of a velvet-walled room in Italy with the grittier velours of the mind of Thelonius Monk. He filled the room with Monk's own jazz (Monk's Music Riverside OJC-5084, 1957) sounding from a boombox on tiny wheels.

To live in the heart of Western ethnocentrism yet press home debate on the alternative importance of the Afro-Atlantic world is no mean accomplishment. Conversely, had Hammons not lived in Italy, he might not have discovered the material—if that is the word for glow-in-the-dark images of Jesus—with which he would come to build one of the most memorable installations of his career.

In 1989 in a flea market in Rome, Porta Portese, on a narrow, crowded street that reminded him of Harlem, Hammons purchased one hundred miniature images of Jesus. He comments, "Porta Portese, that's the only place where you'd find that many images of Jesus." Later, he was to use them to satirize elitist pomp while, at the same time, honoring the human quest for moral wisdom that Jesus, like Lord Buddha, so richly represents.

In Roman churches, Hammons noted there were "about twenty chandeliers to one icon of Jesus." He determined to correct this equation. His ambition was to turn Jesus into one vast chandelier, to show the heavens opening up in light.

Assessing space for his retrospective of December 1990 [not to be confused with *David Hammons: The Unauthorized Retrospective* in New York City at Triple Candie], Hammons discovered one room without windows. It was the perfect setting for realizing his vision. Seventy-five luminescent, miniature images of Jesus from his Roman hoard were soon suspended from the ceiling on threads of different lengths. The effect was startling and direct. "Jesus flyin' rather than dyin'." Gospel music, Aretha's "Jesus Is the Light of the World," subtitled the space while lights went on and off.

When the room went dark, the images turned to stars. The universe became a chandelier. Black Illinois and Rome were one. There were several persons on opening afternoon, December 16, 1990, who did not move when the lights went on. They stayed for multiple immersions in the darkness redeemed by figurated light.

Bakongo see meteors as the flashing spirits of the noblest dead, *bisimbi*. Christians read into a single star the birth of Jesus. In Hammons's orchestration, the one-point Western Jesus fused with an African-constellated Jesus, intense and all-including, like the multiple avatars of a single *orisha*, like the subsets of a single healing Kongo charm.

This room captured, then, the essence of his art-wager on an heroic scale. The Harlem artist is betting on spirit and meaning sensed in ordinary things to be our armor in the twenty-first century.

Wreaking Havoc on the Signified

Coco Fusco

On entering David Hammons's recent show in a TriBeCa shop, one was handed a list of works. The roster served to orient those who preferred not to take on the test of art world savvy posed by the exhibition. One's grasp of things could be measured by whether one knew, for example, that the stack of toilet paper on the table was not the store manager's weekly supply, but one of the artist's trademark sardonic one-liners. Lodged within and between exotic artefacts from Africa and Asia were more than a dozen of Hammons's conceptual sight-gags. A ragged kimono was draped over a soiled slip, complete with protruding, bloody tampon. Nestled among the miniatures was a doll-sized lounge chair with a greying wad of gum stuck to its underside. On a wall hung a row of beef bones still held together by dried flesh, wryly titled *Marimba Ribs* (1994). Peeping out of a handsome wooden dresser was a wooden mallard adorned with bits of white bandaging tape entitled *Tape Duck* (1994). Through these and other pieces that both clashed with and played off the shop's own eclectic fare, Hammons eloquently commented on the kind of spectatorial desire that binds him and his increasingly fetishized work to the regular collectibles at Knobkerry, the boutique.

The message was conveyed with humor; jokes were there for those who could decipher them. No viewing of Hammons's work would be complete without a thorough reading of the network of relationships between his culturally loaded titles and jarringly juxtaposed found objects. The artist has often been characterized as a sophisticated junk dealer who breathes new life into paper bags, bottle caps, frizzy hair, snowballs, rocks,

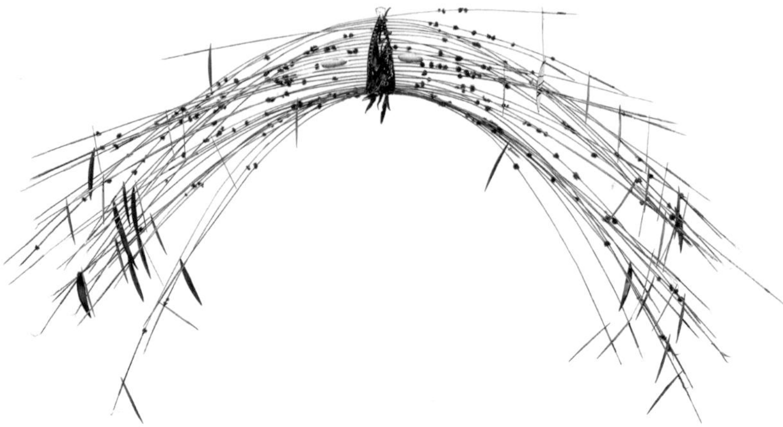

David Hammons, *Flight Fantasy*, 1978, phonograph record fragments, hair, clay, plaster, feathers, bamboo, colored string, 38 × 56 in. Collection Walker Art Center, Minneapolis, T. B. Walker Acquisition Fund, 1995.

broken appliances, old clothes, rugs, grease and half-eaten ribs. He is, in actuality, a masterful investigator of how an oppositional black cultural identity can be generated through a dialogue with "high" culture, particularly as it is articulated through standard English. His method relies on punning and other kinds of word games that short-circuit the dominant cultural interpretation of any given object or term to be redirected for his own purpose.

Hammons's artful play transports the black linguistic act of "signifyin'" analyzed by literary critic Henry Louis Gates in his landmark study, *The Signifying Monkey*, into the realm of the visual.[1] Charting the evolution of this approach to language from its origins in Yoruba and Fon cultures in Africa to its many diasporic transmutations in the New World, Gates defines *signifyin'* and its archetypal representation in the mythology of the signifyin' monkey as the quintessential form of black creativity. Operating in homonymic relation to the standard English term *signifying*, the black variant, even in its own materiality, stakes out a space for a culturally specific practice of creating new meaning through an alteration of the relationship between a given term (signifier) and its usual meaning (signified). Beginning with early references to this practice in slave testimony,

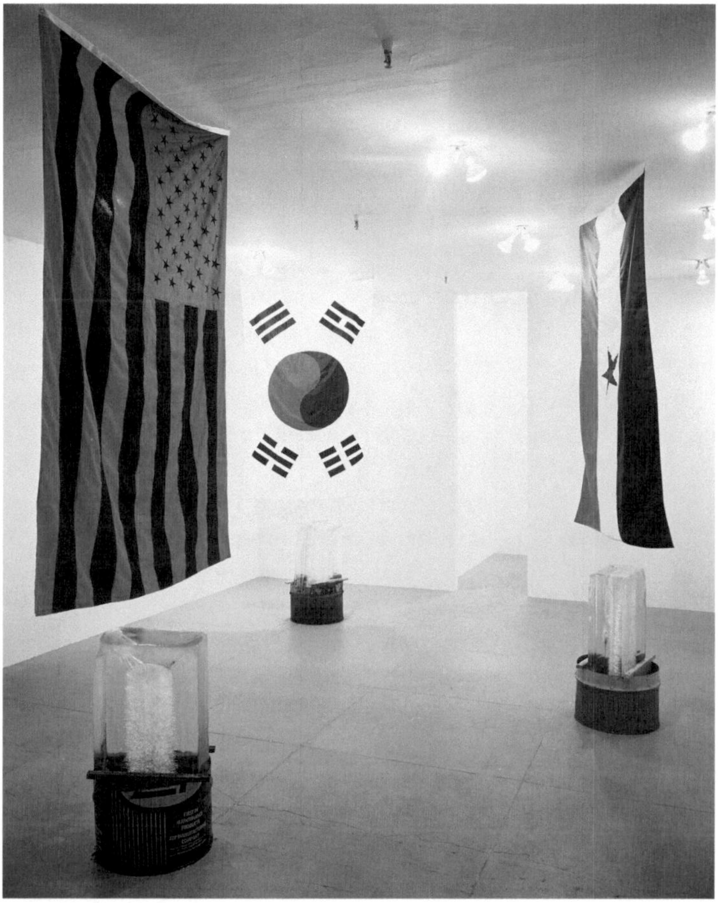

David Hammons, *Whose Ice Is Colder?*, 1990, Jack Tilton Art Gallery.

Gates finds evidence of signifyin' in black oral and written literature, black performative speech, and black music. Within the context of his analysis, the oft-cited techniques of jazz, which involve the constant realignment of already existent musical signifiers, take on a particularly powerful cultural resonance.

Signifyin', according to Gates, involves taking, twisting and transforming English to make it otherwise. It implicitly revindicates *imitation* as a creative gesture, over and against a legacy of negative, Eurocentric appraisal of black literature and culture as unoriginal. To signify is to rework received meanings; the difference between the literal and the metaphorical is thrust into the foreground by an approach that operates by implication, indirect communication, imagistic rendering, rhythmic delivery, and parody. Noting how this method is rooted in vernacular speech patterns and is passed on from generation to generation, Gates cites numerous examples of how signifyin' relies on shared black experience for the evocation of its double entendres; he also emphasizes how this black expressivity is immanently performative.

Designating signifyin' as the "trope of tropes." Gates suggests that its stress on the materiality of the signifier provides a critical rationale for shifting the interpretations of black cultural production away from an exclusively social and political matter of content, to a close reading of the interplay of form, style, context, referencing and subject. Black cultural production, be it oral, written or visual, Gates argues, is experienced most fruitfully when appreciated intertextually, as it relies heavily on its referencing of other texts, both western (white) forms and black literature, legacies and histories. The signifyin' monkey, incarnating the performative dimension of the reinterpretative utterance, occupies the crucial mediating position in this paradigm.

David Hammons is as inextricable from his work as Gates' monkey is from the signifyin' practice. No account of Hammons's art is entirely devoid of references to his streetwise, resolutely anti-elitist persona. He has become infamous for his acerbic appraisals of high art, and his willed cultivation of a split between a black interpretative community to which he directs his messages, and a now admiring (once indifferent) white art world he loves to snub, tease and confuse. This approach is carried over into his artwork. Hammons is one of the few human beings in the world who can sell snowballs and doll's shoes on the street as performance and make money, or urinate on another artist's work—also as performance and social commentary. Like the signifyin' monkey and the practice he enacts, Hammons's performative presence shines through his funky rearrangements of urban debris and cultural icons. His visualization of signifyin' involves several interrelated key strategies. He works off familiar, highly charged iconography; he creates parodies that deflate pretension and conservatism; and his puns conjure up some of the more contradictory and even painful aspects of contemporary black life.

Hammons's own explanation of his motives foregrounds the role of language in circumscribing black identity and experience. "I was trying to figure out why Black people were called spades as opposed to clubs . . . So I took the shape, and started painting it," he noted in a 1986 interview with Kellie Jones.[2] Significantly, his exploration of the epithet came precisely at a point when members of the flowering Black Arts Movement were encouraged, if not compelled, to celebrate blackness, a call to which his works form an abject counterpoint. His *Spade* series of the mid-70s exploits the manifold meanings ascribed to the term as a means of chipping away at its negative inscription of black identity. In his 1974 print *Spade*, he shoves his face against the shape leaving a caricature-like imprint of his Negroid features. Hammons literally deflates the impact of the verbal insult by flattening it. In various sculptures, he recasts the word's derogatory meaning by stressing its literal one. *Spade with Chains* (1973) transforms rusted, wasted shovels into ironic allusions to slavery and incarceration; and Charlie Parker becomes a spade spouting from a saxophone in *Bird* (1973). Not only was Hammons here diverging from a larger trend toward unequivocally positive views of blackness, but this use of culturally resonant found objects signals an absolutely fundamental shift in black aesthetic experimentation from mimetic representational forms to more oblique, metaphorical renderings of black experience.

Hammons's continuing reworking of the relationship between materials, images and their meanings focuses on two primary targets—the pretense and commercialism of "high" art and its exclusionary milieu, and the misguided, even limiting objectives and values of sectors of the black middle class. Works such as *Flying Carpet* (1990) in which fried chicken wings are arranged on a suspended Persian rug, or *Hairpiece* (1975), in which hair cuttings are woven onto free standing wire rods, are coy send-ups of minimalism, and of dominant cultural constructions of exoticizing clichés about otherness. Hammons's many works using brown paper bags smeared with grease and chewed over rib bones push such investigations a few steps further, calling into question which substances can legitimately represent blackness within the context of art. These pieces poke fun at the aspirations of a kind of social posturing and art making (engaged in by both blacks and whites) that attempts to obfuscate its connection to their roots in popular culture.

Other works take swipes at short-sighted materialist values in American life. Indeed, part of Hammons's way of tempering his own success has been to play the role of the sly jester, pointing to the hypocrisies and contradictions implicit in whatever context he finds himself. His oversized basketball hoops, exquisitely adorned with bottle caps in mock-Islamic designs, become blistering critiques of black youths' obsession with financial success through sports stardom as the admonitory title, *Higher Goals* (1986), comes into focus. Equally critical of their white counterparts, Hammons caused a public relations scandal in 1993 with his pranksterish send-up of the preppy tastes of Williams College's student body—a mundane looking boulder topped with broken ventilators, set in the middle of the school's main lawn entitled *Rock Fan*. In a sardonic homage to that generation's parents, Hammons had already draped a *Venus de Milo* with fake Louis Vuitton bags and re-baptized her as *Bag Lady*, lampooning the consumerist style of aesthetic reception at the 1990 Venice Biennale. Finally, his balloon-festooned barricading of a reproduction of a Teddy Roosevelt monument flanked by a docile Indian and a black servant, aptly dubbed *Public Enemy* (1991), forced the social contradictions implicit in his own presence in a Museum of Modern Art out into the open. Hammons refused to be dislocated for the *Dislocations* show—instead, he relocated and subverted the racist pomp in both the monument he appropriated and the paternalist attitudes of the mainstream multiculturalist policies that affect him.

As Hammons's work in particular and Black American contemporary art in general have gained international recognition in the past decade, critical interpretations of the artist's work have begun to include more attention to the cultural specificity of his practice, rather than assuming that his content is black while his method comes largely from Duchamp and Arte Povera. While the "authenticity" of his expression has often ridden on his "location"—that is, his history of operating out of Harlem—and on his material referencing of black culture, it has nonetheless been the artworks that have evoked an inter- and intra-ethnic struggle over recognizable political icons and have facilitated Hammons's "crossing-over," garnering him national notoriety. The most recent upsurge in his popularity began in 1988 with a public-art scandal involving his piece, *How Ya Like Me Now?* Hammons's billboard of a blond, pale-faced Jesse Jackson incurred the wrath of a group of Washington, D.C., youths, whose response to the artist's wry appraisal of the black political leader was to bludgeon it with sledgehammers.

Nearly two decades earlier, at the beginning of his career, his body prints incorporating the American flag and allusions to black unrest in the late 60s and early 70s, thrust Hammons into the art scene in Los Angeles, where he then lived. At the time, the artist was somewhat unsure about the implications of achieving commercial success through the representation of such events as the binding and gagging of Black Panther Bobby Seale during the Chicago Eight trial, works such as *Injustice Case* (1973) (whose title carries Hammons's signature word play) are singularly powerful renderings of the frustration, rage and skepticism about unfulfilled promises in black communities during the period just after the Civil Rights movement. Hammons has continued to work with flags since that time, recoloring the American banner to remake it as an African-American hybrid, and sometimes hanging it outside his exhibitions to demarcate a black symbolic and geo-political territory.

Signifyin's primary purpose, Henry Louis Gate asserts, is to redress the balance of power between white and black cultures through the recasting of an imposed nomenclature. Throughout his career, Hammons has deployed those signifyin' strategies to straddle two worlds. His visual experiments with "non-traditional" materials are much more than simple formal gestures, for he strategically chooses the detritus with which he works to evoke aspects, attitudes and sensibilities of Black American culture. His work is an absolutely critical bridge that links the radical populism of the late 30s and 60s, which influenced his earlier development as a black artist, the experimental vocabularies of the 70s, and the resurgence of interest in vernacular culture in the 80s and 90s. More than a sophisticated junk dealer, Hammons sifts through our society's waste to show us just how powerfully it can speak to the unfinished business of troubled race relations in America, which continues to irk us as we approach the millennium.

Notes

1. Henry Louis Gates Jr., *The Signifying Monkey: A Theory of African-American Literary Criticism* (New York: Oxford University Press, 1988).

2. Kellie Jones, "The Structure of Myth and the Potency of Magic," in *David Hammons: Rousing the Rubble* (New York: The Institute of Contemporary Art and Cambridge, MA: MIT Press, 1991), p. 24.

In the Thick of It: David Hammons and Hair Culture in the 1970s

Kellie Jones

After a decade of success with works on paper (the popular Body Prints), David Hammons walked away from these framed and easily saleable objects. A growing interest in the works of Marcel Duchamp revealed the allusive and metaphoric power of everyday items. The stance of the Dada movement—at once critical, or politically charged and playful—also pointed to another way one could combine art-making with an interest in the world from which it sprang. Hammons's immersion in the southern California art scene, home to strong currents of Funk and assemblage, was another impetus for the change of practice.

Since his arrival in Los Angeles in the early 1960s, a critical mass of African American artists had increasingly worked in this manner, lacing their constructions with an edge of African American cultural symbolism.[1]

Hair—that tangible crown of African American "difference"—was one such common item that Hammons submitted to this new active and all-encompassing approach to art-making, and through which his work moved more clearly into the realm of the environmental.

Kobena Mercer, Judith Wilson, and Lisa Jones have all recently jumped into and furthered the debate about the cultural and political significance of African American and African diasporic approaches to the "hair question." As Mercer has pointed out, hair is a naturally occurring organic bodily matter that is "socialized . . . constantly processed by cultural practices which thus invest it with meaning and value."[2] Or in Jones's words, "hair is never left 'as is.' Hair exists to be worked."[3] And "working it," with all the sense of exertion, effort, and performance that the verbal

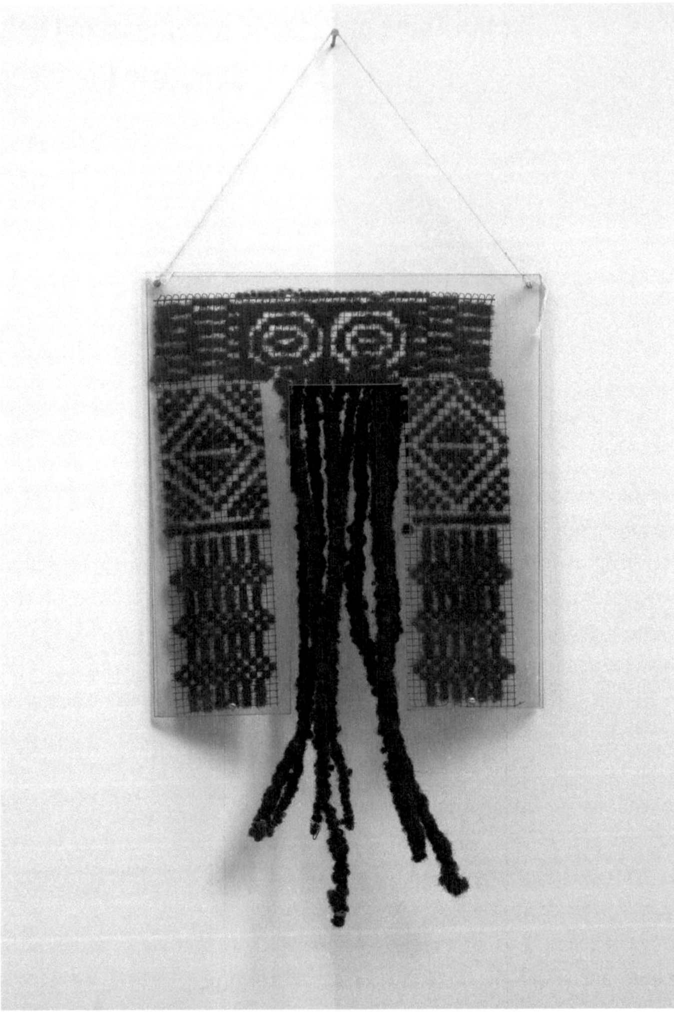

David Hammons, *Nap Tapestry*, ca. 1976, hair, metal wire, plexiglass, 24 × 14½ × 3 in. Hudgins Family Collection.

root conjures, is certainly what is done; indeed, "styling" may be a tad too polite, dainty, and hands-off approximation for what is staged on and in black hair. Wilson's investigations of African approaches to the care and cultivation of hair have revealed an esteem for "abundance" and "mass and volume" as signs of "strength and fertility."[4] The idea of opulence is also paired with artifice:

> [W]here western culture generally condemns most forms of body adornment or alteration as vain, deceitful, grotesque, tasteless, or at best merely frivolous, Africans tend to view *failure* to supplement, transform, or otherwise improve on nature as a lapse of character or a breach of decorum.[5]

Wilson sees this passion for formal invention and innovation as another aspect of the aesthetics of abstraction, one that we easily recognize in traditional African sculpture.

Hair thus becomes an important vehicle for expression. And in African-diasporic practice, as a "popular *art form*," it is a method through which Black people have been able to convey their sense of the beautiful and their creative aspirations, in the face of historical exclusion "from access to official social institutions of representation."[6]

There are dreadlocks, afros or naturals, relaxed dos, conks, close cuts, Jheri curls, braids, and various styles of each and numerous stages in between. Jones's description of braided creations speaks lovingly of the art that she sees, particularly on women's heads: "[T]hese are not simply hair-dos; these are elaborate constructions, with hair piled high, woven with ornaments and shaped like fans, wedding cakes, hourglasses, and halos. Maybe they're crowns, maybe they're altars. Extensions here are used not to showcase length or 'naturalness.' This is hair as textile, fiber art, as nothing less than sculpture."[7]

African American hair initially appeared in David Hammons's work in a series of two-dimensional constructions for the wall. These were first shown in New York in 1975 at the Just Above Midtown Gallery under the title *Greasy Bags and Barbecue Bones*. The fan-like pieces were collages that had escaped the traditional rectangular format and seemed to revel in their movement across space. Constructed from discarded brown paper bags, and lacquered erratically with common household oil, they were then embellished with tufts of hair, spare-rib bones, and glitter. Originally the hair and the glitter provided only decorative touches. They were applied sparingly, in geometric patterns, and appeared at first glance as areas painted on each piece.

These become most visible in a sporadic series of sculptural arrangements Hammons installed along Los Angeles beaches between 1975 and 1977. An array of nappy hair balls, approximately a half inch or less in diameter, were threaded on lengths of flexible wire standing three to five feet high. The wires were curved and bent in places, and the tufts followed their lines, creating irregular dashes and dots like some new-found system of counting—an African-Americanized version of Morse code, abacuses, or quipus.

The artist cultivated his new gardens at the shoreline, taking advantage of the solidity of the wet sand for planting the wires, and the drama of the crashing waves on the horizon and the mirror-like reflective ground, to add to the work's potency. Hammons planted and replanted his temporary and ephemeral hair gardens in a variety of Los Angeles beach sites over the two- year period.

For his second solo New York outing at Just Above Midtown in 1976, he presented a full show of works in which black hair was the principal medium. The exhibition, titled *Dreadlock Series*, was inspired by the "hairstyles of Rastafarians," a press release proclaimed. Along with indoor "sculpture gardens" of hair and wire, the gallery also presented wall "drawings" composed primarily from "the interweavings of hair and rubber bands."[8]

While today, dread—or African or Nubian—locks can be found gracing the pages of women's magazines, or the characters of daytime television, in the mid-seventies 70s this seemingly unkempt hairstyle was the preserve of cultural rebels.

If American process works and European arte povera used all sorts of materials, from felt to hay and chalk to dirt, no one had worked with black hair in such a manner. And certainly it was not just Hammons's simple use of this fiber that made it new and different, but its positioning as an allegorical statement, and one that spoke of redemption and self-love. Hammons's exhibition of the *Dreadlock Series*, during the hoopla of the Bicentennial year, was both a celebration of the incredible facets of black hair and by extension the black self, and a subtle reminder of the place of the black body as commodity in the making of the United States.

Two further solo exhibitions of hair pieces took place in 1977, in the spring at Just Above Midtown, and later that fall at the Neighborhood Art

Center in Atlanta, Georgia, with the title, *Nap Tapestry: Wire and Wiry Hair*. Along with free-standing gardens and rubber-band-based wall drawings, these shows also contained ersatz quilts or textiles Hammons created by stuffing hair into wire screens. There were also new floor-based sculptures of molded hair, such as *Hair Pyramids*.

Writing in the *Soho Weekly News*, John Perreault was intrigued by the work's construction and struck by the power and beauty of the New York show. At one point the critic asks, "[H]ow does one go about making abstract art and still have it come out distinctly Afro-American? Hammons's hair sculpture is his answer. It is an 'outrageous' answer but it works."[9]

Like so many artists of his generation—Jack Whitten, William T. Williams, and Sam Gilliam all come to mind—Hammons was, indeed, searching for an abstract voice—like jazz—that could be identified as distinctly African American; something that could be non-objective in form and coded with (self-) reference, without relying on representation. In hair he seemed to have found his holy grail. As he commented in 1991, "I got to a visual object and medium that was pure [and] nonsexual, which spoke everything I wanted to say."[10]

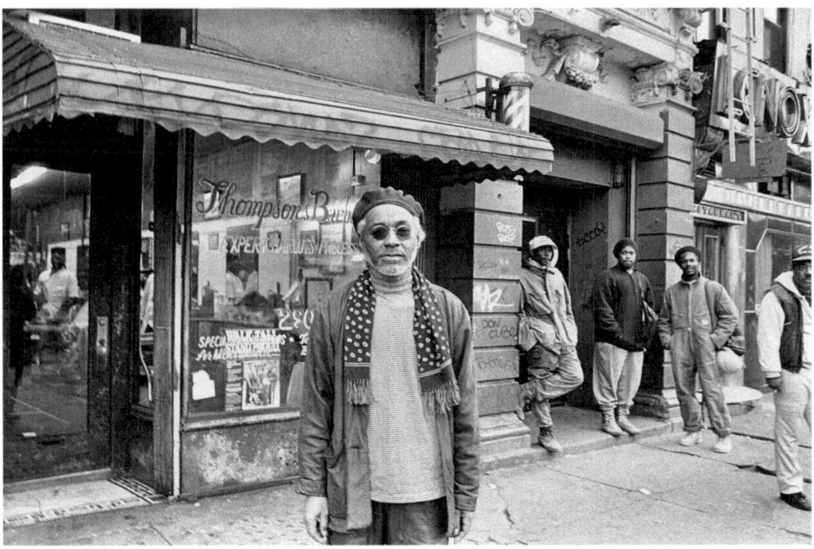

David Hammons, *Haircut*, 1992, performance in Harlem.
Photograph © Coreen Simpson.

Hammons had discovered a way to articulate "blackness" without relying on the painted or sculpted figure. His use of hair as an artistic medium allowed him to create culturally defined meaning while still working within the arena of late-twentieth-century Western form and style. However, in part because this organic matter was an actual physical piece of a human being, these works remained inscribed within the highly charged terrain of the black body. As Judith Wilson has noted, the "use of kinky hair as an ethno-cultural signified fail[ed] to dismantle the stable, biologically-determined classificatory systems . . ." that had adversely defined Black people for centuries.[11]

Hammons's quest for his own abstract visual language has brought him back again and again to the jazz paradigm. Throughout his career he has incorporated it into his work either as homage, or as an actual performative element. He has counted musicians like Charlie Parker and Sun Ra as his creative mentors rather than an earlier generation of African American artists because he felt his break with that tradition was so complete.[12]

For Hammons, jazz musicians, not visual artists, are the keepers of the black avant-garde tradition. From Bessie Smith's blues to Duke Ellington's suites, from be-boppers like Dizzy Gillespie to the "free-jazz" of Ornette Coleman, it is a large and rich trajectory. Yet, it is not only the structural intricacy of the music that Hammons admires, but the enigma of the creative being, the nattily dressed virtuoso cutting a mean figure out in the world, the brilliance that refuses to be categorized or controlled. It is the mythology of the Jazzman as transgressor; and, yes, it is almost an exclusively male club.

If Hammons has endeavored to model himself in the image of the jazz master, the material sources and reality of his installations with hair speak of other origins. He has collected hair from barber-shops and even staged a performance in one where a rock with hair attached has been shaved, thus intentionally locating the site of his practice within a masculine arena. His use of dreadlocks as a motif also draws on the sphere of male culture within the Rastafarian movement.

But let's get real: who has more salons dedicated to this practice, pays more attention to these aesthetics, has more styling options and usually just more hair—WOMEN. As much as Hammons would insist on the non-gendered role of hair in his work, the manipulation of hair is largely identified with a female creative space.

Lisa Jones may sound a bit fanatic when she states, ". . . everything I've done with my hair explains everything I've done with my life and my art. . . . Hair is the be-all and end-all."[13] But what her book and passions pay tribute to is the place of women's imagination and ingenuity. The orchestration of hair as art-form becomes both the embodiment of and a shorthand for this feminist vision. For Jones, the essential, driving force of her feminism, outside of the "big political issues," springs from

> . . . a passion for the creative culture of women and a belief that communion with other women [is] a bread and water necessity . . . what [keeps] me interested in feminism and *identifying* is the pleasure.[14]

Hair is thus a tangible symbol of African American women's creativity and joy. As bell hooks has written:

> [G]etting our hair pressed . . . is not a sign of our longing to be white. . . . It is a sign of our desire to be women. . . . It is a rite of passage. . . . There is a deeper intimacy in the kitchen on Saturday when hair is pressed, when fish is fried, when sodas are passed around, when soul music drifts over the talk. We are women together. This is our ritual and our time.[15]

While hair culture represents inventiveness and pleasure, through it African American women are also able to realize their own sense of ceremony as well as space, by establishing a place where hair rites can be enacted.

So what are men like David Hammons doing there in the first place?

What indeed. If we look at Jones's take on an exchange between black men and black women on this topic we find that, in many instances, it is not a party to which they have been invited: "Then the moment we'd all been waiting for; *Essence* [magazine] invited men to comment on women's hair practice. Men gave thumbs-down to weaves and drippy curls. Women wrote back telling the men to mind their business. As if today, this ain't about y'all and this ain't about The Man, this is our creative space, best you stay out."[16]

This matters little to Hammons, who clearly wades right into the fray. Though he may claim jazz (and its players) as its intellectual guiding force, it is, in fact, the culture of women that provides the material underpinnings of Hammons's installation work.

Alice Walker and bell hooks both have essays which discuss their search for artistic foremothers.[17] Does the heritage of slavery and then back- (and perhaps soul-) breaking manual labor foreclose the possibility of a legacy of African American women's creativity, they ask? While the history of such cultural traditions may have been a bit more difficult to locate than the jazzmen that inspired Hammons, Walker and hooks found them nonetheless.

This inheritance of imagination came through Walker's mother, the gardener, and hooks's grandmother, the quilter. Using the tools of flowers and fabric, these women were able to create aesthetic arenas of meditation, domains in which each could "cease attending to the needs of others" and as hooks's grandmother would say, "come back to herself."[18] Walker has remarked that her mother was "involved in work her soul must have. Ordering the universe in the image of her personal conception of Beauty."[19]

Gardens and quilts. These are tropes David Hammons returns to again and again in his installations using African American hair. Particularly in the 1970s, these works are like fecund vegetation that replicates itself seemingly without end, or cloths to which pieces are continually added. They are all planting and weaving, hair sifting like dirt through the artist's fingers. As with the vivid imagery of hair culture, these sources too cast beauty as cultivation and maintenance; they are also "popular art-forms," performed as daily tasks, as everyday infusions of splendor and grace.

In rejecting and then transforming the white box of the modernist exhibition space through installation, Hammons sought to create a realm that could both symbolize and, to an extent, sustain the culture of commonplace and street life. Hammons's reverence for the everyday is connected to his veneration of "folk" or "naive" art and functional aesthetics found primarily in the South. In many ways this is the tradition of the *bricoleur*. And doesn't this practice include the quilter who constructs a wholly new object from a fleet of scraps?

It is interesting to note as well that both the quilter and the gardener carve out real physical space—as well as the intellectual and spiritual variety—in their creative processes. Hooks recounts how her grandmother added a room for quilting and sewing to her home as soon as she was financially able. The gardens and yards of flowers definitely insinuated themselves as part of both the Walker homestead and the larger Georgia landscape. The interiors that these women created and in which they lived and worked could even be seen as forms of what we know to be installation: hooks's grandmother's chamber filled with baskets, scraps, and material in various stages of piecing; Walker's mother in the act of "cover[ing] the holes in [the] walls with sunflowers."[20] In both cases each marked space is able to signify: to attest to the inventiveness of its maker, and to impart a narrative tied to its construction.

When hooks eventually visited a "real" artist's studio, she was struck by how much that workplace had in common with the one her grandmother had built. With installation the mystical realm of the artist's studio is in effect transformed into a public space, since materially it seems to disclose the working method as well as the necessary tools. In this way it effects the decentering of the authorial role of the artist, and the parallel centralization of the position of the spectator. With this act, the place of installation (and art) is revealed as a space of constructed narrative. It is also acknowledged as a domain of intimacy, a place where not only the maker but the viewer can "come back to herself," exercise her own critical reasoning, and project her own history.

In his work from the 1970s, David Hammons clearly draws on common, everyday rituals of African American communities to create an artistic statement on and through culture. By way of installations, he fabricates sites of familiarity, and it is by evoking the cultural practices of black women—from hair to gardens to quilts—that he is able to invent spaces of experience and of intimacy.

Notes

1. See Lizzetta LaFalle-Collins and Cecil Ferguson, *19 SIXTIES: A Cultural Awakening Re-evaluated, 1965–1975* (Los Angeles: California Afro-American Museum, 1989).
2. Kobena Mercer, "Black Hair/Style Politics," in *Welcome to the Jungle* (New York: Routledge, 1994), pp. 100–101.
3. Lisa Jones, *Bulletproof Diva: Tales of Race, Sex, and Hair* (New York: Anchor Books, 1995, originally published 1994), p. 297.
4. Judith Wilson, "Beauty Rites: Towards an Anatomy of Culture in African American Women's Art," *International Review of African American Art*, vol. 11 no. 3 (1994): 13.
5. Wilson, p. 13.
6. Mercer, "Black Hair/Style Politics," p. 100.
7. Jones, *Bulletproof Diva*, pp. 296–297.
8. *David Hammons: Dreadlock Series*, Just Above Midtown Gallery, April 6–April 26, 1976.
9. John Perreault, "David Hammons," *Soho Weekly News*, April 21, 1977, p. 27.
10. David Hammons and Louise Neri, "No Wonder," *Parkett* no. 31 (March 1992): 53.
11. Wilson, "Beauty Rites," p. 17.
12. Perreault, "David Hammons," p. 27.

13. Jones, *Bulletproof Diva*, p. 11.

14. Jones, p. 139.

15. bell hooks, "Black Is a Woman's Color," *Callaloo*, vol. 12, no. 2 (1989): 382, cited in Wilson, "Beauty Rites," p. 15.

16. Jones, *Bulletproof Diva*, p. 304.

17. Alice Walker, "In Search of Our Mothers' Gardens," in *In Search of Our Mothers' Gardens* (San Diego: Harcourt, Brace, Jovanovich, 1983), pp. 231–243; and bell hooks, "Aesthetic Inheritances: History Worked by Hand," in *Yearning* (Boston: South End Press, 1990), pp. 115–122.

18. hooks, *Yearning*, p. 116.

19. Walker, "In Search of Our Mothers' Gardens," p. 241.

20. Walker, p. 242.

Black Light: David Hammons and the Poetics of Emptiness

Glenn Ligon

1. MY UNCLE TOSSY USED TO SAY THAT THERE are two kinds of Niggers in the world: Niggers and Crazy Niggers. Tossy was in the latter category. Handsome in a rough kind of way, he was highly opinionated, always funny, and frequently drunk. For Tossy, style was content, and he *was* stylish in a Pierre Cardin suit, Stacy Adams shoes, Kangol hat, Kojak sort of way—so fresh and so clean. Tossy (his real name was Elton, but nobody ever called him that) lived in my grandparents' basement, which was set up as a kind of mock bachelor pad with a sofa bed covered in gray-pink mohair, a teak coffee table with blue tile inlays, and a console radio/record player that miraculously picked up long-wave transmissions from Europe. It was on that machine that my older cousins introduced me to James Brown, Parliament/Funkadelic, and Richard Pryor, and it was in that basement that they introduced me to "practice" kissing. Tossy's favorite song was "Come Spy with Me" by Smokey Robinson and the Miracles. He would sing it in a kind of slowed-down bass voice punctuated with staccato laughs and swigs of the whiskey du jour.

I was crazy about Tossy even though he was disdainful of my budding artistic talents: To the gift of a handmade Christmas card he muttered, "The boy needs to get outside more." But even as a child I knew that Tossy's life was not a model of how to live my own. His indifference to the niceties of lower-middle-class black life scared me and challenged my other relatives' messages of uplift and racial pride. At heart, Tossy was a nomad, although he had lived in that basement for twenty years, worked at the Bureau of Printing and Engraving for even longer, and essentially

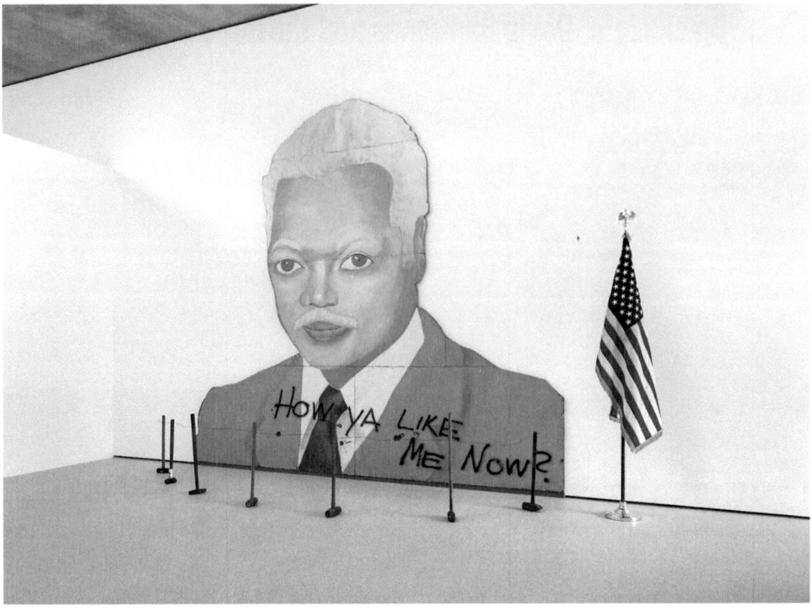

David Hammons, *How Ya Like Me Now?*, 1988, tin, plywood, sledgehammers, Lucky Strike cigarette wrapper, and American flag, 158 × 222 × 48 in. (401 × 564 × 122 cm) overall.

had never left his parents' house. He fascinated me because he took what he had, which was almost nothing, and made something fabulous out of it, made it seem to encompass the whole world. When I first saw the work of David Hammons, with its attention to the poetics of emptiness, I saw in it echoes of my Uncle Tossy's life.

2. A PASSAGE FROM A 1991 INTERVIEW WITH David Hammons by Robert Storr, then curator in the Department of Painting and Sculpture at the Museum of Modern Art, New York:

STORR: How does the question of race affect the reading of your work and the scope of its development?

HAMMONS: I'm trying to get away with the redundancy of being an African-American or making African-American art. It's like a double negative, a double noun. So I'm trying to figure it out. Everyone knows that I am black, so my work doesn't have to shout it out anymore. . . . I am black. The work will automatically be thought of as a part of my African-American culture.

Being black, Hammons says, the work will automatically be thought of as coming from African-American culture. To be sure, Hammons uses materials that are culturally specific: fried chicken wings, cotton plants, gold chains, black hair, jazz, Night Train bottles, hoodies, and basketballs. And a Chinese gong. And spades. And snowballs, burning cigarettes, grease, cardboard boxes, blue cellophane, and "How you like me now?" But it's more difficult than that. "African-American" or "African-American Art" has always been a complicated place to live. A noisy cul-de-sac at the end of a long and winding road that lots of folks are curious about but only want to visit during the summertime. I have always gotten stuck on Hammons's "double negative." I think I know what he means, but the words make me uneasy, with their echoes of DuBoisian double consciousness and "If you're black, get back." In the 1990 film *Paris Is Burning* Dorian Corey says, "When you're all the same then you have to go to the fine point. In other words, if I'm a black queen, and you're a black queen, we can't call each other 'black queens.' . . . That's not a read, that's just a fact." So really it is about how the terms "African-American" and "African-American Art" are used—and by whom. We need to go to the fine point. "African-American" or "African-American Art," they're part of the conversation, not the end of it.

3. ANOTHER QUOTATION BY HAMMONS—This time from a 1993 interview with Deborah Rothschild, curator at the Williams College Museum of Art. In reference to James Turrell, Hammons says:

> Turrell, he's on a different wavelength. He's got a completely different vision. Different than mine, but it's beautiful to see people who have a vision that has nothing to do with presentation in a gallery. I wish I could make art like that, but we're too oppressed for me to be dabbling out there. . . . I would love to do that because that also could be very black. You know, as a black artist, dealing just with light. They would say, "How in the hell could he deal with that, coming from where he did?" I want to get to that, I'm trying to get to that, but I'm not free enough yet. I still feel I have to get my message out.

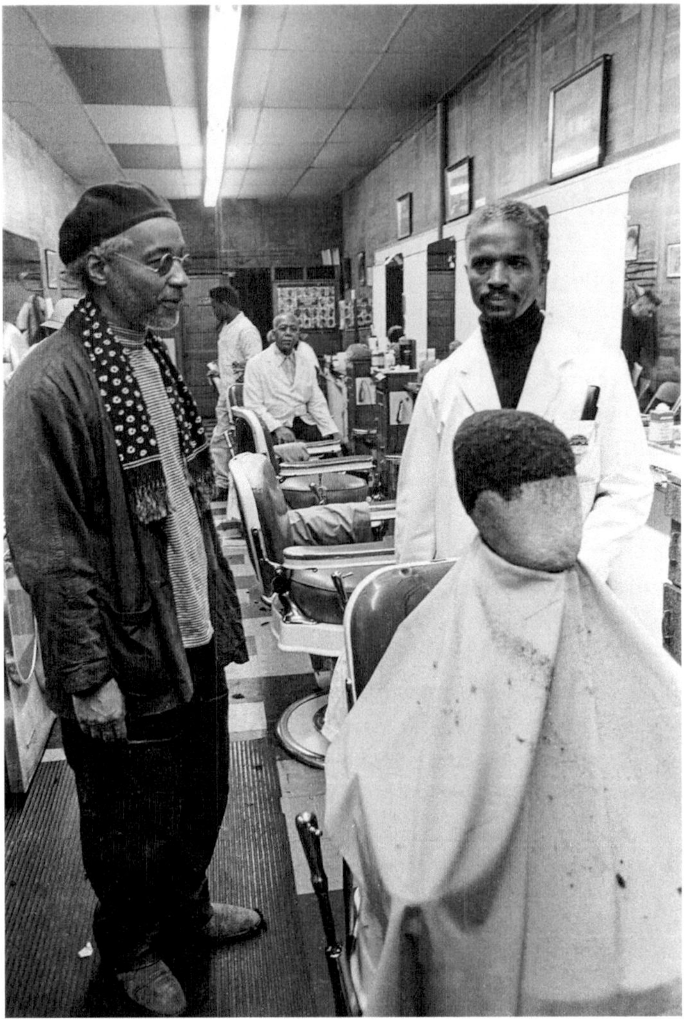

David Hammons, *Haircut*, 1992, performance in Harlem.
Photograph © Coreen Simpson.

Ten years after that interview Hammons indeed figured out how to make light "very black" for *Concerto in Black and Blue*, 2002, his exhibition at Ace Gallery in New York. At the entrance to the gallery visitors were given tiny pressure-activated LED flashlights no bigger than gumballs. When the flashlights were clicked on they gave off a blue light, which lasted until the pressure was released. Visitors were ushered through a door into the main gallery space, which comprised more than twenty thousand square feet spread over several rooms with twenty-five-foot ceilings. The gallery was completely dark. And what was in that twenty-thousand-square-foot space? Nothing. It was completely empty except for the blue light emitted from your flashlight and from those of other people walking around in the space with you.

When talking about Turrell, Hammons said, "We're too oppressed for me to be dabbling out there," and "I want to get to that, I'm trying to get to that, but I'm not free enough yet." The movement to "get free," to cross boundaries, is what's interesting in Hammons's recent work, in particular its radical dematerialization over the last several years. But let me reject a reading of Hammons's project that sets up too strict an opposition between "free" and "not free," "message" and "post-message," objects and dematerialization, "white" work (Turrell) and "black" work (Hammons). For one, Hammons's work has never been "on point" because it's always too Fellini, too carnivalesque, too damn freaky-deke to be useful as a set of cheering fictions, an expression of an essential, unchanging blackness, or a standard-bearer for some multiculturalist agenda. What to make, for example, of a work like *Flying Carpet*, 1990, where fried chicken wings are attached with fish hooks to a Persian carpet hanging on the wall? Or *Traveling*, 2002, a drawing made by bouncing a basketball covered in Harlem dirt on a piece of paper with a suitcase stuck behind the frame pushing the drawing off the wall: playground virtuosity, nomadism, performance art, and Rauschenberg's tire print, all elegantly rolled into one? Also, it would be a misreading of Hammons's project to describe it as a linear movement toward dematerialization, for that doesn't take into consideration earlier pieces like *Cold Shoulders*, 1990, giant blocks of ice with coats thrown over them, or *Bliz-aard Ball Sale*, 1983, where the artist sold snowballs on the streets of New York, or more recent pieces like *Global Fax Festival*, 2000, an empty exhibition hall with ceiling-mounted machines spewing faxes, or his *Flashlight Drawing*, 2000, which records the movement of a flashlight in a darkened room. Process, ephemerality, and transformation have always been part of Hammons's work. In a word: Lightness.

4. OVERHEARD CONVERSATION AT AN EXHIBITION of Lorna Simpson's work:

CURATOR TO SIMPSON: What does your work have to do with black women and our lives?

SIMPSON'S REPLY: [*Silence.*]

The desires, possibilities, and deferred dreams of the black community as expressed through the work: the Message. But those desires, possibilities, and deferred dreams present a difficulty. Message, formulated in this way, equals a kind of restraint, a Bantustan policed from both sides of the fence. When thinking about working with light, Hammons anticipated one kind of response, wherein race delimits the scope of his artistic practice: "They would say, 'How in the hell could he deal with that, coming from where he did?'" Simpson's work generates another response: "What does this have to do with us?" Black bodies, yes, but apparently not "black" enough, because these bodies refuse to "represent." They remain mute, which is not even a representation of silencing but a theater of refusal, a thwarting of legibility. For example, in the two-channel video *Corridor*, 2003, we see the same actress moving through a modernist house and a seventeenth-century house. In each space she does household chores: washes up, gets dressed, sets the table. Husband and Master are out, and she is alone with her thoughts. And while colonial and mid-twentieth-century America were not the happiest of times for my people, one still had to eat and wash under one's arms. Simpson's video presents a decidedly nonmorbid depiction of black life, where Black people are not "representing oppression" but are allowed to just be "people."

The impulse to resist overdetermined readings of the black body is also evident in Steve McQueen's video *Deadpan*, 1997, a complex restaging of a scene from the Buster Keaton movie *Steamboat Bill, Jr.* in which a house facade falls over a standing man. James Baldwin famously said that "the black man has functioned in the white man's world as a fixed star, as an immovable pillar: and as he moves out of his place, heaven and earth are shaken to their foundations." What does it mean, then, to try not to move at all, not to speak, for a body to be unreadable? Stillness and interiority can function as a critical stance, a kind of resistance.

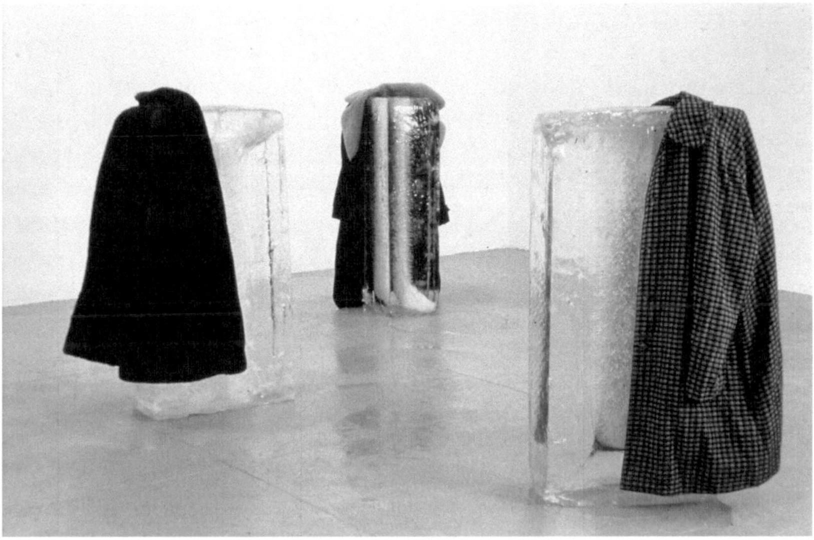

David Hammons, *Cold Shoulders*, 1990, Jack Tilton Art Gallery, New York.

5. ANOTHER HAMMONS QUOTATION: "I'm not interested in who I am. I'm just a force on the planet who plays with these things and has no identity and no personality."

It's hard to leave your body behind, especially when your body is always being thrown up in your face. But being heavy is a motherfucker. The question is: How to remove weight, to move toward lightness, as Hammons has? How to do this while still acknowledging the particular history of a body that has been used, as Stuart Hall suggests, "as if it was, and often it was, the only cultural capital we had"? These questions now occupy several young artists who walk the threshold between a dematerialized and a historicized body.

In works such as *Dispersion*, 2002, and *Excerpt (riot)*, 2003, Julie Mehretu figures the body as a collection of networks. She creates canvases full of incident: records of memories, places, historical events, time, symbols, at once exploded and collapsed on themselves, dynamic, spiraling in and out of control, nonsensical, and coherent. They're a visual equivalent of Borges's "The Library of Babel," except in this library the books are on tape and all talking to you at once. Mehretu's paintings are neural maps, flowcharts describing the processes by which what is exterior becomes interior (and vice versa). They're representations of the dizzying simultaneity and juxtaposition that characterizes this particular moment.

Camille Norment's installations are concerned with the moment the body becomes a stranger to itself. In pieces like *Dead Room*, 2000, and *Notes from the Undermind*, 2001, she creates architectural settings that distort your voice, project unheard frequencies through your body, create spatial disorientation, and generally mess with you. In *Driftglass*, 2004, the theme of the body's estrangement continues. The piece consists of a mirror distorted so that it reflects bodies only at oblique angles to its surface. Standing in front of the mirror, one sees other bodies, but one's own reflection is a blur. As the viewer moves toward the mirror, a motion detector triggers an audio component that intensifies as he or she approaches—sound standing in for the present but fugitive body.

Adam Pendleton's silk-screen paintings and wall-text/spoken-word installations also work with sound, placing our bodies in the space between text and voice. Texts by writers such as Audre Lorde, Adrienne Rich, June Jordan, John Rechy, and Toni Morrison are the raw material that he alters by adding his own text, creating Babel words, adding breaths and pauses, and constantly directing those texts toward questions of love. "TWOPEOPLETOGETHERISAMIRACLE" begins one piece, and the collapsing of identities that love enables is conflated with the collapsing of sexualities, of voice and object, of text and image. In Pendleton's work, as in the work of Mehretu and Norment, the dissolution of the body's boundaries is seen as a productive moment, where the fusion of the body to history, to space, to sound, and to language points toward new possibilities.

6. THE ARTIST MARC ROBINSON STANDS IN A gallery in front of a portrait of Malcolm X with red lipstick and blue eye shadow. A woman sees the painting through the window and comes inside. "Are you the artist?" she says. He is not, but he nods yes anyway. Pointing at the work, she asks, "How can you do that?"

In Robinson's video *I'm The Man You Think You Are*, 2002, a love poem to a bust the artist has sculpted of Malcolm X, this question is asked again. With Nina Simone songs playing in the background, Robinson caresses Malcolm's face, adjusts his glasses, dresses him up in a suit and tie, and makes him slide and shake as if dancing at a house party. This is not Malcolm at the window with a rifle, a figure of hypermasculinity. This is

Malcolm as an object of desire; partygoing Malcolm, good-time Malcolm, Malcolm from the block. Wayne Koestenbaum has noted that "iconicity is a form of makeover, a color scheme laid over a neutral surface." Watching Robinson interact with the bust, we realize that there is no single Malcolm X, no solitary identity or even body, only approaches to Malcolm, only the Malcolm that we make and remake.

The problem with black families, they say, is absent fathers. Malcolm X is absent because he's dead. What's Bill Clinton's excuse? Much was made of the former president's decision to locate his office on 125th Street, a kind of performance piece called "I Like Harlem and Harlem Likes Me." But Clinton's actual presence in the hood has been scarce. In David McKenzie's video *We Shall Overcome*, 2004, this absence is rectified. The artist is seen walking up and down 125th Street wearing a suit and tie and an oversize Bill Clinton mask. Set to a score of Louis Armstrong singing a civil rights anthem, we watch as people respond with curiosity, indifference, amusement, and outrage to McKenzie's Clinton—equal parts Santa Claus and Jesus Christ. The impulse behind the video is a simple and generous one: Bring The Man to The People. But this is not Clinton. It is someone in a Clinton mask, and the lack the performance seeks to address ends up being amplified rather than filled. Ultimately, McKenzie is not interested in Clinton at all (trifling men are all alike!). He's interested in the spooking. Clinton, like Malcolm X, is a void we inhabit, a repository for our desires, possibilities, and deferred dreams. McKenzie's video positions icons as figures of intense identification that our bodies move into and out of and that speak to us in voices we happily misrecognize as our own.

7. ONE LAST DAVID HAMMONS QUOTE:

> I like being from nowhere; it's a beautiful place. That means I can look at anyone who's from somewhere and see how really caught they are.

Sun Ra wasn't from here either—"here" meaning Earth. He also wasn't human. "I'm not real," he says in a 1974 film, to a group of black children. "I'm just like you. You don't exist, in this society. If you did, your people wouldn't be seeking equal rights." For Sun Ra—and for Hammons—not being from *here* is a movement toward placelessness, toward the utopic, the posthuman, *and* a deep critique of American society. Their genius was to employ a postmodern concern with the emptying out of the self as a critical strategy, one that might have particular resonance with a people historically positioned at the margin of what was considered human.

Hammons says light could be "very black," but how to reconcile the desire to be from nowhere, to have no identity and no personality, with the desire to make light "very black," when "black" is suggestive of a particular history, culture, and practices? What, for example, made *Concerto in Black and Blue* "very black" as opposed to merely "dark"? Well, nothing really, at first. But then I remembered a friend of mine's suggestion that Hammons could write a masterpiece with one-syllable words, and it pointed me toward the one-syllable words in the work's title: "black" and "blue." "What did I do to be so black and blue," or "the blues," or Amiri Baraka's *Blues People*, or *Kind of Blue*, or "Say It Loud . . . ," or *Fugitive Blue*, or "Blue on Blue," or "Black is the color of my true love's hair," or "I wear black on the outside, as black as I feel on the inside," and on and on and on. You went into the show looking for the art, but you came out having been the art. What's there is what we bring to the space. Blackness is a transient hotel, as a drawing by William Pope.L suggests. If blackness is a construct, then we are all construction workers, and what Hammons has done is to provide the space in which blackness can be constructed in light, like the famous photo of Picasso drawing a centaur in the air with a flashlight, except this time it's us with our little blue flashlights, signaling one another in the dark. What was black about *Concerto in Black and Blue* is whatever you think blackness is, whatever you brought to it, and what you did with what you brought when you got there.

An Elective Affinity: David Hammons's *Hidden from View* and *Made in the People's Republic of Harlem*

Claire Tancons

I

> We owe primarily to the convictions of the pioneer modern artists [tribal objects'] promotion from the rank of curiosities and artifacts to that of major art, indeed, to the status of art at all.
>
> —William Rubin[1]

James Clifford once referred to tribal objects as "travelers" who "have been around." In *Hidden from View*, David Hammons shows the travelers on a precarious journey. Down from the pedestals that granted them visibility, they have vacated their vitrines and have gone underground. As they hide from view, only their naked feet remain to be seen, and although they are immobile, their scattered positions suggest that they are on the move again.

Clifford tracked down the travelers at the Museum of Modern Art New York in 1984 and wrote his observations in *The Predicament of Culture*, his *carnet de voyage* to ethnography, literature, and art in the twentieth century.[2] All of them went by the name Tribal. Most had an enviable background: they were polished and patinated, and did not shy away from the brightest lights. Some belonged to the lowest classes, as attested to by the clothes they wore. These rags were made, at best, of mended fabric, at worst of dried vegetal matters. Other Tribals bore the stigmas of the hardships of their travels. Others yet got lost on arrival, or simply never

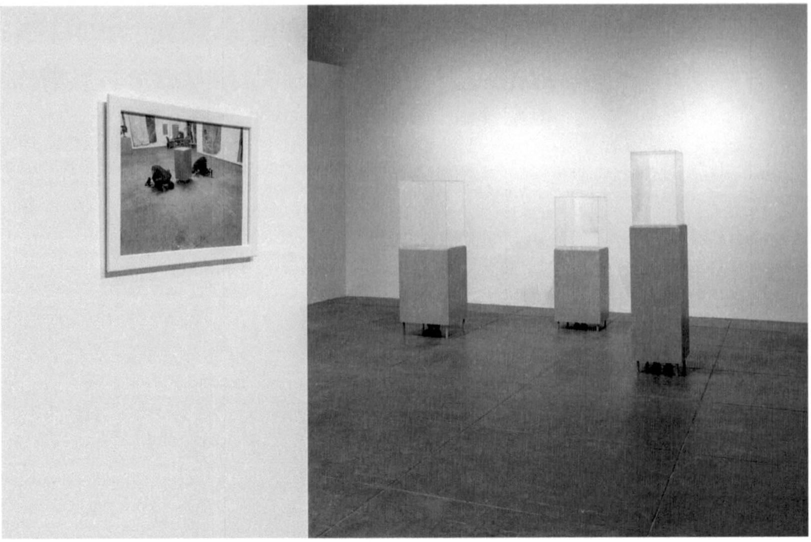

David Hammons. *Hidden from View*, 2003, mixed media, dimensions variable. Shown as part of installation view at Hauser & Wirth, Los Angeles, 2019.

made it. A gathering hosted by William Rubin prompted the Tribals to call at MoMA; it was a celebration of their kinship with their more sedentary cousins, the Moderns. The Tribals and the Moderns rubbed shoulders for a few weeks and then the Tribals took to the road again. The event, remembered under the title *"Primitivism" in Twentieth Century Art: Affinity of the Tribal and the Modern* had a long-lasting impact. It enshrined in history the myth of the modern origin of tribal art.

By the time they reached Galerie Hauser & Wirth in the summer of 2003, the travelers carried a heavy burden of wood and plexiglas. They had known many different situations, on a shelf or on a pedestal, with or without a vitrine, in the dark or under bright spotlights, but they had never been—had never dared go—under their pedestals. From Surrealist *cabinets de curiosités* and cubist *ateliers* to ethnographic reserves and museum galleries, the Tribals had been left to collect dust atop shelves or were conscientiously protected from dust under vitrines. Often they were stripped bare of their clothes or vegetal ornaments. But never had they been left on the ground. They had also known many a rechristening. Once considered curios, alongside shells and other wonders from the natural world, they became artefacts next to the remnants of other material cultures, and finally reached the status of art in the company of Picasso's painted prostitutes and Max Ernst's fabulous figures. Their semantic upgrade was concurrent with the taxonomic shift they underwent, from artefact to art. The possibility of a metonymic shift from objects to subjects nowhere is made more visually pregnant than in *Hidden from View*. Because of the sculptures' anthropomorphic qualities, and the emphasis placed on their feet, the statues call to mind images of maroon slaves in disguise. The African slaves to whom the statues seem to allude certainly made a long journey. They also underwent a semantic upgrade—from "niggers" and "Negroes" to "Afro-Americans" and "African-Americans"—concurrently with their taxonomic shift from commodities to citizens. The fact is that the aesthetic appreciation and cultural assimilation of tribal objects as *objets d'art* was consonant with changes in scientific discourses around race. Evolutionary theory saw Africans as inferior, and cultural anthropology eventually granted them full humanity; their material productions followed a similar path in the realm of objecthood.[3]

On both sides of the metonymy, whether on the side of subjecthood or of objecthood, displacement applies. For the tribal objects, displacement is a strategy of display that follows modern art museums' standards of aesthetic presentation yet runs counter to their purposes. The display at Galerie Hauser & Wirth is a paragon of the modernist setting pushed to its very extreme—a vast expanse of space with polished wooden floors and neutral-colored walls untarnished by obstructive texts of any kind. By hiding the Tribals under their vitrines and pedestals, Hammons subverts the orthodoxy of the museum using its own tools and techniques, turning the apparatus of display into a hindrance rather than an enhancement. He also defines for the viewer the conditions of an unusual encounter. By setting the sculptures off base, Hammons operates a debasement of the gaze, if not of the visitor. Expecting to meet an object of timeless beauty at eye-level, the viewer finds him- or herself looking down onto the wooden bases of the *vitrines*, if not crawling on the floor on all fours, only to face the unsettling vision of wooden feet. The face-to-face on offer is not quite the one a viewer might expect. It is not the representation of the Other and the exotic in the guise of a little statuette from an unknown foreign setting. Rather, the confrontation is with the viewer, or rather the viewer's own reflection. Once he or she is again upright and wants to make sure that nothing on view has been missed, he or she gazes at the voided glass, inspects it further, and catches sight of his or her own likeness. The debasement of the viewer, more metaphorical than real, goes hand in hand with the denial, and even the temporary neutralization, of the ethnographic gaze as it is trapped for seconds inside the translucent display case.

Instigating displacements inside the museum or its commercial equivalent, the gallery, and challenging the traditional viewing experience are not new to Hammons. Two examples of his earlier work are particularly relevant when considering *Hidden from View*. One of these is especially apt particularly when considering the title of the exhibition in which it was featured, *Dislocations*, organized by Robert Storr in 1991 at the Museum of Modern Art. The work itself was called *Public Enemy* and consisted of a large-size photograph of the equestrian statue of Theodore Roosevelt and his Native American and African-American acolytes, complete with police barricades. By bringing the outside inside, Hammons "dislocate(d) the very site-specific institutional traditions of the Museum of Modern Art" and frontally confronted the viewer with ideological and political statements rarely seen at the Modern, the standard-setting institutional reference in terms of museum display and the definition of Modern art itself.[4] Hammons also notoriously brought the inside outside, by setting performances and ephemeral objects in the street, not so much turning the street into an open-air museum as rejecting the museum altogether. More recently, Hammons did go back inside, even though he didn't bring much to it. He notably created a series of works on the phenomenological, social, and racial experiences of light, color, and music, which culminated in 2003 in the presentation of *Concerto in Black and Blue* at Ace Gallery.[5] But the series had started with *House with Blue Light* at *A Gathering of the Tribes* (1993), went on at Kunsthalle Bern with *Blues and the Abstract Truth* (1997), and on again at Ujazdowski Castle with *Real Time* (2000). Each time, Hammons did bring a few small objects and devices to those spaces, whether light bulbs, blue gels, or flashlights, but he mainly removed objects or left spaces empty in those subtle exercises in nothingness. His tactics of removal and emptiness in the museum and the gallery have given way in Hammons's new work to a strategy of displacement on the scale of the glass case, a similarly confining and artificial setting.

Regarding the more specific issue of the display of African art that is at play in *Hidden from View*, Hammons inscribes himself within the lineage of other African-American artists who have made critical use of African art. In *Colonial Collection* (1990), for instance, Fred Wilson featured a Dan mask blindfolded and muted by fragments of the British flag, eloquently pointing to the silencing of the people of Ivory Coast by Great Britain's colonial power.[6] In her 1991 series of black-and-white photographs, including *Flipside* and *Vantage Point*, Lorna Simpson juxtaposed the backs of black women with the backs of African masks. By doing so, Simpson resorted to an "anti-portrait strategy" as a way to deny the ethnographic gaze access to its favorite objects of consumption: primitive art and the black female body.[7] Like Wilson and Simpson, Hammons is well aware of the economy of the gaze and attempts to disrupt it. Where Wilson blindfolds a mask and Simpson turns it inside out, Hammons hides a statue under its pedestal. Like them, he also challenges the tradition of the medium he uses for his formal and conceptual subversions. For Wilson, whose medium is the museum, the reorganization of collections results in institutional critique.[8] For Simpson, the colonial ideology inherent in Western photographic practices is dissected and exposed. In the work of Hammons, the history of Modern sculpture is revisited in light of its different and at times clashing historical traditions.

II

> [Western connoisseurs] essentially see themselves as doing for African sculpture (for example) what Andy Warhol did for Brillo boxes or, more strictly speaking, Marcel Duchamp for urinals.
>
> —Sally Price[9]

It may seem that the story of *Hidden from View* has become only about the Tribals and their perilous progression in the world of museums, leaving the Moderns alone in their settled ways of masterpieces. But it is still very much about the Moderns and their progeny, the Postmoderns. The myth of the modern origin of African art is well established and is retraced above. It is not without its false starts and dark spots, but it is basically the story of an ascending movement. As African artefacts are literally lifted from the ground, they are also elevated to the rank of art objects. The myth of the African origin of modern art is much muddier, the stuff of scavengers of flea-markets and adorers of tribal fetishes. It is basically the story of a descending movement, a metaphorical return to darkness and an actual descent to the floor as artists believe in the redemptive power of the primitive and rid their sculptures of their pedestals.

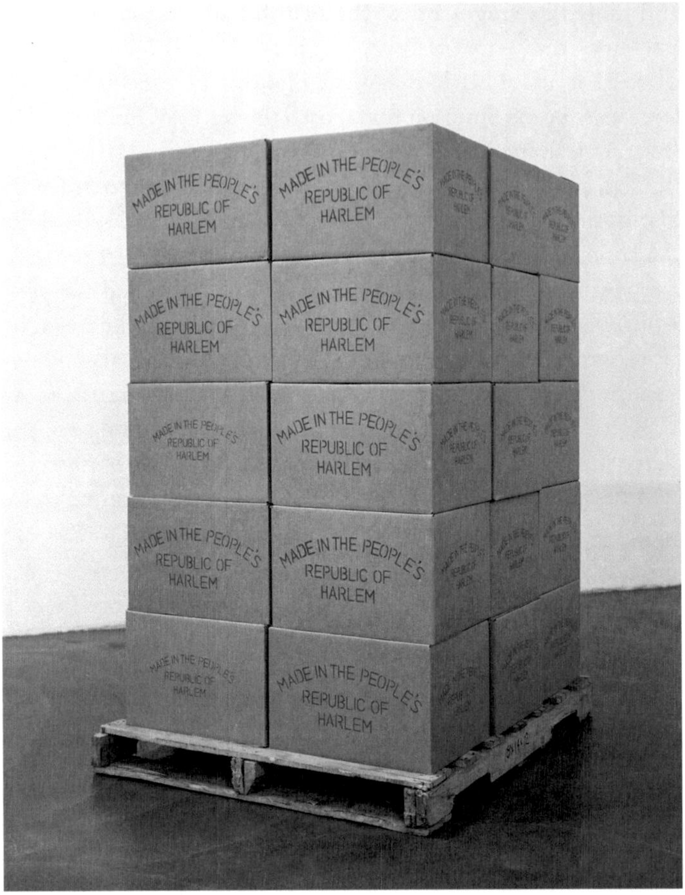

David Hammons, *Untitled (Made in the People's Republic of Harlem)*, 2003, silkscreened cardboard boxes on pallet, 60¼ × 48 × 48 in. (153 × 122 × 122 cm).

In both accounts, the pedestal is central to the refashioning of African art and Western art. At the same time that it was placed underneath African artefacts to grant them the sacred status of artworks, the pedestal was removed from under Western sculptures in a countermovement of desacralization of the art object. Before it was removed, however, the pedestal was integrated with the body of the sculpture itself. Brancusi is the modern master who, learning from African sculpture as a result of his era's general enthusiasm for things primitive, rooted his sculptures in the real world by integrating their bases to them. The results of Brancusi's African lessons cannot be seen anywhere better than in a sculpture from 1914–26 aptly titled *Caryatid*.[10] Like *Hidden from View*, *Caryatid* is an anthropomorphic sculpture with an African touch, made of a pedestal. *Caryatid* has clearly gouged-out legs protruding from a more compact capital and entablature and the reference to African sculpture is diffused, conceptual as much as formal. In *Hidden from View*, the reference to African statuary is very pointed. What Brancusi tried to hide, Hammons reveals with humor as he revisits the Primitivist origins of modern art.[11]

If the joint mythical origins of African and Modern art are more or less known, the myth of the postmodern origin of African art is not widely acknowledged at all. It is true that it follows a different tradition, that of the ready-made, a tradition that remains problematic to this day. Yet, the Duchampian ready-made trend in sculpture is chronologically contemporary with the Brancusian primitivist impulse and of equal if not superior importance for understanding the affinity of the Tribal and the Modern. But the ready-made had to wait until the 1960s to have a conceptual impact on the way sculpture was made—or rather not made—and experienced. It may not be a matter of chronology alone, but rather one more piece of evidence that postmodernism is contained wholly in modernism. Indeed, when William Rubin states that "we owe . . . modern artists [tribal objects] promotion from the rank of curiosity to . . . the status of art" he strongly echoes André Breton's classical definition of the readymade in the *Abridged Dictionary of Surrealism* (1938) according to which a readymade is "an ordinary object elevated to the dignity of a work of art by the mere choice of an artist."[12] Sally Price only goes a step further when, establishing a direct relationship between *Fountain* (1917), Marcel Duchamp's most famous ready-made, and Andy Warhol's *Brillo Boxes* (1964), she proposes the idea of African art as ready-made.

Contiguous to *Hidden from View*, Hammons had installed another work, consisting of identical cardboard boxes reading *Made in the People's Republic of Harlem* in red lettering. The stacked boxes of *Untitled (Made in the People's Republic of Harlem)* were left on their pallets, as if in transit, in a space closer in feel to a loading dock than to a proper gallery—a trend, that of the rough warehouse-like space, very much in fashion for the display of contemporary art.[13] There the floor was concrete, the ceiling supported by obtrusive white-tiled pillars, and the light harsher, not as homogeneously diffused. The boxes were reportedly filled with used garments purchased by Hammons in Harlem. The people of the Republic of Harlem are well known for their spirit of recycling, so it should come as no surprise that their products of exportation would be, so to speak, second-hand ready-mades, as opposed to brand-new manufactured objects. One should not be surprised by the fact that Hammons declares the secession of the people of Harlem from the rest of the United States. In 1990, he had designed the *African American Flag* bearing the colors of Marcus Garvey's Pan-Africanism—red for the blood that was shed, black for the people who died, green for the land that was lost—making clear his non-alignment with mainstream U.S. politics. That in 2003 the geographical entity he proclaims as an independent country follows China's communism, rather than the U.S. capitalist model, is not only another jab at the political establishment. His cardboard boxes filled with invisible clothing found in Harlem seem to bring to a close the promise of a less hierarchical relationship to objects in the realm of art, a promise contained in Andy Warhol's *Brillo Boxes*, which they so clearly reference. With this reference in mind, one starts to envision how, taken together, *Hidden from View* and *Untitled (Made in the People's Republic of Harlem)* retrace a history of sculpture in the form of a visual essay whose central articulation may be what links traditional African art to Brillo Boxes: ready-mades.

African art is ready-made as surely as Duchamp's urinal is. If, unlike most ready-mades, African objects have kept their functional names, they have lost their original functions as surely as Duchamp's have. Caged in by a plexiglas *vitrine*, the typewriter's cover no longer protects the Underwood against dust (*. . . pliant . . . de voyage*, 1916) nor do Akan gold weights weigh gold dust or provide busy traders with proverbial advice. The loss of functionality is one of the key traits by which to discern an artwork from a mere object in an increasingly commercialized art world where consumable products of all sorts find their ways into galleries and museums alike. Plexiglas cases and other display apparatuses that freeze an object in time and space by defining it as unique and authentic and removing it from the realm of the utilitarian have been used to legitimize African objects as art, as opposed to mere artefact. But since Duchamp's ready-mades, techniques of display have also been useful cues for distinguishing artworks that bear a resemblance to (or actually are) banal mass-produced objects from mere functional objects. With *Hidden from View* and *Untitled (Made in the People's Republic of Harlem)*, Hammons interrogates the status of the art object, not just traditional African art, under modern strategies of display. The fate

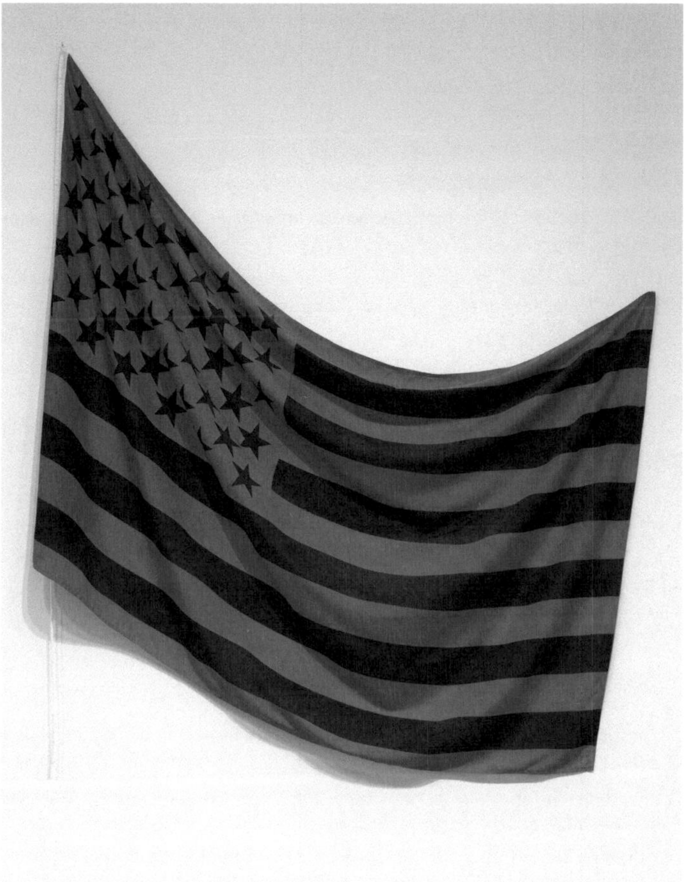

David Hammons, *African American Flag*, 1990, dyed cotton, 56 in. × 7 ft. 4 in. (142.2 × 223.5 cm). The Museum of Modern Art, New York, Gift of The Over Holland Foundation, AR6110563.

shared by traditional African art, modern art, and postmodern artistic practices is not the least of the ironies that Hammons reveals in *Hidden from View*. Articulating the concussion of the postmodern with the postcolonial, he questions the increasing commodification of art and suggests that the Tribals, hiding as they do in *Hidden from View*, may ultimately escape more successfully than can the Moderns and the Postmoderns, who have become so dependent on their apparatus of display—or lack thereof—that they are caught in their own game of make-believe. No one should indeed be fooled: the elective affinity between the tribal and the modern is none other than the rule of the market.

Notes

1. William Rubin, *"Primitivism" in Twentieth Century Art: Affinity of the Tribal and the Modern*, vols. I and II, Museum of Modern Art, New York, 1984, p. 7.

2. James Clifford, *The Predicament of Culture. Twentieth-Century Ethnography, Literature, and Art*, Harvard University Press, Cambridge, MA, and London, 1988, pp. 189–191.

3. Mary Anne Staniszewski, *The Power of Display: A History of Exhibition Installations at the Museum of Modern Art*, MIT Press, Cambridge, MA, and London, 1988, pp. 124–125.

4. Staniszewski, pp. 304–306.

5. See Claire Tancons, "David Hammons: *Concerto in Black and Blue*," in *NKA: Journal of Contemporary African Art*, no 18, Spring/Summer 2003, pp. 94–95.

6. Daniel Shapiro, *Western Artists/African Art*, exhibition catalogue, Museum for African Art, New York, 1994, p. 93.

7. Lauri Firstenberg, "Autonomy and the Archive in America: Reexamining the Intersection of Photography and Stereotype," in *Only Skin Deep: Changing Visions of the American Self*, ed. Coco Fusco and Brian Wallis, exhibition catalogue, Harry N. Abrams, Inc, New York, 2003, p. 320.

8. Kynaston McShine, *The Museum as Muse: Artists Reflect*, exhibition catalogue, Museum of Modern Art, New York, 1999.

9. Sally Price, *Primitive Art in Civilized Places*, University of Chicago Press, Chicago and London, 1989, p. 104.

10. Friedrich Teja Bach et al., *Constantin Brancusi 1876–1957*, exhibition catalogue, Philadelphia Museum of Art, Philadelphia, 1995, pp. 234–235.

11. Bach et al., p. 45. Like Picasso, Brancusi always denied any direct influence from African art, going as far as destroying one of his sculptures, *The First Step* 1913–1914—in actuality an unlikely mix-match of different African sculptural styles—which he felt made that influence too obvious. Brancusi did not destroy *Caryatid* but in 1926 he shortened its legs, allegedly to attenuate its African look.

12. André Breton and Paul Eluard, *Dictionnaire Abrége du Surréalisme* (ref.), 1938, p. 23.

13. I have made no distinction between the museum and the gallery, seeing the latter as the commercial counterpart of the former; both share the same modernist tactics of display. However, I do believe that Hammons's choice of a gallery setting for some of his works is not the result of chance and that the influence of commercial galleries on contemporary artistic practices could be analyzed in the same way that Kynaston McShine analyzed the influence of the museum on the artistic practices of the twentieth century. I also see Hammons's choice of the more traditional gallery space for *Hidden from View* and of the rougher, more contemporary one for *Untitled (Made in the People's Republic of Harlem)* as intentional. The former is wholly governed by the paradigm of the Modern while the latter is ruled by the Postmodern.

David Hammons's *Sheep Raffle* at Dak'Art 2004: Reading Black Art through Léopold Sédar Senghor's Négritude

Manthia Diawara

Prelude

> No sooner did Sango enter the town than he demanded the sacrifice of a ram.
>
> —Yoruba saying

In March 2004, I was invited by my friend Salah Hassan to write an article on David Hammons's contribution to the Dak'Art Biennale.[1] I then invited the artist to lunch in the Village, in New York City, to talk about his installation. Soon after we sat down in Il Buco restaurant, David informed me that he was going to do a sheep raffle as his contribution to Africa's biggest art show.

"A Sheep Raffle?" I asked. "But why?"

"Oh, for no reason in particular," he said.

Knowing David, I told myself that I must remain cool; that it would serve no purpose to push him to say more, right away, about his project. So I told him that it was a great idea, and changed the subject of the conversation. Fortunately, it did not take David too long to return to the topic.

"You know," he said, "people in Dakar do not go to exhibitions. They think that the Dak'Art is for white people. And, considering the state of the art world today, I can't blame them for not showing up. At least with the Sheep Raffle, I'll give them something that they can relate to. They'll come, and at the end of the day, the lucky winners will take home a sheep."

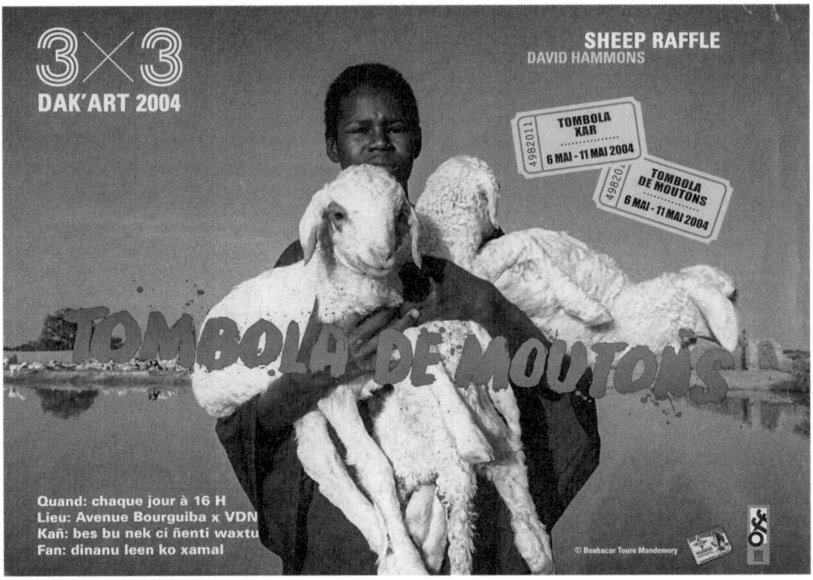

Boubacar Touré Mandémory, Poster for David Hammons, *Sheep Raffle*, 2004, performance. Dakar, Senegal.

I asked David if he had any idea of both the symbolic and literal significance of the ram in West African cultures—from the Yoruba to the Baule and the Dogon. In my desire to impress David, I said that the ram was central to life in West Africa, whether one looked at it from an Islamic point of view or an Animist system of thought. At the end of the Ramadan fast tradition emanating from Abraham and Isaac—the ram is the most important sacrifice for every Moslem household. Still today, in many villages in Mali and Senegal, one can see a white ram roaming around. It is considered a kind of safeguard from evil spirits, a sort of *pharmakon* or caretaker that keeps an eye on the village. The ram is the symbol of purity, of innocence, and it is therefore sacred.

In the West African spiritual imaginary, the ram is both Moslem and Animist. It has survived in many cultures as both a totem of the ancestors and a metaphor for human sacrifice in monotheism. More importantly, it is a signifier of religious syncretism and cultural hybridity. As more and more Africans migrate from the village to the city, the ram has also become cosmopolitan. For example, in the Medina districts of such capital cities as Dakar and Bamako, the traffic often stops to let a herd of white sheep—wearing gris-gris on their necks—cross the street. I have often wondered, why the gris-gris? To protect the rams, or to scare taxi drivers from running over them? But it is clear that while these sheep wait for the Tabaski feast, a Moslem holiday, to be slaughtered, they receive special treatment in the city. In Dakar, they are well fed and bathed in the ocean by young men.

Could David Hammons's *Sheep Raffle* be a signifyin' practice on some of these uses of the ram? I reminded him of the sheep symbolism behind his own name. The Bible says that King David returned to caring for the sheep and "The Spirit of The Lord came upon [him] . . . from that day forward."[2] It was also the same David who challenged Goliath the Philistine,[3] just as he, David Hammons, is now challenging the art world. Finally, I asked, is David signifyin' on Picasso's *The Man with a Lamb* (1943)? A friend of Léopold Sédar Senghor's—poet and first president of Senegal—Picasso had once visited Dakar. David said that he did not know about all of that. All he wanted to do was to be useful while in Africa. He wanted to communicate with the people at a spiritual level. That was what mattered to him. The art world did not matter to him.

Left on my own, I went over my conversation with David, attempting to give meaning to the silences, David's body language, and how many times he had repeated the words—*the art world, art and politics, spirituality, emotion, secrecy,* and *the arbitrariness of the market value of a work of art.* I knew the anarchic side of David—one who was always testy and provocative. The seeming banality of the *Sheep Raffle* calls to mind Gianni Vattimo's concept of weak thought, or what David himself calls the art of "dumbing down."

But I also knew that he was working within a tradition; that everything he did was a commentary on a stereotype or a piece of common sense into which he invested new and provocative signifiers. More than any other contemporary artist's, David Hammons's work questions the mode of existence of African American art; its relations to the art of the black diaspora and of Africa; and its capacity to transform people spiritually. I believe therefore that whatever David does, in spite of his critique of art and the art world, is strongly grounded in black aesthetics. By that, I mean that his work sets in motion the essential elements of black aesthetics—collective memory, vital force, emotion, rhythm, image, recognition of pleasure and terror, and the disposition of the black body. So, given this definition of black art, what could a performance of a David Hammons *Sheep Raffle* at the Dak'Art tell me? To be more precise, what else could it signify in both the Saussurian and the Black Vernacular senses of the term?

The Dak'Art Biennale: May 2004

I arrived in Dakar on the night of the eighth of May, a full day after the opening ceremony of the official Biennale. The catalogue was still not out, and many of the installations were not ready at the main sites: the Foire Internationale des Expositions, the Chamber of Commerce, and the Musée de l'IFAN. I had therefore the time to go and see the secondary shows called the *Off Biennale*. David Hammons's *Sheep Raffle* was part of an "Off Show," entitled *3 × 3*, and curated by Salah Hassan and Cheryl Finley.

The *Sheep Raffle, or Tombola de moutons*, took place outdoors by the main street going past the Sumbejun fish market and toward the university Cheick Anta Diop. It was like a typical crowd gathering around a platform with drummers, singers, and dancers. The master of ceremonies, with a loudspeaker in his hand, announced the sheep raffle and enunciated the rules for participants. At the sound of the drums, the local crowd gathered spontaneously. There were also David Hammons fans who had come from America and Europe, as well as curious foreigners who were attracted by what seemed to be a strange and incomprehensible event.

There were banners and flyers advertising both the event and a brand of soy sauce called Maggi, with which the Senegalese like to season their favorite dish, Cebu Jen. The sheep were tied to a pole nearby, and David himself sat on top of the platform, surveying the performance, or came down the ladder to film certain scenes with a small digital camera. Every once in a while there was a winner—a man or a woman who pulled the sheep away with a rope tied on its neck. Then a taxi was hailed and a fare negotiated, whereupon the lucky winner put the sheep in the trunk and said goodbye to the envious crowd. David then returned to the drummers and singers to watch over the proceedings of the last raffle of the day. All in all, he gave away twelve sheep in six days.

The *Sheep Raffle* contrasted nicely with everything going on in the official Biennale. The more the one was popular and grounded in the tradition of West African masquerade and performance, the more the other was steeped in the contemporary fashion of video and sculpture installations. The installations, paintings, and sculptures in the official show mimicked sheepishly, excuse the pun, the conceptual artists in London, New York, and Berlin. Okwi Enwezor put it aptly in a talk he delivered at the Dakar Conference Center, when he compared the official selection to a second dance in the Yoruba tradition. According to Enwezor, the first dance was the best for the Yoruba. Any performance that was cutting edge belonged to this category, in contradistinction to diluted performances, mimicry, and repetitions, which are called second dances.

I realize that I may be taking Enwezor's nice metaphor of the first dance out of context here, by linking it to the literal and essentialist meanings of such words as mimicry and repetition. For we all know what original thought a Homi Bhabha or James Snead is capable of deriving from these concepts. In Négritude aesthetics, there is also Senghor's notion of a repetition that does not repeat itself, or what Amiri Baraka calls the changing same in the Black Arts Movement.

My point is that David Hammons's return to African ritual practices through the *Sheep Raffle* constitutes an important critique of the limits that the art world has put on artistic productions in Africa and the world. A similar critique was voiced at the École des Beaux Arts of Dakar during the Biennale. A student whose submission to the Biennale was rejected complained that he could not afford a digital video camera, and therefore could not compete with African artists living in Europe and America. The student echoed a general feeling at the École des Beaux Arts of Dakar, when he stated that the future of African art was no longer based in Africa, but rather in Europe and America. "Every artist must do a video installation or be excluded," he said. It is in this sense that I quoted Enwezor's statement about first and second dances among the Yoruba.

For me, the *Sheep Raffle* by David Hammons, a project produced in Africa with local material, provides an invaluable instruction not only to the students at the Beaux Arts, but also to the Dak'Art Biennale as a whole. How can African art find a relative autonomy vis-à-vis the tyranny of the art world, curators, and cultural imperialists? How might one use art at the Dak'Art Biennale to say that there is no art here? In other words, David Hammons's ambition, in the battle between David and Goliath, is to save the soul of Black Art. He had come with the sacrifice, as an ancestor figure, to exorcize the Biennale, to give it strength, and to make it universal, instead of the product of a second dance. If performance art can be compared to a sacrificial object and to a masquerade, then let's look for a moment at the sacrificer and the sacrificed in David Hammons's *Sheep Raffle*.

The Sacrificed

> The sacrifice creates a relationship between the Ancestor and the sacrificer; it is the dialogue between the You and the I.
>
> —L. S. Senghor, *Présence Africaine*, 1956

In some sense, the sheep is literally the signified in Hammons's performance. If you take part in the commerce of the *Sheep Raffle*, you may win a sheep; but also you may not. Either way, you have participated in the performance and you know the rules of the game. Similarly, the one who accepts the sacrifice carries with her/him the burden of the sacrifice—she/he becomes the scapegoat. But as the Senghor quote above shows, the sacrifice is a means to enter a relation with the Ancestor. The sheep is therefore a way to communicate with the Ancestor, and to bring change in the lives of the living. The first purpose of the David Hammons *Sheep Raffle* was to use art and bring people to have confidence in themselves. Hammons accomplished this by grounding it in a public space, for collective participation. Every time there is a winner, the sacrificed brings the sacrificer closer to the ancestors. According to the rules of ritual performance, somebody wins when the ancestors have accepted the sacrifice. Otherwise, the whole afternoon will be spent without a winner. This reminds me of a scene of sacrifice in Chinua Achebe's *Arrow of God (*1964). In this masterpiece of African literature there is a sacrifice ritual carried out before the yam harvest and the priest must accept the gift before the farmers can begin to harvest. In this particular scene, Ezeulu, the priest who is the link between the ancestors and the living, refuses to take the sacrifice. The yams lie rotting until a Christian priest comes to receive the gift in Ezeulu's stead. And this leads the farmers to choose Christianity over the tradition of their ancestors.

David Hammons's *Sheep Raffle*, and the significance of the sacrifice, recall other representations of the sheep for similar purposes in African art, literature, and film. For me, one of the most memorable scenes in African literature concerns the battle between Ramatoulaye and Vendredi, the white ram, in Sembene Ousmane's *God's Bits of Wood* (1960). Vendredi is described as a robust ram belonging to El Hadji Mabigué, a collaborator for the French in the battle that pitted the colonial administration against the striking railroad workers. The book depicts Mabigué as a pseudo-community and -religious leader who participates in the oppression of the people. Vendredi, the ram, is a signifier for Mabigué's wealth, arrogance, yet powerlessness in front of the colonizer. Vendredi is fat, white, and castrated. It roams freely in the neighborhood, from compound to compound. It goes into peoples' kitchens and bedrooms and, like its owner, it feeds off the people, without fear of retribution. Its whiteness and castrated state represent Mabigué's own assimilation into the white colonial system, which occurs without the acquisition of real power.

In contrast to Vendredi and its owner, there is Ramatoulaye, who supports the strike and works in solidarity with the community. One day, as Ramatoulaye returns home from the store where she was turned down for credit, she is told that Vendredi has gone to her kitchen and eaten the only rice left for her famished family. At that moment, Vendredi emerges from her bedroom with pieces of cloth in its mouth. Ramatoulaye meets it with a knife in her hand and they engage in an epic battle. It is a battle of life and death: who will be sacrificed for the strike—the community or the ram? The sacrificial battle between Ramatoulaye and Vendredi is therefore a battle for the success or failure of the strike and the survival of the community. To put it in Ramatoulaye's own words, "When we know that the life and courage of others depend on our lives and courage, we no longer have the right to be afraid."[4] Thus, Ramatoulaye defeats Vendredi. She slaughters it and distributes the meat among the strikers. The sacrifice of Vendredi becomes a moral and literal victory for the spouses of the men on strike. The whole community comes to realize, through this ritual of sacrifice, that they can defeat colonialism if they have confidence in themselves.

Another great moment of political and aesthetic representation of the sacrifice of a ram in African art occurs in Souleymane Cissé's award-winning film *Finyé* (*The Wind*, Mali, 1982). The story of *The Wind*, like that of *God's Bits of Wood*, revolves around a strike. The film depicts the conflict between the student resistance movement and the military dictatorship in Mali in the 1970s. When students go on strike to protest against corruption and the soldiers' abuse of power, the soldiers beat them up and throw them in jail. The colonel of the army, who is also the governor, threatens that the students must return to school or be killed.

In the film, the students' resistance is defined through the character of a young man, called Bah, whose innocence and love for democracy contrast with the dictatorship of the colonel/governor. Bah defies him by choosing to die in prison. Bah's grandfather, a traditional figure in the film, then decides to confront the colonel governor. However, before the confrontation, Kansaye, the grandfather, goes to the shrine and offers a ram as sacrifice to his ancestors in return for advice and protection. But, soon after the ritualistic greetings, the ancestors advise Kansaye to listen to the winds of change; to find new ways of handling the present situation; to follow the stars and the youth. At that point in the film, we see a magnificent-looking white ram running toward Kansaye, who waves at the animal to keep going. The ram's horns match the shape of the hat Kansaye is wearing, creating an identification between the two, the human and the animal. There is no doubt at that moment in the film that Kansaye and the ram, sacrificer and sacrificed, have become one with the ancestors. Now they must all fight together to survive in a modern world. The film implies that the message of the ancestors is that Kansaye must have confidence in the youth. Thus he returns to the city and follows the youth in their civil disobedience, which eventually brings down the military dictatorship.

The political and aesthetic lessons we learn in all these performances in literature and film concern the transformative power and modernity of the sacrifice in contemporary African art. Far from being static and primitive, the purpose of sacrifice is to teach people the modern techniques, the new aesthetic languages and political strategies that enable the sacrificer to transcend obstacles in her/his environment. In *God's Bits of Wood*, the sacrifice of Vendredi enables women to acquire agency, and transform their role in the struggle for self-determination. In *The Wind*, the sacrifice of the ram is seen as a sign that the old generation should give way to the young.

To return again to the Senghor quote above, the sacrifice is a means to enter a relation with the ancestors, a dialogue between the "You" and the "I." The radical emotional and terrifying moment in *The Wind* comes when the ancestors follow the youth, instead of guiding them, as we are used to seeing in traditional African society. Similarly, in David Hammons's *Sheep Raffle* the sacrificed brings more vital force from the ancestors to the art world at Dak'Art. As Senghor puts it, in Baule ritual, the dancer who is wearing the ram mask, and the audience in attendance, identify with the ram-symbol of Nyamie, the Sun King. It is through this identification that the spirit of the ancestors finds an outlet and then flows in the bodies of the audience attending the ritual.[5] David Hammons's *Sheep Raffle* therefore provides a new energy to the Dak'Art Biennale through the sacrificed.

The Sacrificer

> Everything sacred, that intends to remain so, must cover itself in mystery.
>
> —L. S. Senghor, *Liberté 5*, 1993

> I once saw the Sun-King-Ram dance in Côte d'Ivoire. The dancer expressed with his steps the sacred furor of the Ram, and the orchestra followed with musical phrases.
>
> —L. S. Senghor, *Présence Africaine*, 1956

One way of reading David Hammons's *Sheep Raffle* is to look at it through a detour to Léopold Sédar Senghor and the Négritude movement. It is well known that when the movement was under attack in the 1950s and 1960s by such young Turks as Frantz Fanon, Wole Soyinka, and Ezekiel Mphahlele, Senghor defended himself by hiding behind the writers of the Harlem Renaissance. For example, when Wole Soyinka brashly dismissed Négritude in a now famous statement—"The tiger does not go about boasting of its tigritude"—Senghor's response was both surprising and revealing. He stated that if Négritude's poems were perceived as self-celebratory, it was because they were influenced by the poets of Harlem. He cited Langston Hughes, who said: "We younger Negro artists, who create now, intend to express our individual dark skinned selves without fear and shame."[6]

Unfortunately for Senghor, most people, including this author, preferring to see Négritude only as an instance of Francophone imperialism and assimilation, did not hear or see the strong echoes of the Harlem Renaissance in the definition of the movement. We also missed the strong racial consciousness in black poetry from America to France and Africa which today defines the African diaspora aesthetics. In retrospect, one can see that Soyinka's position was more appealing as a critique of the Négritude movement not only because of the pun which linked Négritude to Tigritude, but also because Soyinka had dismissed the essentialist claim to racial solidarity that was at the core of the Négritude movement and the Harlem Renaissance.

But if we were to take Senghor seriously today, and consider the influence of Harlem on Dakar, then the David Hammons's *Sheep Raffle* becomes more relevant at the Dak'Art Biennale. Senghor was the translator into French of the poetry of Langston Hughes. In the work of Hughes and other Harlem Renaissance writers like Claude McKay and Countee Cullen, Senghor and his Négritude peers discovered "a whole network of ties and relations, images and archetypes that had been dormant at the bottom of memory."[7] The deep-seated memory in question is that of Africa before slavery and colonialism. Islam and Christianity combined forces to destroy its social, religious, and economic systems. When Harlem comes to Dakar, it brings back to life this memory, it awakens the gods and the ancestors for the homecoming ceremony.

David Hammons, the sacrificer, knows his role in the dance of this homecoming. According to Senghor, "the sacrificer as the oldest member of the community is closest to the ancestors, can even be considered as part of them. He is the one who offers the sacrifice to the Ancestor. In exchange the latter makes the vital force flow through the sacrificer to the entire participating community."[8]

I attended several performances of the *Sheep Raffle* in Dakar. I tried to observe from a distance as much as I could. But one day I could not resist the temptation to interview David. After all, I felt confident of our friendship in New York. I was also feeling confident that I had a privileged relationship with David and I knew that he was pleased that I was writing this article on him. But he completely ignored my presence and continued with his performance. Surely, David must have incarnated the body of the Ancestor in Dakar during the Biennale. I felt that he was not himself in the way that he was relating to people.

It is important to return to Senghor's theory of African art to make my point here. It is well known that Senghor's theory of Négritude was more drawn toward the primacy of "emotions," "feelings," rhythms," and "repetitions." For him African art, unlike Western art, was not a discourse with a beginning, middle and end."[9] So, instead of being an art of imitation, African art is an art of invention, and a visionary art; instead of an art of re-presentation, it is a production, a spiritual transference that "guides the creator all along her/his performance."[10] It was for this reason that Senghor believed that African art obtains its full meaning only during performance. He writes: "Hence, these rituals or prayers and sacrifices, music and song, dance and masquerade are at the same time artistic manifestations. It is the way they partake of art that they are meaningful."[11]

When I met David during his *Sheep Raffle*, he was possessed by the performance, and therefore was not himself. He had, as Senghor puts it,

> taken hold of the world outside and made it respond to him. He was one with the world he had created, with its shapes, colors, movements, sounds, and rhythms—both musical and plastic—taste and smell. . . . He had begun to live at the pace of this world, beyond the pleasure of the sensory systems. He had identified with the object, and had become the Other [creator, ancestor, God?] in the happiness of communion, a feeling of total presence, of beyond-being.[12]

What could one say about David Hammons's sheep raffle, by way of conclusion? Some people thought that it was arrogant on the part of a Black American to come to Africa and make fun of African art. A *Sheep Raffle* during Africa's most prestigious art meeting is a kind of Afro-pessimism that foreigners project onto the African landscape. In this sense David's *Sheep Raffle* resumes recent racist representations of Africa by journalists such as Keith Richburg's *Out of America* (1998) and Stephen Smith's *Négrologie* (2003). It is also possible to see the exotic side of the *Sheep Raffle* that is so much a part of tourist art. Many African artists, for this reason, stayed away from the performance. They argued that it was not art, and that David was able to get away with it only because he is David. In fact, some found the whole thing misleading and dangerous because the craft of art was missing in it. Even as I write this last sentence, I am still thinking about all these assessments of David Hammons's *Sheep Raffle*. But, putting aside the artist's mastery of modernism, the place of blackness in the Western imaginary, the art market, the minstrelsy of contemporary black artists, and my own fascination with the artist—I wonder?

Notes

1. David Hammons (born in Springfield, Illinois, in 1943) is a well-known African American installation artist. His works can be found at the Museum of Modern Art in New York and in most contemporary art galleries in the U.S. and Europe. Salah Hassan is Chair of the Department of History of Art and Professor of African and African Diaspora art history and visual culture in the Africana Studies Department at Cornell University. He is also a curator and art critic, and founder and editor of *NKA: Journal of Contemporary African Art*.

2. 1 Samuel, 16:13.

3. 1 Samuel, 17:1–58.

4. "Quand on sait que la vie et le courage des autres dépend de votre vie et de votre courage on a plus le droit d'avoir peur." [Ousmane] Sembène, *God's Bits of Wood* (Garden City, NY: 1962), p. 117 [originally published in 1960 as *Les bouts de bois de Dieu*].

5. [Léopold Sédar] Senghor, "L'esprit de la civilisation [ou les lois de la culture négro-africaine]," [*Présence Africaine* (September 19–22, 1956):] 56.

6. [Léopold Sédar] Senghor, *Liberté: Le dialogue des cultures*, volume 5 (Paris: Éditions du Seuil, 1964), p. 15.

7. Senghor, *Liberté: Le dialogue des cultures*, p. 18.

8. Senghor, *Liberté: Le dialogue des cultures*, p. 19.

9. [Léopold Sédar] Senghor, *Liberté: Négritude et civilisation de l'universelle*, volume 3 (Paris: Éditions du Seuil, 1964), p. 326.

10. Senghor, *Liberté: Négritude et civilisation de l'universelle*, p. 327.

11. [Léopold Sédar] Senghor, *Léopold Sédar Senghor et la revue* Présence Africaine (Paris: Présence Africaine, 1996), p. 126.

12. Senghor, *Léopold Sédar Senghor et la revue* Présence Africaine, p. 123.

The Joke of Painting: On David Hammons at L&M Arts, New York

Alexander Alberro

Artworks are often analogous to jokes. Their initially puzzling or ridiculous propositions discharge psychic energy and produce pleasurable effects. The main condition is that the generated tensions reach their highest level at the end. Like jokes, too, which allow their tellers to articulate impolite thoughts that they ought not introduce into public speech, many artworks expose that which dominant codes and social conventions prefer to mystify.

The work of New York–based artist David Hammons has long traded in a sly sense of humor with a sharp polemical edge. From early sculptures and performance pieces such as *Spade in Chains*, 1973, which puns on racism and slavery, and *Pissed Off*, 1981, for which he urinated on a large-scale Richard Serra steel sculpture, to more recent installations such as *Which Mike Would You Like to Be Like?*, 2003, featuring three microphones (i.e., three "mikes") representing three Michaels (Jordan, Tyson, and Jackson), Hammons formulates ironic commentary on the lived experience of urban life in the U.S. and the operation of contemporary art. The tongue-in-cheek puns, word plays, and jokes his artworks mobilize undermine the authority of prevailing rules and norms. This derisiveness is their political force.

Hammons's recent suite of untitled assemblages at the L&M Arts gallery in Manhattan's snooty Upper East Side operates along similar lines.[1] However, this time the focus is on one of the central myths of modernist painting, which the assemblages at once restage and explode with the same kind of irreverent wit that has characterized the artist's work. L&M Arts

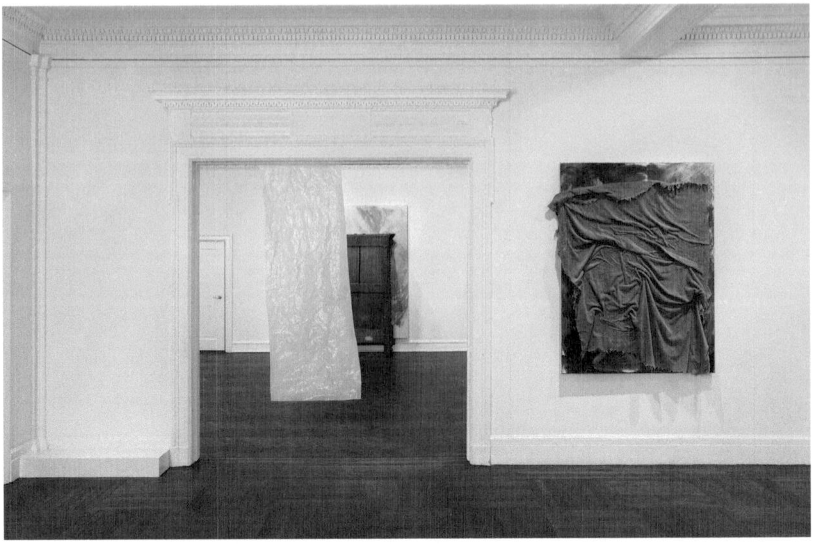

David Hammons, exhibition view, L&M Arts, New York, 2011.

is a secondary-market gallery, with its primary source of income coming from reselling paintings by members of the New York School, the first made-in-the-U.S.A. artistic avant-garde. *Village Voice* critic Jerry Saltz reported that Hammons initially approached the proprietors of L&M Arts "out of the blue" with an idea the artist claimed "would perfectly fit the gallery's space and history."[2] The result was a much-talked-about 2007 show of six vintage dress forms, each outfitted with a fabulously expensive, segmented, and tailored full-length mink, wolf, fox, and sable coat (*Fur Coat*, 2007). Hammons and his partner, Chie, sullied the backs of five of these garments with broad strokes of thick paint and varnish, turning them into paintings, and the paintings, in turn, into a reflection on the marketing of luxury objects. They also partially torched one coat, an exquisitely puffed chinchilla, rendering a large hole through the middle. The artists offered to pay production costs but refused to allow the gallery to sell any of the artworks. Their provocative gesture brought together questions of class and what it means to be humane with questions of symbolic and economic value.

For this year's exhibition, his second at L&M Arts, Hammons draped ten or so big, abstract oil canvases composed in a luminous palette and all-over style with large sections of various grungy materials. The latter include crumpled plastic garbage bags, an old and ragged terrycloth towel, and industrial tarpaulins of the type housepainters typically use to protect furniture and floors from stray drips of pigment. Aggressively gouged, bitten, or scorched holes here and there in the cheap plastic or tarps allow glimpses of the generic abstract expressionist compositions beneath. Some of the trappings that shroud the paintings are stitched together by hand, others appear to be machine-sewn, and yet others glued or pressed onto the canvas, seemingly while the paint was still wet. The multiple folds and crinkles of the banal materials hung in layers over the compositions double as expressionistic gestures and produce dramatic effects. In one instance, the tarp is missing, and Hammons shoved a castoff, decrepit wooden wardrobe up against the canvas instead, obscuring the splotches of lavender magentas, mint greens, pastel reds, and turquoise blues. And two pieces on the gallery's second floor consist of just the vandalized industrial elements—translucent plastic tarpaulins and opaque black trash bags ripped, torn, and nailed to the wall through embedded grommets—with no "paintings" underneath.

Hammons's compositions are as dependent on the history of nonrepresentational painting as they are on the Duchampian readymade, Dada collage, and Arte Povera sculpture. The works integrate and turn these legacies, thereby corrupting the machine-made elements with abject refuse and investing the painterly aspect with a renewed sense of aesthetic desublimation that the whole repertory of rips, scratches, gouging, and abrasions implies. The resulting assemblages recall the iconoclastic form of self-expression with trash materials that characterized the work of mid-twentieth century *informel* painters such as Alberto Burri or Antoni Tàpies, though they conspicuously lack the existential, humanist-driven impulse of these European abstract artists.

The big scale, garish colors, and thick, spontaneous-seeming brushstrokes of most of the paintings Hammons installed at L&M Arts directly relate to the work of the New York School and hence to the gallery's commercial "history." Where we can see them, Hammons's canvases restage Abstract Expressionism's strange synthesis of formal rigor and idiosyncratic passion, as well as its play on figure-ground versus all-over compositions and stained versus impastoed surfaces. Hammons surely knew that the Museum of Modern Art's blockbuster exhibition, *Abstract Expressionist New York*, prominently featured the apotheosis of this heroic art movement during the run of his show.[3] He was also aware of the fact that L&M Arts has been the site of no less than seven solo exhibitions of the work of the New York School painter Willem de Kooning. Indeed, it is the oeuvre of the latter that Hammons's abstract pictures resemble the most. The paintings derive their ludicrously vulgar colors and emotional high heat whole cloth from de Kooning. And as if that was not enough, Hammons produced the broad sweeps that dominate his canvases with the help of the type of large brush de Kooning often employed to endow his expressionistic compositions with a virile swagger. But if the reference is de Kooning, it is not as much an homage to the intuitive and technically gifted painter as an oblique revamp of Robert Rauschenberg's outrageous 1953 gambit *Erased de Kooning Drawing*. Hammons's riff, it seems, is more one of derision than of eulogy, a parody of de Kooning's medium and style rather than an embrace.

The compositions at L&M Arts are as sculptural as they are painterly. Their draped membranes often touch the ground, establishing a continuity between the walls and the floor. By linking the two axes in a position of apparent correspondence and parity, the artist erodes the boundaries of painting and sculpture and makes the work, in its evident flow and self-determination, directly respond to the viewers' own bodily experiences. Not only are spectators discouraged from lifting the veils of trash that obscure the ostensibly pristine canvases beneath, but they must also be attentive not to trample on the sculptural elements of the compositions that flow into the space of the room.

Twentieth-century viewers embraced abstract art as the shortest route to universal meaning and significance, a phenomenon that has waned but not entirely disappeared. Many of the abstract compositions of Kasimir Malevich and Piet Mondrian, for instance, or those of Dan Flavin, Lygia Clark, Agnes Martin, and, more recently, artists such as Olafur Eliasson and Paul Chan, claim (to a greater or lesser degree) a relevance and subject beyond representation, a meaning unspeakable otherwise, yet held in and made concrete by the organization of form and color (and increasingly sound). The emphasis is alternately on liberation, transcendence, and foundational experience. Spectators, in turn, are assured that concentrated speculation about the interior, virtual space of the artwork will lead to moments of sudden intuitive understanding. In order to maintain this belief when confronted with the testimony of their own eyes, viewers often have to act as if there is much more there than there actually is; as

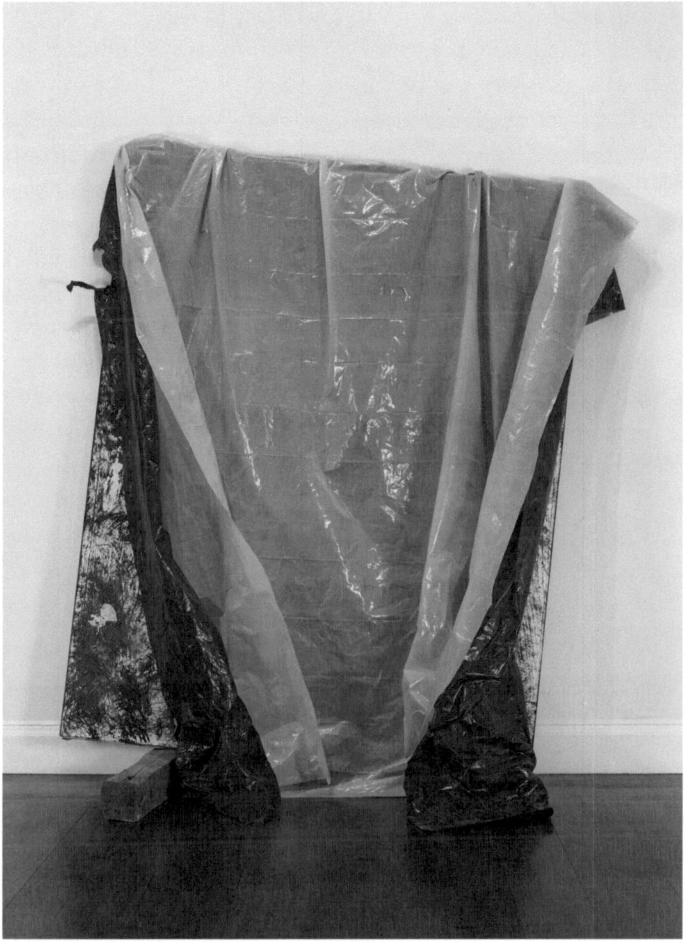

David Hammons, *Untitled*, 2008, mixed media painting.

if, to borrow from the classic tale, the emperor is decked out in exquisite new clothes.

Hammons's compositions offer little in the way of mythical experience. On the contrary, they represent a kind of fervid literalness, one befitting an art surviving the death of art. In their attempts to solve the riddle by peering through the tears and gapes in the tarpaulins or around the edges and margins of the compositions, spectators cannot escape the fact that there is little of substance beneath the damaged facades. This reality is nowhere more apparent than in the two stunning assemblages on the second floor of L&M Arts, the last in the exhibition narrative's order, that consist solely of double, canvas-size curtains of mutilated industrial plastic affixed to the gallery wall. Here, painting's bare truth confronts the viewer; the problem posed by the bewildering objects is solved. The emperor is naked, after all.

Some will undoubtedly quibble that there is nothing new about this insight. The negation of interiority, of any solid, plotted depth, is as central to the history of modern art as is the passage from content and the division of signification to a phenomenology of the surface, from the figural to the literal, from representation to presentation. But Hammons's insistence is not on the work's facticity. His recent assemblages go beyond a refusal of inner necessity and presentness. They even exceed the late-twentieth-century notion of art as a field within what conceptual artist Daniel Buren once called "critical limits." For Hammons, art is a mischievous game beyond limits. It perverts the logic of forms of belief, conventions of knowledge, and ways of seeing to make the repressed visible in a manner only an excellent joke could accomplish.

Notes

This chapter has been revised since originally published.

1. *David Hammons*, L&M Arts, New York City, January 26–March 4, 2011.

2. Jerry Saltz, "Fur What It's Worth," *Village Voice* (February 27, 2007), at https://www.villagevoice.com/2007/02/27/fur-what-its-worth/.

3. "Abstract Expressionist New York," Museum of Modern Art, New York City, October 3, 2010–April 25, 2011.

Dark Angels of Dust: David Hammons and the Art of Streetwise Transcendentalism

Greg Tate

In the continuum of Black American interventions into spaces culturally marked "Whites Only," David Hammons's emergence and tactical maneuvering in the American and international realms of the modern art world seem as voluble as Nat Turner's and as inevitable as Miles Davis's. Educated in the sixties—in the Los Angeles of the Watts riots—Hammons follows in the footsteps of activists and artists such as Malcolm X, Amiri Baraka, James Brown, and the Black Panthers, who made manifest the degree to which being Black and Black forms of being, especially those found in the urban streets, could be erotically and politically poeticized and positioned as countersupremacist provocations to Black American self-renovation and agency. Martin Luther King Jr. and the civil rights movement mobilized the Black American desire to end legalized racism; more radical figures sought to awaken the community's perception of its innate beauty, genius, and power of vernacular disruption. Inspired by this sentiment as much as by the technocratic funk and erudition of jazz icons Thelonious Monk and John Coltrane, Hammons proceeded from the notion that Black American culture readily contained an inexhaustible wealth of gestural, metaphorical, and material resources. He then went about developing a practice that pursued street cred and modernist cred with equal authority (and intensity), and with sly, shamanistic wiles. The influence of the Black experience on modern art has been well documented—how African art acquired by intrepid anthropologists found its way to ravenous European artists, such as Picasso, in search of antibourgeois, antiauthoritarian inspiration from outside the institutional cosseting of museums, universities, and the church.

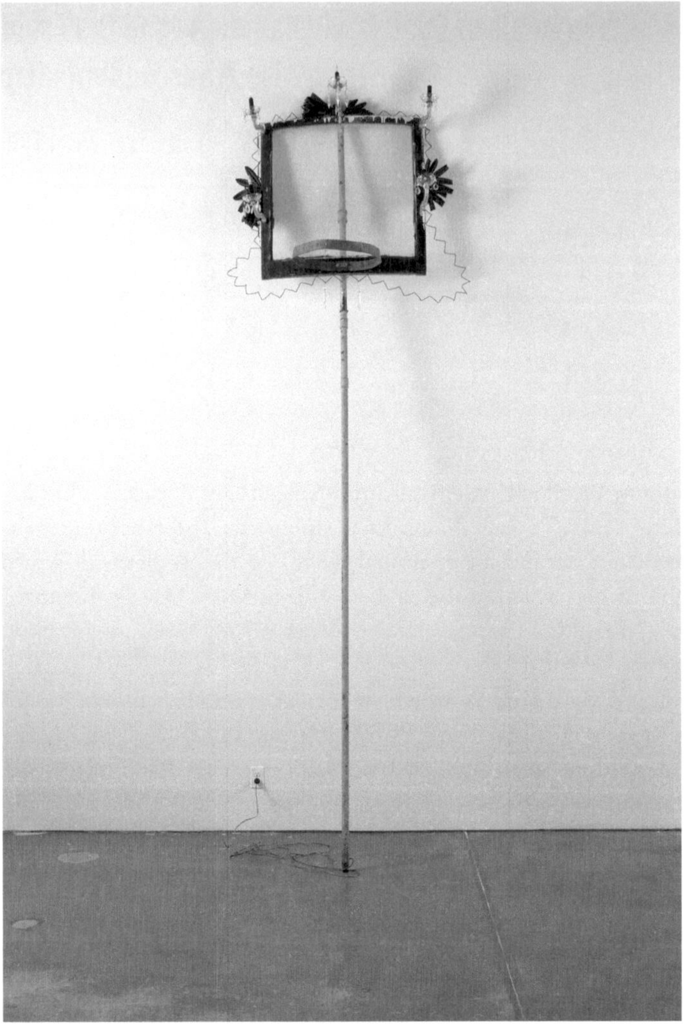

David Hammons, *High Falutin'*, 1990, metal (some parts painted with oil), oil on wood, glass, rubber, velvet, plastic, and electric light bulbs, 13 ft. 2 in. × 48 in. × 30½ in. (396 × 122 × 77.5 cm). The Museum of Modern Art, New York, Robert and Meryl Meltzer Fund and purchase.

The midcentury pursuit of African formal expressivity as a counterforce to rationalist modernity became manifest in the impact that Thelonious Monk's and Charlie Parker's virtuosic improvisations on the blues and Tin Pan Alley ballads had on the aesthetics of artists Jackson Pollock, John Cage, and Andy Warhol. The notion that an "America first" formalism and classicism could emerge from fetishization of the pop-familiar had long coursed through the post-African paramodernity of Black American music and dance. The increasing desire among American creatives for a visual modernity of their own gave rise to the dominant categories of postwar American visual art: abstract expressionism, pop, minimalism, conceptualism, performance art, video art. However, postwar American visual culture was equally influenced by the liberatory political actions of the African American body politic in this period. The mass mobilizations and theatrical staging of protest and self-determination politics by the civil rights and Black Power movements in the sixties and seventies, those movements' grassroots creation of personality cults proved as viral as the Hollywood machine. They produced the notion of an American public sphere that could be artfully and anarchically occupied and manipulated.

Black American political action provoked other repressed American constituencies to take dramatic street action for their constitutionally guaranteed due—Hispanic, female, gay, antiwar. The organized counterattack and overreach of the federal branch against all those contesting constituencies turned America's urban centers into battlegrounds, real and symbolic, where not only opposing political passions but opposing representations of American cultural style and identity were challenged or destroyed by fire. American notions of the spectacular and the prophetic shifted from the silver screen to the television, from the gallery wall to the street in the 1960s, because the dark gods in the street started doing more than just shouting back and made "Black" and "street" synonymous in the American psyche. The movement and school of American street painting we know as graffiti—but among hip-hop devotees more correctly understood as writing, tagging, and bombing—is thought to have begun in Philadelphia in the late sixties by an intrepid teenager named Cornbread (Darryl McCray), who not only tagged his name but a levitating crown (presaging Basquiat by a decade and visually predicting that artist's well-known encomium that his work was about "royalty, heroism and the streets"). After tagging up his reform school, McCray would go on to tag an elephant in the Philly zoo and the Jackson 5's private jet. A stylish bombing of the biggest and baddest targets, these acts also mark a self-authorized assault on private property rights and state control of public space. The proliferation of writing, tagging, and bombing on the world's biggest rolling canvas, the New York City subway system, continued the combative tradition of artfully Africanizing jihad by stylish, gladiatorial degrees. Bombing's mobilization of the repressed energies in the city's guerilla creative core eventually produced several early masters of war—Crash, Futura 2000, and Rammellzee among them. Hammons is a generation older than these writers, and by the seventies, he was showing in L.A. galleries with a community of fellow travelers such as John Outterbridge, Betye Saar, and Noah Purifoy—a group as much influenced by Arte Povera as by the Watts Towers. What is evident in the most stellar work Hammons produced at this time, his legendary *Body Print* series, is his interest in representing both the materiality and the ephemerality of blues and jazz, and Black folk, especially Black street folk. The creation of this series required actual Black bodies and Vaseline—a skin product of particular cosmetic significance to Black Americans—marked the last time that graphic figuration would be a dominant feature of the artist's work, it was not the last time he would articulate an inherent tension between Black conceptual bodies and negative white space.

Despite the commercial success of the *Body Prints*, Hammons decided he'd exhausted that vein and stopped making them in the 1970s. In that refusal, Hammons established himself as the Duchamp of America's streetwise artists, an elusive illusionist whose practice became focused on creating a body of work the art world could not easily ignore, categorize, claim, or disclaim, either. Hammons spent the next twenty years making his relationship to the street the essence of his practice, which extended beyond the various and multifarious works he created. Joseph Beuys became another valued point of reference alongside Duchamp. For Hammons, whatever an artist did outside the white cube—or found and transformed out there—was art too, whether or not it was ever exhibited. Having already experienced success inside the art world when he was barely twenty, Hammons committed himself to proving how little validation an artist needed from that world to be significant, productive, prolific, and influential. In a 1986 interview in *REALLIFE* magazine, Hammons told art historian Kellie Jones why he preferred the streets to galleries for his work: "The worst thing in the world is to say, 'well I'm going to see this exhibition.' The work should instead be somewhere in between your house and where you're going to see it, it shouldn't be at the gallery. Because when you get there you're already prepared, your eyes are ready, your glands, your whole body is ready to receive this art. By that time, you've probably seen more art getting to the spot than you do when you get there. That's why I like better doing stuff on the street—because the art becomes just one of the objects that's in the path of your everyday existence. It's what you move through, and it doesn't have seniority over anything else."

Hammons's tactical evasion of art world fame and fortune reached its pinnacle in correspondence with that eighties moment in New York when many graffiti artists were hungry for gallery legitimacy, and the pursuit of celebrity beset the city's art world like a plague. While the meteoric and doomed Basquiat was being fêted in princely fashion by dealers from Berlin to Beverly Hills, Hammons was selling immaculately white and perfectly round snowballs in the company of squatters and junkies on the Lower East Side (*Bliz-aard Ball Sale*, 1983); bagging elephant dung from the Bronx Zoo; collecting greasy brown paper bags from Harlem BBQ joints; and catching lice from the hair he swept and saved for the wire-sculptural work that would eventually produce his dreadlock colossus (*Untitled*, 1992). During this period, Hammons built a shanty house in Battery Park City for a 1985 work called *Delta Spirit*. A shrine of sorts, in the tradition of self-constructed habitats in the Mississippi Delta, it was made from discarded lumber, evoking similar rickety shelters still visible there and in South Africa. That *Delta Spirit* was erected near Wall Street, where auction blocks selling enslaved Africans once thrived, only heightens the site specificity and poignancy of the work. Later would come his short film collaboration *Phat Free* (1995), a recording of a performance in which Hammons goes kicking a bucket around Harlem—one of Hammons's many oppositional asides about the mentality of hip-hop culture. If one had to name two Hammons works that epitomize and provocatively strike a balance between his love for Black American street folk and his critical intentions toward that community, they would be 1986's *Higher Goals*—a fifty-foot-high basketball pole and hoop encrusted with African-esque decorations composed of discarded soda bottle caps bent to resemble cowrie shells—and his 1989 circular assemblage *Night Train*, made from trashed bottles of Night Train and Thunderbird wine (legendary Harlem wino favorites).

Like the Alabama painter/sculptor/assemblage artist Thornton Dial, Hammons believes there is a magical and even dangerous aura specific to organic and industrial materials that have been touched by Blackfolk. Hammons told Jones, "I have information on Black people's hair that no

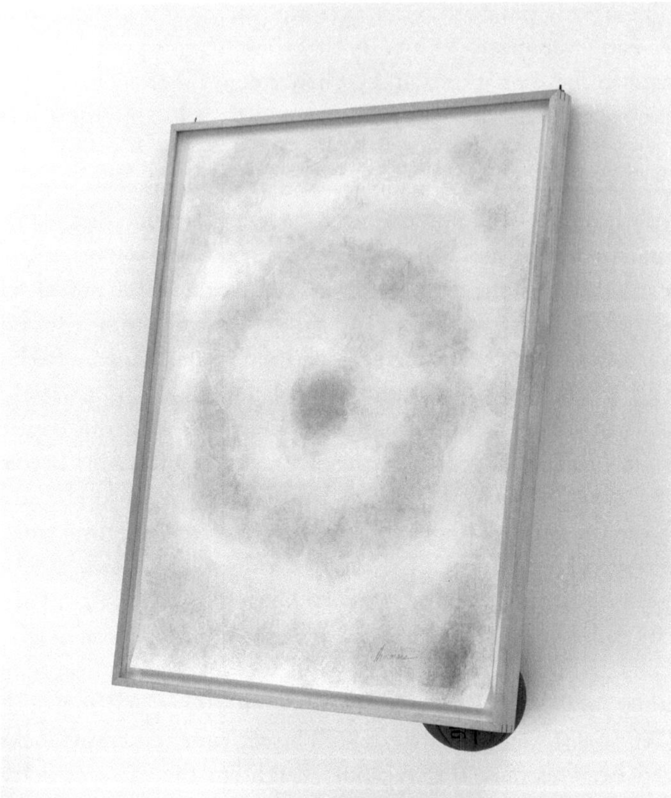

David Hammons, *Out of Bounds*, 1995–1996, dirt on paper in artist's frame, with basketball. 53¼ × 41½ × 11½ in. (131.2 × 105.4 × 29.2 cm). The Museum of Modern Art, New York, Gift of the Friends of Contemporary Drawing, The Friends of Education of The Museum of Modern Art, and Peter and Eileen Norton.

one else in the world has. It's the most unbelievable fiber that I've ever run across. I was actually going insane working with that hair so I had to stop. That's just how potent it is. You've got tons of people's spirits in your hands when you work with that stuff. The same with the wine bottles. A Black person's lips have touched each one of those bottles so you have to be very, very careful."

In Basquiat's and Hammons's work, one recognizes a shared obsession with bringing visual recognition to the aspects of Black life that elegantly and eloquently teeter between functionality and dysfunction, form and chaos, vision and apocalypse. In light of Basquiat's fate, it's impossible not to read the apparitions in his work as possessing a marked-for-death aura. With Hammons, you also get fatalism and sly gallows humor, but because his works often take their complex feelings about race, death, and desire into the public square, they presume no transcendence or representation of folks' circumstances that cannot be critiqued by the folk themselves. This was never more apparent than in 1988, when his installation *How Ya Like Me Now?* was attacked by Black men with sledgehammers. The work in question, shown in a vacant lot in Washington, DC, near the National Portrait Gallery (which had no representation of Black Americans on display at the time), depicted a billboard-sized drawing of Jesse Jackson that Hammons had given blue eyes, blond hair, and pink skin, along with the taunting inscription of the title (taken from a popular song by hip-hop lyricist Kool Moe Dee).

The piece's street critics, not in on the joke, interpreted Hammons as an alien interloper out to insult a Black hero rather than to expose an American electorate for whom Jackson's primary disqualification as a presidential candidate was his skin color. Hammons took the assault in his usual acerbic stride: When the work was moved inside, he placed several sledgehammers on the floor in front of it, sardonically attaching the defacers' toolkit (and brutal misreadings) into the work.

Having become an art historical figure and an unpretentious and unaffected art world star on his own savvy outlier terms in the nineties, Hammons has become more familiar to regular gallery-goers, curators, and collectors, but he remains an elusive trickster-figure. He exhibits more inside these days, albeit with his own arch twists on what coming in from the cold can mean for the adoring hordes who now show up to see his work.

In 2002, before the opening of his exhibition *Concerto in Black and Blue* at New York's Ace Gallery, idle chatter speculated on whether Hammons might use the Lascaux-scale rooms to install a major retrospective. Instead, gallery visitors were given slight plastic objects which emitted a faint blue light, and then entered a space of near-total darkness. Once there we were only able to make out the silhouettes of our fellow blue-glinting spectators. Hammons had evaded and avoided the obvious once again. In works such as 1989's *Highfalutin*—a recombinant construction that morphs a basketball hoop into a crystal chandelier—and *Hail Mary*, 2006—from a series of seventy-two dusty drawings that record the impressions of a dribbled basketball—the artist continues to mine, mock, and memorialize the streets.

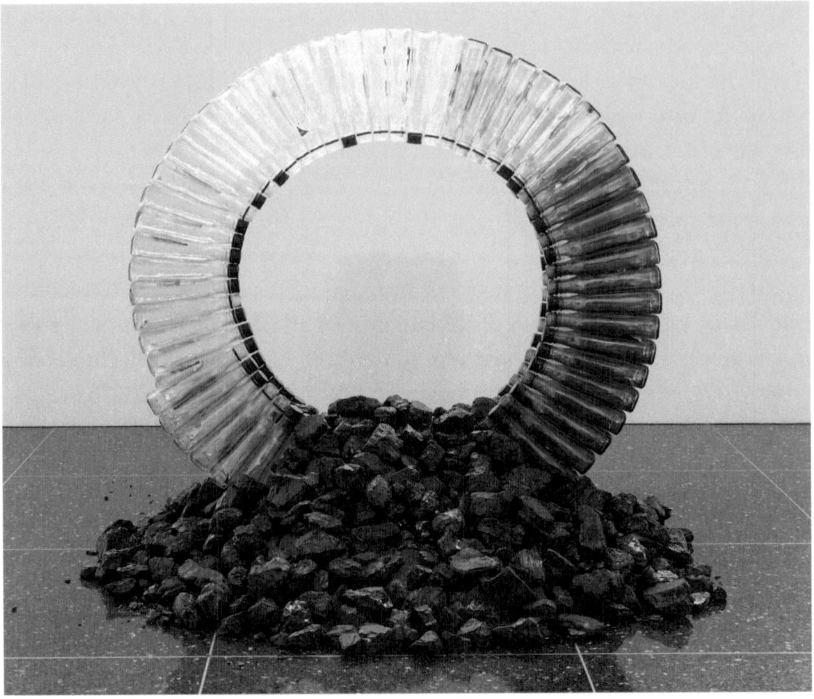

David Hammons, *Untitled (Night Train)*, 1989, glass, silicone glue, and coal, 42 × 42 × 30 in. (106.7 × 106.7 × 76.2 cm), depth and width variable. The Museum of Modern Art, New York, Gift of the Hudgins Family in memory of Lawrence D. "Butch" Morris.

In 2006, proving he's lost none of his desire to set the bourgeoisie aflame, Hammons and his wife, Chie, exhibited two floors of expensive fur coats that they'd torched to ruined perfection. The show occurred at an otherwise barren townhouse atelier on the Upper East Side. Clearly, Hammons's street ethos and 'hood-elevating aesthetics continue to repel the domestication that's expected to follow rebel artists into respectability. What Hammons's practice has bequeathed the modern scene more than anything is a nomadic sense of the street as not just a canvas but a carnival in constant tumult to which attention must be paid and for which argumentative translations will be made. Concomitant has been his commitment to taking the art world down to ground level every chance-operation he gets. In the realm of so-called street art, Hammons looms large as the field's philosopher–king and most agile demolitions expert.

Can You Dig It? Signifying Race in David Hammons's *Spade* Series

Tobias Wofford

In the spring of 2001, the Studio Museum in Harlem held the groundbreaking exhibition *Freestyle*, which introduced a new generation of black artists to the American art world. Though somewhat united along the lines of racial identity, the work of the twenty-eight exhibited artists displayed a surprising diversity of media and subject matter. In the introductory essay to *Freestyle*'s catalogue, curator Thelma Golden proclaimed the advent of "post-black." The term was simultaneously an ironic addition to the excessive use of the "post" prefix in scholarship on contemporary culture and a serious prognosis of a tangible shift in African American cultural production. Post-black drew attention to the often nebulous symptoms of a new relationship between African American artists and the representation of identity. "For me," wrote Golden, "to approach a conversation about 'black art,' ultimately meant embracing and rejecting the notion of such a thing at the same time."[1] The artists grouped under the "post-black" banner share a similarly complicated relationship to the term "black art" as a category in which their work can be grouped. "(Post-black) was characterized by artists who were adamant about not being labeled as 'black' artists, though their work was steeped, in fact deeply interested, in redefining complex notions of blackness."[2]

If a conversation about black art is one wrought with ambivalence, a conversation about post-black art seems nearly impossible. One need only look to the uneasy role race has played in recent media coverage and policymaking of the Obama administration to see that the notion of a post-racial society is hardly a resolution to racial inequity in America, but a condition

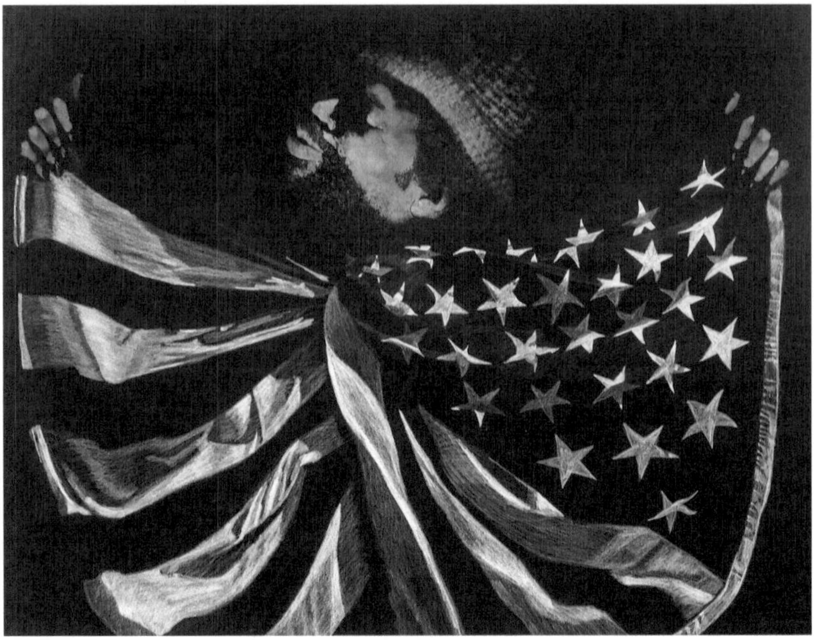

David Hammons, *Untitled (Man with Flag)*, n.d., body print—grease, pigment, and white crayon on paper, 29¾ × 39¾ in. (76 × 101 cm). Glenstone Museum, Potomac, Maryland.

that requires new tools for understanding it. Thus, the emergence of post-black as a term is symptomatic of a crisis in theorizing the representation of identity in contemporary African American art. It emerges amidst a long and charged debate over the representation of black identity and poses the difficult question of how to come to terms with the elusive role of identity in contemporary art. Yet the issues that arise around the term "post-black" are not new. Implicit within the work of many artists that brought about a "Black art" in the 1960s, and those who championed identity politics in the 1970s and 1980s, was the critical relationship to identity that defines post-black. A return to these earlier artists, then, may give a better understanding to the elusive practices of a younger generation of African American artists.

This essay picks up the conversation with the signifying strategies of African American artist David Hammons, whose career has played an important role in the evolving tradition of African American art since his entrance into the American art scene in the 1960s. Even in these early years, Hammons's work explored the problems of representation, language and identity that continue to confront African American artists today. For example, in his *Spade* series of the early 1970s which incorporates the derogatory term "spade," Hammons employed a strategy of representation that interrogated stereotypes and black identity. Through his interest in language and a clever manipulation of racial signs, Hammons questions the ability of the language of race to represent black subjectivity.

While Hammons moved on to create a vast and complex body of work after the *Spade* series, many of the strategies of representation developed through it have informed his later career as well as that of some contemporary African American artists grouped under the banner of "post-black." Hammons's early work offers a vital perspective on a long and charged debate over the representation of blackness in the arts and ultimately engages with the difficult question of how to come to terms with the role of identity in contemporary African American art. This essay explores the ways in which Hammons's art elaborates the complex notions of blackness that have so profoundly eluded the viewer. Further, an exploration of Hammons's practice may ultimately demonstrate why a conversation about black art is wrought with such deep ambivalence.

Hammons made his entrance into the Los Angeles art scene in the late 1960s after attending the Otis Art Institute where he worked under the tutelage of famed African American WPA [Works Progress Administration] artist Charles White. Artistically, the Los Angeles area was an especially fertile ground in the 1960s, having established itself as a major location for those looking for alternatives to the artistic dominance of New York. The early embrace of Pop Art, reflected by Andy Warhol's 1962 one-man show at the Ferus Gallery on La Cienega, as well as the critical celebration of Marcel Duchamp's conceptualism as seen in the large retrospective of the artist held at the Pasadena Art Museum in 1963, reflected the city's unique artistic sensibility. From this context grew the careers of Los Angeles' Pop artists including Ed Ruscha and Edward Kienholz.

The 1960s was a decade charged with social and political turmoil in the United States. The Civil Rights Movement, the Watts rebellions in 1965, the Vietnam War and growing consciousness of marginalized ethnic groups all served as elements that would greatly influence the artistic production of African American artists working in Los Angeles. Hammons joined other Los Angeles–based African American artists such as John

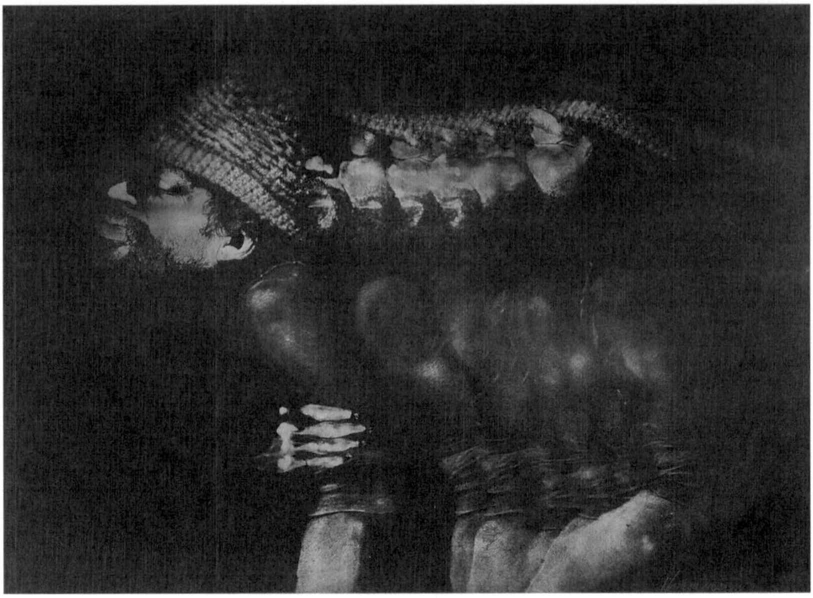

David Hammons, *Defend Your Walk*, 1974, body print, 31½ × 42 in. (80 × 107 cm). Glenstone Museum, Potomac, Maryland.

Outterbridge, John Riddle, Noah Purifoy, Betye Saar, Senga Nengudi and Timothy Washington. These artists worked to articulate new philosophies of art that incorporated an African American aesthetic sensibility. Often, these artists referenced African American folk traditions by using found materials in assemblage and collage. Of course, the assemblage aesthetic favored by many of the major African American artists in Los Angeles did not emerge in a vacuum. While it would take significant space to chart the relation between Los Angeles' Pop artists and the number of innovative African American artists who were also working in the city at the time, certainly, the emphasis on found materials in the funky assemblage works of Saar and Purifoy reflect the ways in which these artists shared many aesthetic and social concerns with artists such as Keinholz.

However, to grasp the context of Hammons's interaction with notions of identity in his early works, one must consider it in relation to the Black Arts Movement and the critical framing of African American artistic production in the 1960s and 1970s. The Black Arts Movement describes a dispersed and complicated shift in African American art discourse to which it is difficult to ascribe any one cohesive aesthetic or artistic program. Like the Harlem Renaissance, it was broad both in terms of geography and in terms of artistic medium. In fact, the most vocal proponents of the Black Arts Movement were poets and playwrights such as Larry Neal and LeRoi Jones (who changed his name to Amiri Baraka in 1968). One of the main concepts that the writers and artists associated with the movement promoted was the notion that art should serve the needs of an African American community, challenging white hegemony and the oppression of African Americans.

Part of the challenge to white hegemony was the development of a black aesthetic. For some, such as Neal, this aesthetic involved a complete rejection of Euro-American ways of seeing. He asserted this point in his 1968 essay "The Black Arts Movement," where he argued that, through Black Power movements, black artists were recognizing that "there are in fact and spirit two Americas—one black one white."[3] He and other critics insisted that black artists abandon dominant aesthetic paradigms in favor of one that allowed Black people to define the world on their own terms—a black aesthetic oriented toward the empowerment of the black community. Neal's assertion of two separate Americas mirrors the increasing disillusionment with American systems of power among African American cultural producers. Yet, this binary relationship between a black and a white America maintains the problematic presumption that the black aesthetic is counter to a white one and thus the black aesthetic relies on the white in order to define itself. A similar conundrum emerged in Elsa Honig Fine's discussion of the tension between what she called "Mainstream vs. Blackstream" artists in her 1971 essay "Mainstream, Blackstream and the Black Arts Movement" which formed a major premise in her 1973 book *The Afro-American Artist*.[4] Further, the insistence that artists engage with a black aesthetic that served the notion of a black community avowed assumptions about identity and community that were inevitably reductive and essentialist. As later theories of identity emerged, the notions of blackness and community that framed the critical reception of the Black Arts Movement seemed problematic at best and entirely insufficient at worst.

Kobena Mercer offered one such critique of the theoretical framing of Black Arts Movement in the 1960s and 1970s, arguing that the essentialist focus on authenticity relied on an ability to claim the right to speak for "the black community." He wrote in his 1990 essay, "Black Art and the Burden of Representation," that an insistence on an aesthetic tied to the notion of a "black community," "risks the unwitting return to a critical slippage, which arises whenever issues of audience become decisive in evaluating what counts as 'black art,' from judgments about the blackness of the text, to judgments about the 'blackness' of its author (and his or her intended audience)."[5] For poststructuralists critical of essentialism in identity, the Black Arts Movement's apparent promotion of authentic notions of blackness as a primary aesthetic criteria raised serious barriers for reading the work of black artists from this period. As Mercer continued, "When the trope of 'authenticity' is used to define the question of aesthetic value, it often reduces to an argument about who does, and who does not, 'belong' in the black communities."[6]

How then do we engage with the art of the Black Arts Movement and the ways in which identity, authenticity and community function in these works? Despite their constructed and mutable nature, identity and community were of central importance for the art of the Black Arts Movement. Yet, in order to assess these works and their contribution, we must not attempt to examine whether the artists and their works are "authentically black" or whether they properly serve a black community. Recent reassessments of the movement in studies such as Lisa Gail Collins' and Margo Natalie Crawford's anthology *New Thoughts on the Black Arts Movement* as well as Daniel Widener's *Black Arts West* have offered new insights about the broad range of responses by visual artists to the cultural and political atmosphere of the Black Arts Movement, especially in Los Angeles.[7]

The opportunity to reassess the artists in Los Angeles, and Hammons's work in particular, during this time shows that much of the claims of essentialism attributed to the Black Arts Movement (even by critics of the day) do not hold when works are given a close reading. The claims of authenticity or essentialist notions of blackness made for artists of the Black Arts Movement seem insufficient in describing Hammons's art in this period. Rather, the Black Arts Movement itself and its particular manifestation in Los Angeles suggest new ways to think through the cultural and historical terrain of race in the 1960s and 1970s.

In Los Angeles, Hammons first produced his well-received body prints, a format for which his early years as an artist are best known. To create these works, Hammons literally used his own body as a printing plate—coating his skin or the printing paper with margarine and then pressing his greased body onto the printing paper. Powdered pigment was then sprinkled onto these stains which clung to the areas sticky with

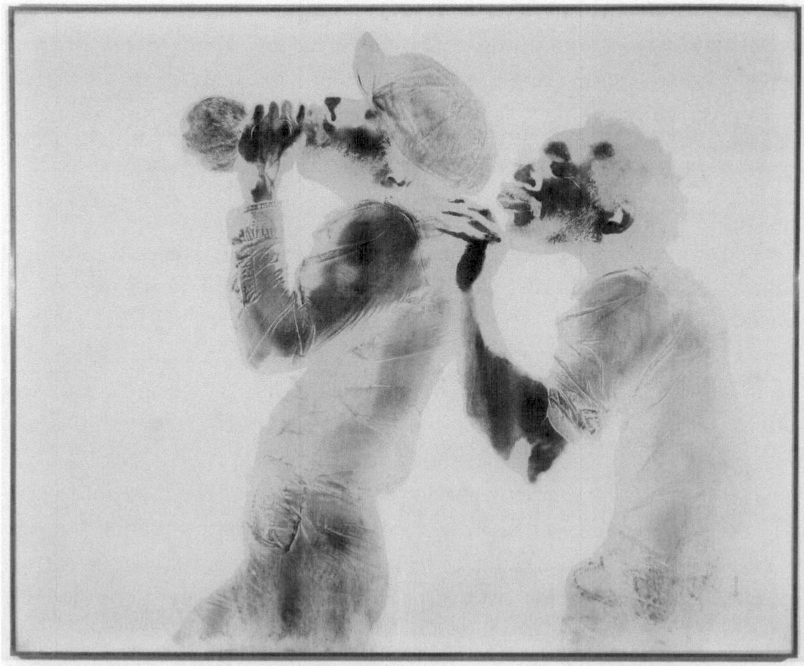

David Hammons, *The Wine Leading the Wine*, c. 1969, body print, 40 × 48¼ in. (101.6 × 122.6 cm). Hudgins Family Collection.

grease, thus revealing the body's impression. The image was subsequently fixed with a fixative and sometimes embellished with silkscreened or collaged elements. This method produced images that record the textures of skin, hair and textiles in surprising detail.[8] Viewers of these images are confronted with distorted but readable representations of the body, often appearing frozen in profile or with entire expanses of flesh unraveled onto the printing surface.

This direct relation to the body that seems so blatantly proclaimed in the body prints lends them an unusual sensuality. Examples like *Untitled* (1974) confront viewers with an impression of a face with a broad nose and full lips pressed against the surface of the print. This impression is framed by black collaged paper that suggests the subtly curving silhouette of a body while the heavily textured background adds to the tactility expressed in the impression of the face. The explicit corporeality of such images, along with the size limited to the actual size of the body that creates them, gives these images a hauntingly physical presence. The mystery of these images perhaps draws from the fact that they make so clear to the viewer the impression of the body. This use of the body print has some reflection in the work of Yves Klein whose famous use of the body as brushstrokes in the early 1960s was a lens through which many viewers must have seen Hammons's interventions.[9] However, Klein's body imprints seemed to emphasize motion and fleeting presence to the point that many of these works appear almost completely abstract. In contrast, the exacting textures of flesh, wooly hair, as well as portrait-like emphasis on faces—broad noses and thick lips—lend Hammons's impressions an undeniable racial specificity that never seemed to be a concern in Klein's work. Hammons's bodies seem to declare their presence, undeniably black while also not didactically so.

Hammons often incorporated other elements layered onto the imprints of the bodies in his work. For example, the use of the flag can be seen repeatedly throughout his early works. Of course, the use of the flag connects to the earlier Pop art precedent of Jasper Johns, and also was widely used among the artists of the Black Arts Movement. These works have an overt political charge. This is especially salient in works such as Hammons's famous *Injustice Case* from 1970. The work depicts a full body print of a man in profile. He is pictured bound to a chair with his mouth gagged and head thrown back, his arm rigid in an apparent struggle against the tight coils of his restraints. The dreadful violence of this image is juxtaposed to the crisp geometric stripes and stars of the American flag that frames the composition. The work is a condemnation of the institutional violence of the American justice system, inspired by the binding and gagging of Black Panther activist Bobby Seale during the "Chicago Eight" trial.[10] Through the incorporation of symbolic elements such as the American flag in his body prints, Hammons engaged with the charged political environment of black culture in the 1960s and 1970s.

However, it is arguably not the use of the flag that lends the work it primary allure or renders the violence in *Injustice Case* so disturbing. The special appeal of the body prints is tied to the fact that the work represents the scene through the body's imprint. In linguistic terms this imprint functions as an index of the body. Representation through the index uses a particular process of creating meaning. Rather than the symbolic sign whose relationship to the referent is arbitrary, or the iconic sign whose relationship is one of similarity, the index is a sign whose causal relationship to the referent can be conceived of in terms of the trace or evidence. The violent scene seems all the more real as the viewer is presented with the testimonial imprint of this tortured body.

Writers such as Alfred Gell have looked to the index as an important aspect of art's social functions.[11] Within Gell's theorization, art objects gain a unique type of agency because the artwork is entangled in a nexus of relationships between artists, viewers and representations. Audiences infer agency to the artwork as an index of an artist's production. Artworks seem like ambassadors who grant viewers access to the genius of an artist, the disposition of a portrait sitter, or the zeitgeist of an era. While this theorization of the index is perhaps a little too broad for our purposes here, the notion of the perceived agency expressed in indexical signs, especially when brought into an art situation, is a helpful way to think through the signifying power of Hammons's body prints. Certainly, Hammons's use of the imprint of the body encourages us as viewers to imagine a presence beyond our own—to project or infer a relation to a presence that is not physically proximate, but whose very existence seem so vehemently insisted upon by the bodies that literally press themselves against the picture plane. The body prints offer an extraordinarily human appeal for recognition, yet they are also evidence of the absence of the represented bodies, suggesting a kind of haunting in which the artwork is a medium for communication.

Like a clue at a crime scene, indexical signs offer the evidence of the referent while simultaneously demonstrating the referent's absence. Yet how do we solve its mysteries? Works like *Injustice Case* seem to have a clear message, yet the black bodies in Hammons's work are still surrounded with a beguiling ambiguity. They are traces of the body that offer a sign that is both as meaningful as it is indeterminate. This is part of the unusual appeal of the index. It mirrors a discussion of indexical signs posed by Rosalind Krauss in her essay "Notes on the Index." In this discussion, the photograph, which maintains an indexical relation to portrayed objects by the literal burning of reflected light onto a photosensitive material, is presented as "a disruption in the autonomy of the sign. A meaninglessness surrounds it which can only be filled by the addition of a text."[12] Photographs need a caption in order for the viewer to interpret the photographer's intent. Photography and all indexical signs, then, present a trace that is a signifier before the establishment of stable meaning, a "message without a code" that requires a supplemental discourse in order to attain intelligibility.

Perhaps the semiotic processes that Hammons's work creates can best be grappled with through his pivotal *Spade* series. By the beginning of the 1970s, Hammons elaborated his explorations of race through an interaction with the word "spade." The term, which has long served as a derogatory slur in reference to Black people, spurred an entire series of works that incorporated the spade. The series expanded beyond the body prints to include a number of performances and assemblage sculptures. Most importantly, the series has often been referred to as marking a move away from the frame format of the body prints to performance, sculpture and installation.[13]

In his essay, "Notes on the Surface: Toward a Genealogy of Flatness," David Joselit provides a compelling account of these early body prints. Tracing a history of flatness through twentieth century American art ranging from Abstract Expressionism to the contemporary art practices of Kara Walker, Joselit explored a relationship between representations of flatness in art and concerns with psychological and subjective depth. For Joselit, flatness in contemporary art has been much more than a formal exploration of the picture plane or a simple concern with the optical. Rather, the artistic engagement with flatness expresses a deep concern with subjectivity. He asserted that:

> . . . flatness may serve as a powerful metaphor for the price we pay on transforming ourselves into images—a compulsory self-spectacularization which is the necessary condition of entering the public sphere in the world of late capitalism.[14]

Focusing on a 1974 body print entitled *Spade*, Joselit discussed the flatness of Hammons's work in the context of stereotype. *Spade* consists of an expanse of flesh out of which emerges a broad and flattened nose and thick lips. A face is made complete with the placement of two thick circles above the nose which become wide owl eyes. The flower-like geometric patterns that stripe across the surface recall scarification patterns and the flesh is further textured with curly hairs that give the figure a bestial appearance. Most striking of all is the fact that this face is confined within the sharp iconic form of a playing card spade. The stereotype of the spade is joined with the bestial furry texture of the skin to create an image of blackness that seems repulsive and animalistic. The two rings that replace the eyes of *Spade* offer only a dead and unseeing stare, an alteration that is especially significant in the representation of eyes, known as windows into the soul and often seen as expressing agency and subjectivity in portraiture. The black person as spade is flattened to an abject object devoid of subjectivity.

Spade presents a scenario in which Hammons's body is inscribed with the racist stereotype of the spade, confining the imprinted body within its cookie-cutter shape. Here, Hammons plays out the conflict between the social stereotype and the self. As Joselit described:

> The encounter between an unwrapped expanse of flesh and precise iconic outline allegorizes the collision of two models of identity: one in which subjectivity is immanent to the body, and one in which the architecture of selfhood is imposed from without.[15]

In Hammons's body prints, the expanses of flesh pressed to the paper's surface generate feelings of a literal imprisonment within the work. The transformation of the self into image in this case is enacted through a brutal confinement of the body within the flattened surface of the paper. Joselit concluded that, in Hammons's work, "flatness signifies identification and identification is a violent process indeed."[16]

Through the allegory of flatness, Joselit seems to point to a process of subjection performed in *Spade*, a process in which the individual becomes a subject through an entrance into a linguistic system of representation. Certainly, language is an essential key to subjectivity because an individual can only become a subject and gain the agency available to a subject when it makes itself intelligible to others. A subject must speak its identity and represent itself to the social world in order to exist at all. As Judith Butler wrote of the process of subjection in her book, *The Psychic Life of Power*, "The subject is the linguistic occasion for the individual to achieve and reproduce intelligibility, the linguistic condition for its existence and agency."[17] Further, this entrance into language necessary to achieve subjectivity should not be conceived of as a singular occasion but rather one that must be continually performed through the constant reproduction of intelligibility. While it is the condition of existence and agency within the realm of the social, in the context of the stereotype and identity, this process of subjection can emerge as a point of great ambivalence.

In *Spade*, one observes the inherent violence of reducing the body into the form of the spade, despite the fact that this form gives the body a defining and intelligible structure. Thus Hammons's project emerges as one in which language is a central concern. He plays out the conflict between the necessary entrance into language and the ambivalence maintained in black communities toward the language of representation available within American culture. In the work, this is enacted through the juxtaposition of an imprint of the body, conceived of as the "self," and the highly coded language of the stereotype presented both in the symbolic form of the caption or title and the iconic form of the spade shape.

In fact, all of Hammons's *Spade* series can be thought of as a project exploring the conflict between self and language. More specifically, this is a conflict between a racially positioned self and the über-codified language of race represented through the spade. In a number of poorly documented performance pieces, Hammons launched interrogations of the spade through performing a number of actions with actual shovels, including running them over with a Volkswagen and burying them with sand.[18] He also created a number of assemblage pieces in which he altered found spades into entirely new objects, reconfiguring the spades into new contexts with new possible readings for them. In his 1973 sculpture, *Bird*, for example, Hammons mounted a rusted and deteriorating spade on an old saxophone whose keys appear to be manipulated by the disembodied hands of a black store mannequin. Here the spade is juxtaposed to the African American musical tradition of jazz represented by famed musician Charlie "Bird" Parker. In another work, entitled *Spade with Chains* (1973), Hammons references the aesthetics of accumulation in African sculpture that so greatly influenced the Black Arts Movement by affixing chains onto the broad blade of a shovel. In an interview with Kellie Jones, Hammons offered the following account of these works:

> . . . I started getting shovels (spades); I got all of these shovels and made masks out of them. It was just like a chain reaction . . . Outrageously magical things happen when you mess around with a symbol. I was running my car over these spades and then photographing them. I was hanging them from trees. Some were made out of leather (they were skins). I would take that symbol and just do dumb stuff with it, tons of dumb ignorant corny things.[19]

These works, both individually and as a body, obsessively play out a traumatic interpellation with the spade as a racial sign—a sign with which Hammons is supposed to identify. Hammons described the genesis of the

Spade series: "I was trying to figure out why Black people were called spades, as opposed to clubs. Because I remember being called a spade once, and I didn't know what it meant; nigger I knew but spade I still don't. So I just took the shape and started painting it."[20] One can imagine this confrontation in the allegorical framework of the Althusserian address. Here, the subject is hailed by an officer and, recognizing itself as subject to the law, the subject turns in response, thus demonstrating the internalization of its subjective position within the society. Yet, in Hammons's account, the reception of this address is characterized by misrecognition—the subject's failure to identify.

This is especially salient in a 1970s photograph by Bruce Talamon of Hammons and his work. The photograph depicts an installation view of the body print entitled *3 Spades* (1971) with Hammons himself presented only as a reflection on the glass surface of the framed work. *3 Spades* portrays a profile impression of Hammons's body. Tucked under his arm is a large, flat playing card spade and another smaller spade is held in his clenched fist. A conflict between the title and image becomes alarmingly apparent as, after searching for the third spade, the viewer comes to the realization that Hammons himself is the missing spade. The photograph capturing Hammons's reflection superimposed within the work mirrors the disrupted identification with the spades in the piece. In it, Hammons appears to be positioned simultaneously within the work and standing in opposition to it. Like his account of being called a spade, Hammons plays out an interpellation with the spade as a representation of the self, yet always this process ends with misrecognition. Thus Hammons's *Spade* series seems to point to a failure in the signifying potential of the stereotype. Spades are made abject, reclaimed or reconfigured and even literally destroyed, but in all cases the spade as a signifier of the black body is placed into doubt.

These works can be thought of as pointing not only to the violence of transforming ourselves into stereotype, or entering into language, but also as demonstrating the inability of the spade as stereotype to represent the black subject. Though, here, the term subject may prove inadequate. Rather the work seems to conceptualize a racially positioned self before an entrance into language, a self which is subsequently reduced into intelligibility by the language of the stereotype. The flatness of the spade, then, is also a flatness of meaning, a lack of depth in the signifying potential of the stereotype that strains to contain its referent. I wish to suggest that through the linguistic games played out where the spade is juxtaposed to indexical imprints of the body and elements culled from African American cultural traditions, Hammons points to a crisis in signification, or a crisis in language. Further, considering the inextricable link between subjectivity and language, one can easily see that a crisis in one realm is necessarily a crisis in the other.

After the *Spade* series, Hammons abandoned the frame format of the body prints and moved to creating art primarily from found materials, due in part to a growing interest in the practices of earlier avant-garde artists such as Marcel Duchamp and the aesthetic innovations of black artists like Noah Purifoy. This period is also marked by the artist's move from Los Angeles to Harlem and an increasing tendency to work outside of gallery venues. Hammons focused on creating performances and sculptural pieces in the communal spaces of the city. His art in the eighties and early nineties is best known for works such as *Higher Goals* (1986). These outdoor installations of basketball hoops mounted onto telephone poles and painstakingly adorned with bottle caps reflected an increasing interest in interacting with the community in Harlem. The new works developed during this time also elaborated on many of the strategies explored in the *Spade* series. Two such strategies are especially significant to this essay: the use of the indexical sign, and an often humorous manipulation of language through the juxtaposition of the index, icon and symbol.

Central to Hammons's strategy in bringing about a crisis in signification was his use of the indexical imprint of the body. Immediately after the *Spade* series, Hammons continued working with indexical signs by creating works that incorporated hair in sculpture and installation. He also used chicken bones, bottles and grease—all remnants of the everyday lives of African Americans. These remains offer traces of cultural practices and economic exchange that circulate and are disseminated along lines of race and class. As refuse, this evidence of the consumption and practices of everyday life can arguably be seen as having an indexical relationship to the community from which they come.

An example can be found in a work entitled *Indoor Hair Garden* (1975). The piece, installed at the Slauson Avenue Studio in Los Angeles, consisted of a network of wires sprouting from the ground in the corner of the room like long blades of grass. On these wires grew hundreds of tiny hairballs made of coarsely textured black hair. Like constellations of little afros, this piece transforms the highly contested and highly codified realm of black hair and black beauty into an abstracted and spatialized art installation.

Kellie Jones offered a compelling analysis of this work: "Like so many artists of his generation . . . Hammons was, indeed, searching for an abstract voice—like jazz—that could be identified as distinctly African American; something that could be non-objective and coded with (self) reference, without relying on representation."[21] That this abstract voice, this reference without representation, is manifest through the strategy of the index is significant. If, in his earlier body prints, the index of Hammons's body could be read as alluding to a self before subjection, like a message before a code, the use of the indexical signs here seems to represent traces of blackness before an entrance into language, an essence of a black community.

The index as employed by Hammons in signifying blackness and notions of a black community exceeds the indexical signs of the body, broadening its focus to traces of relations and practices that create and reinforce community. His use of hair reflects interest in cultural networks as well as the body. The initial use of hair, in fact, was motivated by Hammons's experience of African art adorned with hair,[22] alluding to an interest in signifying an aesthetic patrimony as well as the body. Hammons's later use of bottles, in sculpture and a number of performance pieces in which he walked the streets of Harlem picking up bottles and hanging them inverted on branches of trees, also referenced the African American spiritual practice of bottle trees common to the south which demonstrate strong ties to African spiritual practices. A sense of spirituality permeates much of Hammons's work. Discussing hair and other found materials, Hammons stated, "You've got tons of people's spirits when you handle that stuff. The same with wine bottles. A Black person's lips have touched each one of those bottles, so you have to be very, very careful."[23]

Yet the waste products that Hammons uses as his materials also reflect a deep interest in mapping community through consumption. Just as a bottle signifies a power gained through use, through touching black lips, a community's bond is made evident through the tracing of a network of relations established by the exchange of goods and the practice of cultural traditions. Hammons's interest in the underground economies through which goods circulate has been well documented. His famous performance pieces in which he sold snow balls and other useless objects on the street corners of New York, like a street hawker, are exemplary of this. Community thus creates and is constituted through a number of relations; genetic, spiritual, cultural and economic. His body of works sculpted from hair found in barbershops, from bottles of cheap wine, chicken bones and grease all allude to logics of use and exchange that bond black communities. These communal practices, such as the circulation of goods outside of official economies as well as the practice of spirituality outside of official religions, resist the cooption of official language in a manner similar to the index. The relations they form can only be made present through evidence, through discharge cast off from these relations that is ultimately unintelligible in the realm of representation.

Hammons's use of the index posits a blackness signified by the abject residue of the community, the detritus resulting from the interactions and relations that bond that community. This ambiguous mode points to an elusive nature of blackness that can be mapped only through traces; that can only be represented through its absence. I am reminded of Golden's assertion, ". . . to approach a conversation about 'black art,' ultimately meant embracing and rejecting the notion of such a thing at the same time."[24] In this light, Hammons's explorations become a search for ways of representing blackness that, while it works to signify, also points to the impossibility of that signification. The index here is at once meaningful and devoid of meaning. In reading the work, one can only point to a connection with a notion of blackness, yet the nature of that connection, the meaning of that connection, is always ambiguous; is always in flux.

If Hammons's use of the index offers an illusive notion of black identity and community for his viewers, similar claims can be made for his use of language. In *3 Spades*, Hammons placed the language of race into doubt by juxtaposing the title, *3 Spades*, with a representation of himself holding two spades. The viewer is left to discern the discomfiting punch-line. This visual joke that brings together signs of race in order to expose their inability to signify can be thought of in terms of Michel Foucault's "unraveled calligram."[25] A calligram is a poem whose prose is roughly fit into the shape of its subject. Through the symbolic form of its words and the iconic form of its shape, the calligram reinforces itself through a double signification. However, this reified sign masks its uncertain relationship with its meaning. Foucault points to the art of René Magritte whose painting *The Treason of Images (Ceci n'est pas une pipe)* embodies a calligram whose signs unravel its meaning instead of reinforcing it. In *3 Spades*, the presentation of Hammons's body against the spade can be seen as the unraveling of reified notion of race through the juxtaposition of racial signs. The spade as icon and the imprint of Hammons's body seem jarringly at odds with the assertions of the works caption. The signs of race undo each other, meaning becomes unraveled. In this juxtaposition of blackness to the language that is supposed to represent it, language becomes absurd, ridiculous, and almost humorous in its claims for representation.

The rhetorical power of absurdity and that uneasy humor achieved through the juxtaposition of racial signs as developed in the *Spade* series can be seen throughout Hammons's art. Most of his work hinges on a humorous play of language that undoes notions of race as much as it incorporates the signs of blackness. The 1973 assemblage *Laughing Magic* seems to suggest the power in these visual puns. The piece is among Hammons's reconfigured spade works presenting a shovel broken into segments then reassembled using chains, strips of fabric and patterned neckties. When looking at this work, I personally see it as a face with bright eyes and a gaping, laughing mouth formed by the drooping chain. Perhaps this is the "magic" of Hammons's curious objects, which encourages each viewer to search out a meaning in order to be "in" on the joke. It mirrors the complex processes experienced by art audiences struggling to comprehend and identify a new artwork. However, many of Hammons's works demand more than just a simple reading; they also demand a judgment. This is seen in the example of *3 Spades*. The work, if taken literally, is actually quite offensive as calling someone a spade is neither funny nor aesthetically laudable. Thus, the punch line relies not only on a literal reading, but also an attitude toward that reading (I know it says this and I know it is wrong) and a faith that this reading is shared with the artist (he also knows it says this and he also knows it is wrong). Thus perhaps the joke and the ways in which it imagines one's community with others offer a view into the function of Hammons's art.

Certainly, the pleasure of the joke, the pleasure of "getting it," can be associated with the pleasure felt when confronted by a humorous work. Though the laughter that may result from getting a joke can be very personal, the pleasure of "getting it" is a communal experience. In his essay on the joke, Peter Kivy points to jokes as having a group producing and reinforcing function. The teller of the joke and all those who "get it" are bonded together in a satisfying sense of community. "[T]hat satisfaction can be elicited only when the *joke* calls the audience's attention to their long-held common stock of knowledge, beliefs, and feelings, and, thence, to their community with one another and with the joker."[26] Yet, for Kivy, jokes also have a dark side. Not only does the joke define a community through shared knowledge and feeling, it divides through delineating difference. The joke, he claims, has an aggressive and divisive effect. "For as the group consolidates, in getting the joke . . . it also separates itself from whoever is *not* the group. There can be no insiders without outsiders."[27]

The joke, in this conception, imagines a community that is quite different from many understandings of the art audience. The community drawn together by the joke not only participates in completing the joke through the creation of meaning, this community must internalize an identity in relationship to it, defining itself as either "in on it" or not. This is the imperative of the joke. It demands more than simply being heard, even more than merely being internalized and understood. The joke demands the subject to identify itself in relationship to it, its producer and consumers and that this identity is believed at the core of the subject. Thus, despite the seemingly inherent humor in *3 Spades*, the reading of the joke, and the judging of its humor, is actually a complex process of interpellation.

Unlike the reading of a calligram, the joke in this conception levels an address that focuses on the identity of its consumers and producers. Yet like the intended receiver of its address, these identities are always in question. One observes another's pleasure in a joke, but one must ask whether it is enjoyed for the same reasons. Further, was the joke told with the same intentions? The position of the readers and producers are of central importance in a joke because they often expose the blurry lines between different identities and different communities. This is perhaps why the identity of an artist becomes of such central importance when thinking about art that engages with notions of community. Such lines can be unwittingly crossed with alarming results. An example can be seen in a later work by Hammons. His 1989 work *How Ya Like Me Now?*, for example, was a large 14′ by 16′ portrait of famed African American civil rights leader Jesse Jackson represented with blond hair, blue eyes and white skin. Spray painted across Jackson's chest at the bottom of the work were the words "how ya like me now?" taken from the popular song by rapper Kool Mo Dee. The work was sponsored by the Washington Project for the Arts and installed like a billboard near the Smithsonian Institution's National Portrait Gallery. Hammons describes the portrait as a visual pun. Yet, the controversy that arose around the charge of racism and the physical attack on the work launched by a group of ten African Americans armed with sledgehammers demonstrates the volatile nature of such jokes.

The joke in these instances highlights a field of differently positioned subjects. Yet, in all respects, the joke here is surrounded by an ambiguity, perhaps even a confusion of subjective positions. This is perhaps the most telling aspect of the joke in contemporary art. It is elusive and the laughter it generates is usually ambivalent. As Linda Yablonsky described in an issue of *ARTnews* dedicated to humor in contemporary arts, "First you laugh. Then you wonder why. This is the one-two punch of humor in art today, where laughter is nervous but never cheap, and comic turns are but the gateway into a world of doubt."[28] While funny art may create a community of insiders, almost instantly, it divides it and creates a new one. It becomes obvious that, as soon as Hammons's work builds communities and identities through its humor, these identities and communities are unraveled, rendering them ambiguous and unstable. In the context of race in America, the definitions that have formed around race are so finite that the ambiguity in meaning in Hammons's joke has powerful results. This uncertainty can erupt in nervous laughter as with *3 Spades* or in the violence that defaced *How Ya Like Me Now?*

The works that result from Hammons's play with language as well as those that incorporate indexical signs maintain what I would like to call a productive opacity. They do not represent the complete collapse of meaning. Rather, they stimulate an obsessive production of meaning, insisting that meaning is possible, almost demanding to be read, and yet simultaneously eluding any complete and finite significance. The productively opaque inspires a production that is always in doubt. As soon as meaning can be established it dissolves and must be produced again. The implication of this as far as representing identity is concerned becomes obvious. It points to the unstable nature of subjectivity today.

Can you dig it? The question is not merely an allusion to the spade in Hammons's work, or the 1970s when the term was at its peak of usage. To ask the question "do you dig?" is to pose a question deeply connected to the type of meaning production that I am calling the productively opaque. The question incorporates dominant language and, through slang, reconfigures that language to produce a way of making meaning, a slide in signification, which is uniquely black. "Do you dig?" asks not only do you understand, but do you understand in a certain kind of way that positions you within a particular group, yet does not suggest a closed and stable notion of that group. Tracing the intersections of race and the production of meaning, the question asks its audience to create their blackness leaving the options open for that blackness to proliferate. Now, a blackness that is made unknown and opaque can have some questionable effects, especially in the realm of the political. But I believe that this work points to some truly revolutionary possibilities in reframing the discussion of race today. It is this productive opacity that informs the representational strategies of many contemporary African American artists whose work was exhibited in *Freestyle*. Their work, like that of Hammons, is steeped in ideas of blackness, yet the signs of blackness they employ and the notions of black identity they construct are always ambiguous, are kept just out of reach. This mode of signification concedes that a conversation about blackness will always be one wrought with ambivalence, but simultaneously assures us that we will always keep talking.

Notes

This chapter has been revised since originally published.

1. Thelma Golden, "Post-," *Freestyle* (New York: The Studio Museum in Harlem, 2001), p. 14.

2. Golden, p. 14.

3. Larry Neal, "The Black Arts Movement," in *A Sourcebook of African-American Performance: Plays, People, Movements*, ed. Annemarie Bean (London: Routledge, 1999), p. 55.

4. See: Elsa Honig Fine, "Mainstream, Blackstream and the Black Art Movement," *Art Journal* vol. 30, no. 4 (Summer, 1971), pp. 374–375. See also: Elsa Honig Fine, *The Afro-American Artist* (New York: Holt, Rinehart and Winston, Inc., 1973).

5. Reproduced in: Kobena Mercer, *Welcome to the Jungle: New Positions in Black Cultural Studies* (New York: Routledge, 1994), p. 243.

6. Mercer, p. 243.

7. Lisa Gail Collins and Margo Natalie Crawford, eds., *New Thoughts on the Black Arts Movement* (New Brunswick: Rutgers University Press, 2006); Daniel Widener, *Black Arts West: Culture and Struggle in Postwar Los Angeles* (Durham: Duke University Press, 2010).

8. An excellent account of this process can be found in: Joseph E. Young, *Three Graphic Artists: Charles White, David Hammons and Timothy Washington* (Los Angeles: Los Angeles County Museum of Art, 1971).

9. Two writers from the *Los Angeles Times* both noted the affinity to Yves Klein's work while reviewing two different shows that included the body prints. See: Henry J. Seldis, "Trio Blends Art, Anger in Graphics," *Los Angeles Times*, January 26, 1971; William Wilson, "Hammons Show at Cal State," *Los Angeles Times*, October 7, 1974.

10. Kellie Jones, "Structure of Myth and Potency of Magic," in *David Hammons: Rousing the Rubble* (New York: Institute for Contemporary Art; Cambridge: MIT Press, 1991), p. 17.

11. Alfred Gell, *Art and Agency: An Anthropological Theory* (Oxford: Clarendon Press, 1998).

12. Rosalind Krauss, "Notes on the Index," in *The Originality of the Avant-Garde and Other Modernists Myths* (Cambridge: MIT Press, 1986), p. 205.

13. Kellie Jones, "In the Thick of It: David Hammons and Hair Culture in the 1970s," *Third Text* no. 44 (Autumn, 1998), pp. 17–24.

14. David Joselit, "Notes on Surface: Toward a Genealogy of Flatness," *Art History* vol. 23, no. 1 (March, 2000), p. 20.

15. Joselit, p. 27.

16. Joselit, p. 29.

17. Judith Butler, *The Psychic Life of Power: Theories in Subjection* (Palo Alto: Stanford University Press, 1997), p. 11.

18. Brief accounts of these performances can be found in: Kellie Jones, "David Hammons," *REALLIFE* vol. 16 (Autumn 1986), pp. 2–9; and in David Hammons, *David Hammons: Rousing the Rubble* (New York: Institute for Contemporary Art; Cambridge: MIT Press, 1991).

19. Jones, 1986, p. 4.

20. Jones, 1986, p. 4.

21. Jones, 1998, p. 20.

22. Jones, 1986, p. 4.

23. Jones, 1986, p. 4.

24. Golden, "Post-," p. 14.

25. Michel Foucault, *This Is Not a Pipe* (Berkeley: University of California Press, 1983).

26. Peter Kivy, "Jokes Are a Laughing Matter," *The Journal of Aesthetics and Art Criticism* 61, no. 1 (Winter 2003), p. 6.

27. Kivy, p. 8.

28. Linda Yablonsky, "What's So Funny about Contemporary Art?," *ARTnews* (September 2004), p. 115.

Good Mirrors Ain't Cheap

Kellie Jones

I. Drop the Mic

Traveling back and forth between Los Angeles and New York for much of the 1970s, David Hammons had claimed New York as his home base by 1980, the year he was an artist-in-residence at the Studio Museum in Harlem. However, it would be another decade before most of the artworld caught up with him. In 1990 he was awarded the Prix de Rome, and the following year a MacArthur Fellowship. These prestigious honors were followed by a survey exhibition, organized by Tom Finkelpearl at the P.S.1 Museum, that traveled across the country. By the end of the tour, Hammons, for all intents and purposes, was the hottest household name. He was a postminimalist phenomenon, an artist who cared little for artworld conventions, and one of the few African American artists singled out as an international and artworld star. In an interesting parallel to Romare Bearden's breakout moment, Hammons was in his late forties, having pursued the muse for almost thirty years when he was "discovered."

In the 1960s and 1970s it was Hammons's body prints that first wowed the public. The popularity of these pieces turned on their figurative profiles and unique printing method as well as the quite literal indexing of the black body in themes of love (*Untitled*, ca. 1969; *The Kiss*, 1975), power (*Spade (Power for the Spade)*, 1969), and protest (*Black First, American Second*, 1970; *Injustice Case*, 1970). What also emerges is Hammons's engagement with what Henry Louis Gates, Jr. has designated the "speakerly text."[1] In

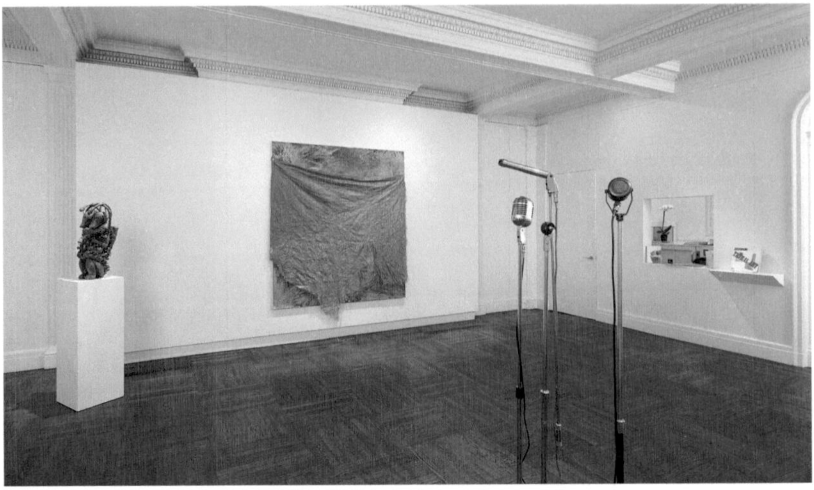

David Hammons: Five Decades, 2016, installation view, Mnuchin Gallery, New York.

the artist's works the language of African America becomes fleshed out in codes of the visual.

Injustice Case, 1970 (purchased by the Los Angeles County Museum of Art the same year) is emblematic of Hammons's investment in the spoken word over the course of five decades. In this large-scale print we see the image of a man in profile, seated on a wooden chair. He is clothed and every inch of the fabric of his jeans, rubber-soled shoes, and workshirt is recorded in minute detail. His face is crowned by an Afro halo. Encircling the figure's ankles, wrists, thighs, torso, shoulders, neck, and mouth are lengths of material which bind him at times to his seat. His arms are fastened together behind him and the back of the chair. A taut line of tension moves from his straining wrists diagonally up to his face which appears to jerk upwards. The cloth tying off his mouth seems to cover half his face as he struggles against his gag.

Injustice Case records an incident in the Chicago Conspiracy trial of the previous year. In that dispute the state of Illinois brought charges against eight defendants, accusing them of crossing state lines to incite riot during the Democratic National Convention of 1968.[2] The trial began in late September 1969, and the defendants were popularly known as the Chicago Eight, however six weeks later that number was reduced to seven.

Bobby Seale, the only African American among the eight defendants, was the National Chairman of the Black Panther Party. While his attorneys were seeking an order to halt his removal to Chicago, he was spirited away by federal marshals and driven across country in shackles; no one knew of his whereabouts for a week until he surfaced at Chicago's infamous Cook County jail.[3] Even before its start, Seale had tried to have the trial postponed because his lawyer had to be hospitalized. The unwilling judge neither permitted the case to be delayed nor allowed Seale to represent himself as he requested. Presiding Judge Hoffman finally did respond to Seale's repeated public condemnations in the courtroom and outcries against the denial of his constitutional rights. Over a four day period between October 29 and November 3, 1969, Hoffman had Seale gagged and bound in the courtroom.[4]

Although such restraint of unruly witnesses was allowed by law, there is no question that its use on an African American in the theater of justice called up vivid images of the country's heritage of slavery, and that system's legal *and* physical control of black human chattel; the looming specter of lynching also floated close at hand.[5] Though a federal judge had initially barred cameras and recording equipment from anywhere near the building housing the Conspiracy trial, that ruling was eventually modified.[6] Yet, as striking as the image of Seale restrained must have been, it was not to be captured on photography or film which was banned from the courtroom. An illustration by at least one commercial artist, however, did circulate in various publications.

The meticulous quality of' Hammons's interpretation of this incident certainly owes much to the body print technique. And because of its ubiquity, Hammons was surely familiar with the published image. Yet there is another source that may have had an even greater impact on the artist. In 1970, the same year that *Injustice Case* was completed, Random House released Bobby Seale's book *Seize the Time*. In the chapter which covers the ordeal of the Chicago Conspiracy trial (titled "Chicago: Kidnapped, Chained, Tried, and Gagged") Seale spends several pages discussing exactly how he was restrained. The particulars are powerful given that some of the tapes were made right after the incident. The picture he draws is also incredibly detailed because he knew that the world at large had not been able to see him via the photographic or televised media.

After first having his mouth taped over and being shackled to a folding chair, yet continuing to comment on the proceedings through the "clanging" of metal against metal, Seale recounts that:

> The next day they strapped me to a wooden armchair, put a lot of padding in front of my mouth and tied a big large rag around it. Another rag came up under my chin. The marshals tied a knot on top of my head. The rag came across my mouth and went around the back of my neck.[7]

Hammons's *Injustice Case* shows Seale tied up with cloth not constrained with handcuffs or leg irons. While it certainly had to have been easier to print fabric rather than metal using the body print method, the image nevertheless stays true to Seale's own account.

The phrase *Injustice Case* made it clear that in the mind of the artist this affair, and the predicament of African Americans at that time, was not about equity or justice but its lack. However, *Injustice Case* starts its life as part of larger assemblage. Parked in a museum-style glass case with a gavel, the body is effectively "In Justice's Case." But Hammons drops that pesky "'s" taking the power away from "justice" and through a grammatical mis—or rather—re-direction gives it back to the people and to the vernacular language of the street.

"Black Dialect," Geneva Smitherman has argued, springs from both a "linguistic-cultural African heritage" and its growth as a separate language formed under "conditions of servitude, oppression" and segregation.[8] Under the exigencies of slavery African Americans developed two kinds of communication systems: one to deal with the master class and the forces of subjugation, the other to commune among themselves. This insider/outsider split continued into the modern and contemporary periods and cannot only be seen in recent debates around "ebonics" but in patterns of humor.

Writing on the African American comedic tradition, Mel Watkins also identifies this same dual behavior, revealing forms focused outward for a larger (white) audience and those which remained directed specifically towards black communities. With this practice comes both a power and an agility to reverse meaning, to turn things (linguistically) to one's advantage. It is a legacy which over time has fostered "indirect wordplay and double edged wit."[9]

Hammons's growing investment in black language also mirrored that of certain African American poets of the 1960s and 1970s who became recognized under the banner of the Black Arts Movement.[10] Intent on making poetry that was intellectually available in the broadest sense to the African American masses, they incorporated the spoken sounds of black "slang" in their verse along with profanity which was thought to reflect popular speech.

This trajectory has continued throughout Hammons's career. We see it, for instance, in *How Ya Like Me Now?*, 1988, a billboard scale installation depicting Jesse Jackson. Created in context of his back to back presidential campaigns (1984, 1988), like any aspect of media strategy it seeks to capture voter imaginations and support. In this portrait Jackson is garbed patriotically, sporting a white shirt topped by a blue jacket and a red tie. But the black activist is also shown with white skin (along with blonde hair and eyes that pick up the hue of his coat), the work's title provocatively scrawled across his chest. Hammons's piece posed the question whether race, not platforms, policies or experience predicted the political outcome. *How Ya Like Me Now?* was shown in Boston and New York throughout 1988 without incident. However, the following year in Washington, D.C., the object was attacked as it was being installed outdoors as part of Richard J. Powell's exhibition *The Blues Aesthetic: Black Artists and Modernism* at the Washington Project for the Arts. Since then Hammons exhibits the piece with the sledgehammers that brought it down along with an American flag.[11]

The title *How Ya Like Me Now?* comes from hip hop artist Kool Moe Dee's 1987 hit of the same name. A battle rap attesting to his facility with language or rhyming skills, Dee speaks of being the "only real mic-aroni" and tells us "rapping is an art and I'm like Picasso."[12] For Hammons such wordplay becomes a signifier of a larger black community and its traditions, an acknowledgement of vernacular culture whose sign is "the street."

It is no accident that an aspect of Hammons' *How Ya Like Me Now?* is rooted in a black music tradition. Kool Moe Dee's 1987 song samples the sounds of funk master James Brown but also boasts a riff from the bebop jazz classic "Salt Peanuts" written and made most famous by trumpeter Dizzy Gillespie. Hammons's obsession with music is constant and seen most notably in his perpetual return to jazz paradigms. For Hammons jazz musicians are sentinels of black avant garde innovation, with the jazz master as at once transgressive and enigmatic. This sense of the black jazz heroic is also most often masculine.

Music historian Guthrie P. Ramsey, Jr. writes about the gendered aspects of jazz in the 1940s, particularly bebop. He contends that on the road to becoming great art music, jazz found the need to "man up" in order to compete with things European. This is embodied in a demand for a certain aesthetic fierceness and found in the intellectual titles that musicians bestowed upon bebop songs (i.e., Charlie Parker's *Ornithology*, 1946). Bebop was, in Ramsey's words, a "patriarchal heroic performance space" for the unfurling of "virtuosic bravado."[13] It was a place to perform black manhood, played out in musical battles where one honed and developed performative skills. It was a site of melodic improvisation and risk, but one where the traditional harmonics of standard songs would still remain recognizable.[14] Jazz as the black heroic performative was also irrefutably modern.

One who is lyrically astute and victorious, particularly in a rap battle, is said to "drop the mic," departing and leaving nothing more to say. Hammons's feats—his facility with language, wordplay and punning—endure. In *Which Mike Do You Want to Be Like?*, 2001, a collection of three vintage microphones conflates the shorthand term for the equipment (mic; a perpetual icon of hip hop culture) with its homonym, "Mike." These are the names of three men—Tyson, Jordan, and Jackson, athletes and musical superstars—who become representative of black communities, their cultural accomplishments as well as their transgressions. Here the interrogative format (as in *How Ya Like Me Now?*) also enlists participation, asking for a response, in the tradition of the parry of the rhyme, rap battle, or the dozens. This is language as a machine of the modern.

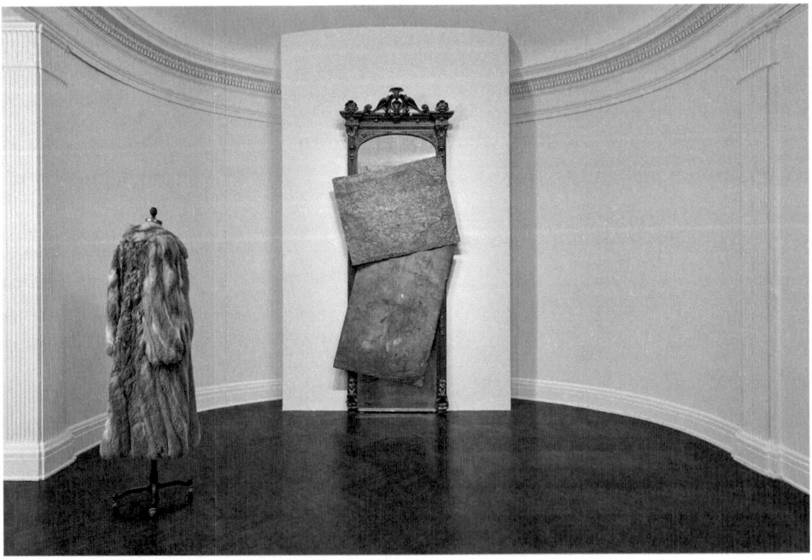

David Hammons: Five Decades, 2016, installation view, Mnuchin Gallery, New York.

II. Dry Every Tear

In a recent series of articles for *Artforum*, scholar Thierry de Duve seeks to drive home the overwhelming importance of Marcel Duchamp, and what his practice and legacy has meant for the history and making of contemporary art, what it authorized and permitted artists to do and be. Enter David Hammons, one of the artists in the 1960s who apparently received the missive sent by Duchamp earlier in the century. He certainly was at the right place at the right time: just outside Pasadena where the elder artist had his first retrospective in 1963; in Los Angeles where Dada had a foothold and Walter Hopps kept the fires burning.

Hammons and someone like Noah Purifoy, for instance, have at times celebrated such legacies. Purifoy exulted in Dada in the 1967 self-published zine *One to One: Quarterly Report on Aspects of Creativity*, and wrapped his practice in the language of its traditions. Hammons went initially for its descendants in his adaptation of Nouveau Realiste Yves Klein's body printing technique and an exploration of Pop in the oeuvre of Jim Dine. As Hammons once intoned,

> I was trying to figure out why Black people were called spades as opposed to clubs. Because I remember being called a spade once, and I didn't know what it meant; nigger I knew but spade I still don't. So, I just took the shape, and started painting it. I started dealing with the spade the way Jim Dine was using the heart . . . then I started getting shovels and made masks out of them. It was just like a chain reaction. . . .[15]

While Dine's work could be found in 1960s L.A., Hammons's extensive thinking about it may have come from his encounter with the artist's retrospective at the Whitney Museum in 1970, while taking in Mel Edwards' influential show there.[16] The hearts that were so suggestive to Hammons were on view. These were not the combines that defined Dine's heart motifs of the early 1970s and 1980s but more clearly transitional works, assemblages of straw (*Nancy and I at Ithaca (Straw Heart)*, 1966–69), chicken wire, refuse, and power tools with snaking cords (*Five Chicken Wire Hearts (James Peto)*, 1969), along with a series of watercolors. Created at a time when he was painting less, in these pieces Dine seemed to reach back to assemblage and to consider materials in a manner more aligned with process art and postminimalism. Other pieces may have turned Hammons's head as well, including a group from 1962 with a "black" theme, *Black Garden Tools, Black Saw, Black Tools in a Landscape*, created in what emerged as Dine's signature: painted items affixed to painted canvases. *Black Garden Tools* featured two spades; from the same year there was also *Shovel*. One is struck by the spareness of Dine's early projects represented in the retrospective—paint, canvas, tool, title—felt even in the installations. For all their autobiographical sheen (or perhaps because of it) they exude a sense of muteness, indecisiveness, and search.[17]

And then there is language, "word and image interchanges," which Robert Pincus-Witten sees as Dine's debt to Jasper Johns.[18] If many critics have seen an ode to Duchamp in Hammons's visual mischief and take on language, it perhaps also comes through neo-Dada running from Johns to Dine. In Hammons's relationship to traditions of the western avant-garde, however, we see something else as well. There is a confrontation with Dine: the language volley becomes a parry. You want to see a black shovel? A black shovel is a spade. There is a turn to the rich semantics of African diasporic communities, one which Richard J. Powell has recognized as an art that is both "commentary" and "oath-taking."[19]

If Hammons and Purifoy did claim legacies of western modernist artmaking, did they do so to empower a different linguistic or perhaps neologistic past? Was it a way to at once privilege the Black South and its inheritance in Hammons's precious formation of "the street"? These are places where, as Grey Gundaker and Judith McWillie have argued, "things [are] thoughts,"[20] and where the most bedraggled bit of everyday life, seemingly non-sensical, is posted as sign, as protection, as a point of meaning. Where to misread is to redirect. Where language, seemingly simple, commonplace, seemingly ungrammatical and anti-intellectual, is spot on. And it inherits a longer and larger custom in which the Black South is bequeathed (and remixes) such gestures and traditions from West and Central Africa. Such signs open onto and invoke the metaphysical. "Can't go by what you see," sings gospel artist Twinkie Clark. "So dry every tear from your eye. There is a word . . ." that will deliver the force of your destiny.[21]

Yet Hammons engages Africa and its aesthetic conventions in another register as well, through what scholar Manthia Diawara sees as a "banalization" of African objects.[22] It is an encounter with these traditions on the level of the quotidian, the routine, the popular and not particularly the epic. We see this in works such as *Standing Room Only*, 1996 in which a taxidermy cat is curled up on Ghanaian peg or Djembe drum. *Untitled*, 1996 from the same year presents a stack of masks from an array of West and Central African civilizations, most likely purchased on the streets of New York City or at a flea market. Curving delicately outward from the wall this assemblage is topped by a small hand mirror, rendering it a single, multinational, Nkisi. Hailing from the Democratic Republic of Congo the traditional Nkisi is activated by language where puns have medicinal and spiritual force, their power driven home with nails to secure an oath.[23] It most often takes the form of the human body with punning materials of authority sited in a central cavity behind a reflective surface. However, it also appears as a Janus-headed dog. In *Orange Is the New Black*, 2014 Hammons lacquers this element with bright paint the color of jailhouse uniforms, its embedded nails and flashing mirror still visible.

This is the same Hammons, however, who gives us *The Holy Bible: Old Testament*, 2002—Duchamp's catalogue raisonné wrapped in the worn leather covers of prayer and on an altar to boot; an apparent warning not to worship the western modernist covenant. He has also styled himself, at times, as the "C.E.O. of the Duchamp Outpatient Clinic" which vaccinates people against artworld clichés.[24] But when we compare pieces such as Hammons's *The Door (Admissions Office)*, 1969 with Duchamp's *Fresh Widow*, 1920 in both composition and the mobilization of language, we can't help wondering, "misdirection or redirection?"

In his review of David Hammons's 2011 exhibition at L&M Arts, Alexander Alberro thinks about art as both "an analogy to a joke" and a "solution to the initially unintelligible;" art introduces that which cannot be said and what is occluded in public speech or polite conversation.[25] This is the action performed by Hammons's tarp paintings: collapsing the usual histories of painting with those of "banal factory made materials" which overlay and obscure while also meshing with the underlying canvases.[26] In these objects the stories of worn and abject commodities and those of contemporary art are one. Constructed paintings such as *Untitled*, 2014 and *Untitled*, 2015 remain upright and wallbound yet continue to kiss the floor, tipping us off to these proximate narratives.[27] They are also Hammons's way into painting, begun with the dense flourishes of the "hotel-style" enamel on Masonite of *Untitled*, ca. 1969, continued decades later in the equally saturated yet washy embellishments of *Untitled (Kool-Aid)*, 2006. The tarps are in one sense protective of the painted image, their obfuscation leaving work for the mind's eye and our own speculative thoughts.

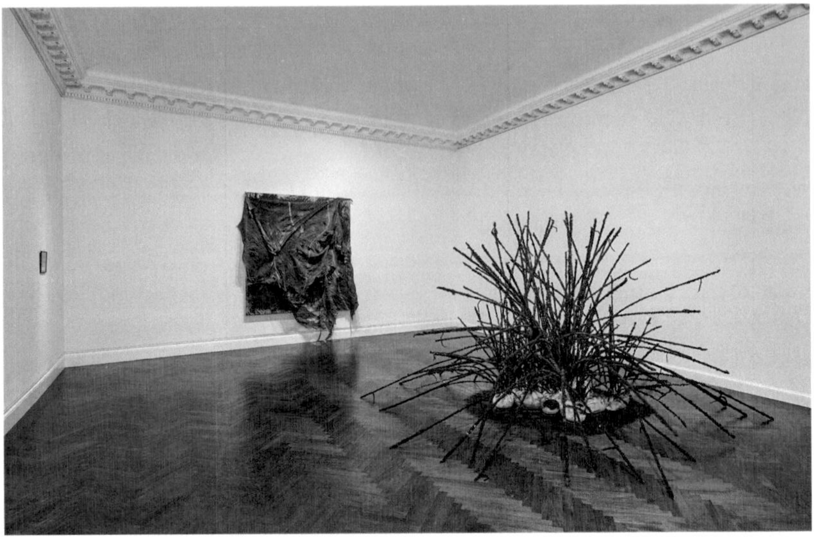

David Hammons: Five Decades, 2016, installation view, Mnuchin Gallery, New York.

Hammons's conscious layering is also interrogative: what do these apparently disparate materials of our environment have to say about our lives on this planet? The mobilization of unexceptional materials also imbricates the bodies that produced them, or even further, as Rizvana Bradley argues, speaks to the exigencies of the flesh, bare life.[28]

The wide splashy brush strokes and loud colors of the tarp paintings, as Alberro points out, access a legacy of the New York School (particularly the example of Willem de Kooning, a stalwart of L&M Arts) but also erase and stand in for the same. Indeed, in *Untitled*, 2014 and *Untitled*, 2015 the literal earth tones of ground in dirt along with painted corals, turquoise, black and silver present themselves (to this viewer at least) as homages to a lesser known figure of the era, New Orleans–born painter, Edward Clark. This same palette goes horizontal and three-dimensional, both constructed and deconstructed, in *A Movable Object*, 2012, where the blasting orange of a home construction supply store cart is loaded with chunks of glistening black asphalt interspersed with luxurious skeins of organza the colors of the ocean.

After Hammons and Ralph Ellison we are reminded that all paintings or art for that matter are "tricksters and confidence men."[29] Audre Lorde continues this thought, beginning her poem *Good Mirrors Are Not Cheap* just so:

It is a waste of time hating a mirror
or its reflection
instead of stopping the hand
that makes glass with distortions

Lorde's reminder to shift our perception away from things that demean us, runs through an article by Lowery Stokes Sims on the circumscribed categories for works of artists who are neither white nor male. Using the writing of Jacques Lacan as a flash point, she invokes the image of distorted artworld mirrors that constrict what or whom is esthetically pleasing and thus reflected. Such action is determined by broader social mirroring that not only suppresses, but rallies hateful propaganda, rendering certain peoples (and artists) deficient; it is the trauma, according to Ellison, of being "reduced to a negative sign that usually appears in a comedy of the grotesque and the unacceptable."[30]

David Hammons's journey has nimbly challenged such equations. In themes of beauty and athletic prowess—hair and basketball—Hammons has played with signs often manipulated as stereotype. Hammons's hair pieces date back to the seventies from site works in Los Angeles to shows in New York at Just Above Midtown Gallery. The later works seen in *David Hammons: Five Decades* are monumental, such as the artificial, wig-like, *Rubber Dread*, 1989. In the Whitney Museum's exquisite *Untitled*, 1992, perhaps Hammons's ultimate statement using human hair, its garbage strewn tendrils appear as the definitive bad object. But we are left to wonder, is its copious expanse a warning to keep us at arm's length, or are its fecund strands meant to draw us closer? The excess of these pieces is contrasted with *Untitled*, 2004, a large rock whose close shaven surface sports sinuous decorative lines, a homage to barbershop style *and* minimalist painting. Hammons's perpetual return to the trope of the black athlete is found in the backboard articulated in bottlecaps of *Untitled* 1987, a street smart hoop-cum-chandelier (*Basketball Chandelier*, 1997), and *Traveling*, 2002, where the dirt of the steady and skilled dribbling ball creates the composition and palette of a drawing. It is literally propped up by a worn suitcase, giving the piece one logic for its title, which is also a term for a baller's patently illegal move.

Musing on his 1966 collaborative exhibition of assemblage or junk art *66 Signs of Neon*, one commemorating L.A.'s Watts Rebellion, Noah Purifoy described his goal as communicating the human potential of Watts to the neighborhood itself as well as the world:

> Its purpose was to reflect the August 11 event on a symbolic level and to demonstrate to the community an existing fact: If the community of Watts found itself in the midst of something—something like junk—value could be placed on it to far exceed the few cents paid at the junk stores on Monday morning.[31]

A decade later David Hammons would build on this, offering another scenario for the context of cast off materials:

> no one will buy . . . outrageous art . . . it will make people think, think about themselves and what that means. You can't sell this . . . they won't buy this . . . old dirty bags, grease, bones, hair . . . it's about us, it's about me . . . it isn't negative . . . we should look at these images and see how positive they are, how strong, how powerful . . . our hair is positive . . . it's powerful, look what it can do. There's nothing negative about our images, it all depends on who is seeing it and we've been depending on someone else's sight . . . We need to look again and decide.[32]

Audre Lorde ends her poem thus:

Because at the same time
down the street
a glassmaker is grinning
turning out new mirrors that lie
Selling us
new clowns
at cut rate.

In the last year Hammons has created a series of mirrors where an overlay of junky materials obscures the reflective surface. Related to the occlusions of the tarp paintings, they ask us to "look again and decide" what constitutes the discarded/image. Using a palette similar to the canvases, the crumbling ornate and gilded flourishes of the assemblages bespeak the failures of classical norms. Yet, as Ellison remarks, artists choose their inspirations from everywhere, "his form is his greatest freedom and his insights are where he finds them."[33]

Through his designation of "the street" Hammons offers a framework of both participation and power. The mobilization of potential is initiated by a change of perception. His ambivalent address sketches the outline of the dream, where freedom is first imagined. It is the site of the otherworldly, brought into view by artists' and onlookers' active collaboration at making things evident. As Alberro prompts us, "For Hammons, art is a mischievous game beyond limits. It perverts the logic of forms of belief, conventions of knowledge, and ways of seeing, to make the repressed visible in a manner that only an excellent joke could accomplish."[34] Hammons himself continually reminds us of the same, today embedded in the title of the sculpture, *Orange Is the New Black*, a gloss on pop culture which nonetheless comments on the ongoing exigencies of Black life.

Notes

1. Henry Louis Gates, Jr., *The Signifying Monkey: A Theory of African-American Literary Criticism* (New York: Oxford University Press, 1988).

2. The defendants included David Dellinger, Rennie Davis, Tom Hayden, Jerry Rubin, Abbie Hoffman, John Froines, Lee Weiner, and Bobby Seale.

3. "U.S. Marshals Move Seale from Coast as Lawyers Appeal," *New York Times*, September 13, 1969, p. 24, and "Seale in Chicago Jail," *New York Times*, September 19, 1969, p. 38. See also Bobby Seale, *Seize the Time* (Baltimore: Black Classic Press, 1991; originally Random House, 1970).

4. J. Anthony Lukas, "Seale Put in Chains at Chicago 8 Trial," *New York Times*, October 30, 1969, pp. 1, 39, and J. Anthony Lukas, "Seale Found in Contempt, Sentenced to Four Years," *New York Times*, November 6, 1969, pp. 1, 54.

5. "Seale Put in Chains at Chicago 8 Trial," p. 39, and Fred P. Graham, "High Court Backs Gagging to Curb Trial Disorders," *New York Times*, April 1, 1970, pp. 1, 19.

6. "Press Curbs Set at Trial of 8 Protesters in Chicago," *New York Times*, September 18, 1969, p. 44, and "U.S. Judge in Chicago Modifies Press Ban," *New York Times*, September 19, 1969, p. 26.

7. Seale, *Seize the Time,* pp. 338–339.

8. Geneva Smitherman, *Talkin and Testifyin: The Language of Black America* (Detroit: Wayne State University Press, 1986; originally Houghton Mifflin, 1977), p. 2.

9. Mel Watkins, *On the Real Side: Laughing Lying and Signifying, The Underground Tradition of African American Humor* (New York: Simon & Schuster, 1994), p. 36.

10. Poets of the Black Arts Movement included Amiri Baraka, Sonia Sanchez, Haki Madhubuti, and Nikki Giovanni among others. See Geneva Smitherman, "The Power of Rap:

The Black Idiom and The New Black Poetry," *Twentieth Century Literature* 19 (1973): 259–274.

11. I showed Hammons's *How Ya Like Me Now?* in the exhibition *Trading Places: An Arts Exchange Exhibition* at the Artists Foundation Boston (Apr. 19–May 21, 1988); it later traveled to Jamaica Arts Center in Queens, NY (Aug. 5–Sept. 17, 1988).

12. Kool Moe Dee, "How Ya Like Me Now?," 1987 was a battle rap against LL Cool J who Dee accused of stealing his lyrical style.

13. Guthrie P. Ramsey, Jr., *The Amazing Bud Powell, Black Genius, Jazz History, and the Challenge of Bebop* (Berkeley: University of California Press, 2013), pp. 121, 122.

14. Ramsey, p. 181.

15. David Hammons interviewed by Kellie Jones, *REALLIFE Magazine* No. 16 (Autumn 1986): 4.

16. *Melvin Edwards: Works* appeared from March 2–29, 1970 and the Jim Dine survey ran from February 27–April 19, 1970, at the Whitney Museum of American Art.

17. David Shapiro, "Jim Dine's Life-in-Progress," *ARTnews* 69 (1) (March 1970): 42–46; Graham W. J. Beal, *Jim Dine: Five Themes* (Minneapolis and New York: Walker Art Center and Abbeville Press, 1984).

18. Robert Pincus-Witten, "Jim Dine," *Artforum* 8 (9) (May 1970), 74–75. However, in considering another piece from that era, *Black Bathroom #2*, 1962, one intuits a commentary, while subtle, on the battle against segregation and inequity in the U.S. See Kellie Jones, "Civil/Rights/Act," in Teresa A. Carbone and Kellie Jones, eds., *Witness, Art and Civil Rights in the Sixties* (New York: Brooklyn Museum and The Monacelli Press, 2014), pp. 11–55, 162–163.

19. Richard J. Powell, "African American Postmodernism and David Hammons: Body and Soul," in David C. Driskell, ed., *African American Visual Aesthetics: A Postmodernist View* (Washington, D.C.: Smithsonian Institution Press, 1995), p. 133.

20. Grey Gundaker and Judith McWillie, *No Space Hidden, The Spirit of African American Yard Work* (Knoxville: The University of Tennessee Press, 2005), 51.

21. Twinkie Clark, "There Is a Word (Dry Every Tear)," *Live and Unplugged* (2013).

22. Manthia Diawara, "Make It Funky: The Art of David Hammons," *Artforum* 36 (9) (May 1998): 120–127.

23. Robert Farris Thompson, *Flash of the Spirit: African and Afro-American Art and Philosophy* (New York: Random House, 1983).

24. Peter Schjeldahl, "The Walker," *The New Yorker*, December 23, 2002.

25. Alexander Alberro, "The Joke of Painting," *Texte Zur Kunst* 82 (June 2011), p. 233.

26. Alberro, p. 234.

27. This wall-to-floor axis is also mobilized by Senga Nengudi (a friend of Hammons's since their days L.A.) in her RSVP works. See Kellie Jones, "Beyond Reverie," in *Senga Nengudi, Alt* (London: White Cube, 2014), pp. 31–34.

28. Rizvana Bradley, "Transferred Flesh, Reflections on Senga Nengudi's RSVP," *TDR: The Drama Review* 59 (1) (Spring 2015): 161–166

29. Ralph Ellison, "Change the Joke and Slip the Yoke," in *Shadow and Act* (New York: Vintage Books, 1972) [essay originally 1958], p. 46.

30. Ellison, p. 48; Lowery Stokes Sims, "The Mirror, The Other, the Politics of Esthetics," *Artforum* 28 (March 1990): 111–115; Jacques Lacan, "The Mirror State as Formative of the Function of the I as Revealed in Psychoanalytic Experience," *Ecrits: A Selection*, trans. Alan Sheridan (New York: W. W. Norton, 1977), pp. 1–7; Audre Lorde, "Good Mirrors Are Not Cheap" (1970), *The Collected Poems of Audre Lorde* (New York: W. W. Norton, 1997), 67. The current essay is inspired, in part, by Thelma Golden's 1992 exhibition of Glenn Ligon banners in dialogue with Lorde's poem. *Good Mirrors Are Not Cheap*, July 17–November 28, 1992, Whitney Museum of American Art at Philip Morris. See also Glenn Ligon, "Notes on a Performance by Kellie Jones," *Triple Canopy* (Aug. 6, 2015). The correct title of my performance/lecture was "'There Is a Word': Absence, Presence, and David Hammons," Museum of Modern Art, Value Talks, curated by Ralph Lemon. March 14, 2014.

31. Noah Purifoy, "'66' Philosophy: Seeing Old Things in New Ways," *One to One: Quarterly Report on Aspects of Creativity* (January–March 1967): 3; Noah Purifoy papers, 1935–1998, Archives of American Art, Smithsonian Institution. The Watts Rebellion began on August 11, 1965.

32. David Hammons from a discussion during August–September 1977 in Linda Goode Bryant and Marcy S. Philips, *Contextures* (New York: Just Above Midtown Gallery, 1978), p. 41.

33. Ellison, "Change the Joke and Slip the Yoke," p. 59.

34. Alberro, "The Joke of Painting," p. 236.

"Those Who Know Don't Tell": David Hammons c. 1981

Abbe Schriber

In the summer of 1983, curator Jeannette Ingberman solicited a statement from David Hammons as part of a forthcoming exhibition called *Performances Not to Be Seen*.[1] She had routed a questionnaire to several artists under consideration for the show, which asked rather bluntly: "Why do a performance that has no audience and is not seen?" The inquiry made the stakes clear. Was performance predicated upon an audience, or could it occur for the maker alone? According to Ingberman, documentation was always already considered part of the work. While physical acts might take place privately, or as an indistinguishable part of commonplace life occurrences, audience perception could only occur in and through the action's record, what Ingberman conceived as the act's "original perception."[2] In response, Hammons offered a single sentence, written in looped scrawl: "Those who know don't tell." Telling, or the oral or written dissemination of knowledge, is tantamount to showing or visual display for Hammons, who has repeated this sentiment in various iterations. According to Manthia Diawara, the artist had a motto: "Those who know, don't show."[3] Apparently for Hammons, performance was predicated on an absence of the stage or frame, never making the work initially legible as art. The "knowledge" of a work as performance would only come with its alleged proof: the photographic documentation.

The Exit Art statement was never published, and *Performances Not to Be Seen* never realized, which is in keeping with the implications of Hammons's answer—and with his broader interest in the unintelligibility of his own practice. "Those who know don't tell" might well serve as a guiding

Why do a performance that has no audience and is not seen?

those who know dont tell

Please return to: EXIT ART 578 Broadway New York City 10012 212 966-7745
This statement will be published in the catalogue. Please return as soon as possible.

David Hammons, Unpublished artist statement, 1983. Exit Art Archives, series III, box 153, folder 15, Fales Library & Special Collections, New York University.

DAVID HAMMONS

"Pissed Off" is about the fact that in New York City a man doesn't have any public access to relieve himself in a decent manner. There is no way for a gentleman to relieve himself in a gentlemanly way without having to buy a drink.

Keeps the rage going.

David Hammons, "Statement for Illegal America," 1990. Exit Art Archives, series I, box 24, folder 24, Fales Library & Special Collections, New York University.

mantra for Hammons's actions and street interventions in early 1980s New York. The retort reflects less a desire to avoid the initial question, than to refuse the terms by which Hammons's artistic production has been conventionally codified. Critics and writers have time and again perceived the artist's actions—or inactions—as evasion, a trait coterminous with his "trickster" persona.[4] Yet they have frequently failed to analyze it as a systematic praxis of refusal, as resistance to the worn grammar of institutional capture. Édouard Glissant has argued that peoples historically relegated to the margins have often used strategies of opacity, whether through local dialects or folk culture, to claim a right to be illegible and ambiguous in the face of totalizing, universalist narratives that presume to speak on their behalf.[5] But my interest lies in a less examined component of opacity that is nevertheless inseparable from it: obscurity, which Glissant acknowledges as a known and accepted risk of opacity.[6] For opaque tactics run the risk of casting those that practice them into obscurity—remaining unseen, unacknowledged, little-known, or misunderstood.[7] In proposing new methods of writing history, Glissant invites the reader to be his "accomplices in obscurity."[8]

By the early 1980s, Hammons began to gesture to the viewer not as author, but as accomplice. In doing so, he implied that minoritized publics might choose to remain "obscure," concerned more with coming into appearance for one another than for a dominant white public sphere.[9] Within a network of Black visual artists, writers, photographers, musicians, and performers—Dawoud Bey, Lorraine O'Grady, Jorge Rodriguez, Charles Abramson, Butch Morris, Senga Nengudi, Candace Hill-Montgomery, George Mingo, and Coreen Simpson, among others—Hammons exhibited in the city's burgeoning alternative spaces, public non-profit organizations, and the street, rather than in larger, established museums and galleries. It was not simply that these were the available options, but that this mode of obscurity refused the didactic integrationist agenda associated with dominant institutional expectations. Hammons's resistance to the trappings of the art institutional apparatus—gallerists, comprehensive CVs, consistent factual information—are part of this fugitive praxis, questioning the elite systems that lend credibility, and refusing the politics of respectability and assimilation that would require open, full participation in systems that for so long foreclosed that possibility to artists of African descent. Here fugitivity is not synonymous with literal departure or escape, given that Hammons remained active amid Black artistic communities in New York more broadly throughout the 1980s. Rather, fugitivity manifests as studied practices of refusal and withdrawal from the status quo, described eloquently by Tina Campt as "practices honed in response to sustained, everyday encounters with exigency and duress that rupture a predictable trajectory of flight."[10] Rather than focus on Hammons's practice as tied up in persona, I ask how such tactics can be located in the performances or street interventions that Hammons made in New York in the early 1980s.[11]

Unofficial Truths

At first it is unclear what the man is doing there as he circumnavigates the structure, a public sculpture, pausing now and then to closely examine its rusted steel surface, or squint up at its soaring height as though to gauge its proximity to his body. He wears a visor and Puma sneakers, loose khakis, and a short-sleeved, tie-dyed dashiki shirt, a patterned bag slung over his shoulder. The look is that of urban forager—mildly eclectic, but in the way that characterizes most New Yorkers. Though it is the middle of the day, not many people are around, and when he is finished inspecting the sculpture he takes advantage of it: shifting the bag further up on his shoulder, he turns his back and empties his bladder in the corner, a steady arc of urine adding to the graffiti, crumpled cans, and peeling posters that deface the steel. An acrid, bitter smell emanating from the semi-enclosed space confirms that the sculpture has already been used for this purpose—perhaps by local homeless people, or drunks from the nearby bars and No Wave venues where Rhys Chatham and Glenn Branca play. After he finishes, the man turns around to find a police officer waiting for him, a summons waiting in his hand. Time, momentarily, stops; a tense anticipation

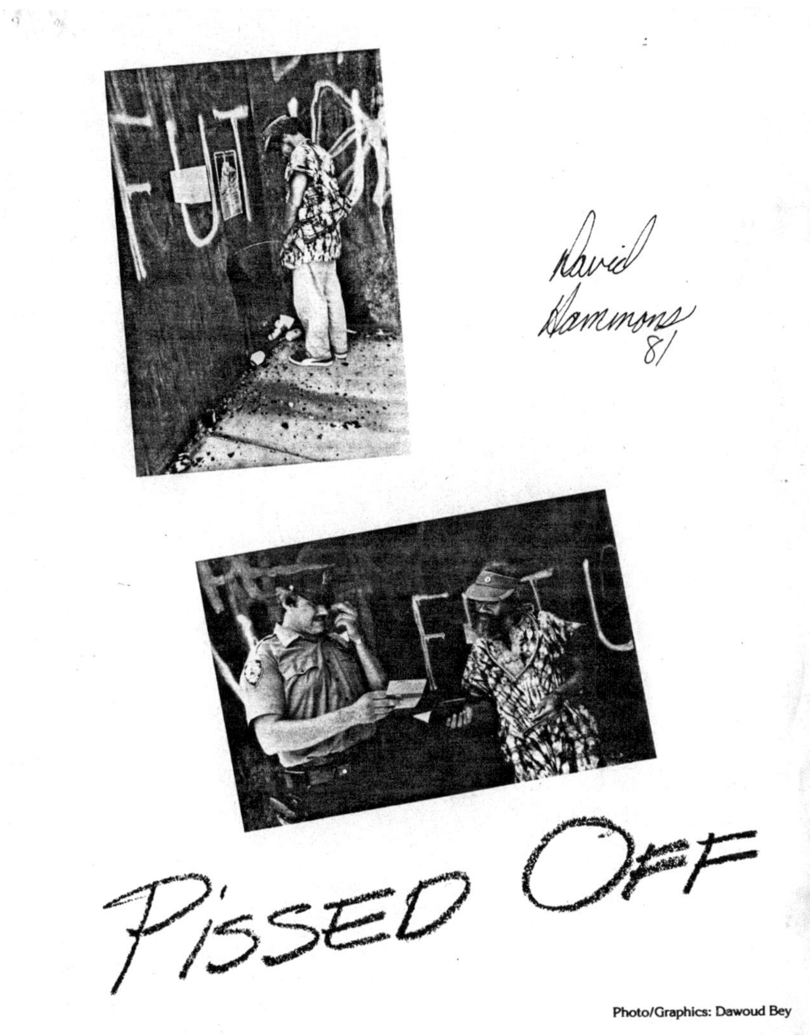

Dawoud Bey and David Hammons, Photocopy of *Pissed Off* collage, 1989. Exit Art Archives, series IV, box 175, folder 2, Fales Library & Special Collections, New York University.

quickens his heartbeat. The policeman asks to see his identification. With no passersby to corroborate what could or could not occur, the man crouches and rummages through his bag to find the passport—he digs through a notebook, an envelope stuffed with papers, a wrinkled paper bag. He rises to hand it to the officer. See that dude, over there? With the camera? He's here taking pictures of me pissing because I asked him to. This is a performance, he says. The officer looks at the other man, who has been standing quietly photographing this whole time. Miraculously, he nods, and backs off.[12]

Or, actually, what happened was that he carefully explained to the officer the injustices of having to urinate on the go, with no public restrooms in sight—at least, none that one might be able to reasonably stomach using. Simply "using the facilities" requires becoming a paying customer in bars, coffee shops, restaurants, or fast food joints in yet another example of the restrictive spatial determinations of the "public" in an increasingly privatized city. In October 1990, the Legal Action Center for the Homeless would sue the city, seeking an increase in public toilets; one year later, a *New York Times* article detailed the varying proposals being considered despite legal and bureaucratic roadblocks, including the quarter-operated self-cleaning toilet "kiosks" prevalent in major European cities.[13] With limited access to the very few free public toilets and facilities available in public space, relief had to be taken wherever possible. However, for a man perceived under the sign of blackness, urinating—whether a basic need, or a literal and symbolic marking of territory—opens up intense vulnerability to the law. Facing the everyday terror of existing on the brink of annihilation, blackness comes into view once again via the presumption of suspicion, then punishment. Yet on this day, with this particular self-explanation in the name of self-survival, the man emerges unscathed save for the violence of having to prove one's identity at any time, of being subject to questioning because one's movements are viewed and marked as furtive, questionable, or aberrant.

These are multiple scenarios for a street performance, now known as *Pissed Off*, imagined both from what is known—and what is not—given that this was a performance without an audience and those that did see it are, of course, careful not to tell.[14] On an as-yet unknown date in 1981, for a currently indeterminable length of time, Hammons urinated on a corner of Richard Serra's Cor-Ten steel public sculpture *T.W.U.* He was documented at various stages, the order of which remain unverified, by his collaborator, the photographer Dawoud Bey. What does it mean that Bey recorded the encounter with the policeman, and that Hammons decided to keep the photograph, indeed, to emphasize it, as part of the work's circulation? In part, it indicates what we are asked to remember about *Pissed Off*. One of the performance's only verifiable audience members, a policeman, threatened Hammons with disciplinary reprimand, shading the encounter with the threat of harm most palpable for Black men in American public space. Though it began as a critique of Richard Serra, *Pissed Off* merged seamlessly into the criminalization of regular behaviors and minor transgressions if carried out by a Black person.[15] While it does not get us any closer to the facts of what "actually" happened, the implicit hierarchy of power captured in Bey's image forces viewers to consider the potential scenarios outside the frame, and relatedly, the call to justice or action that photographs so often fail to engender, despite their utility as evidence.[16]

In a separate performance now referred to as *Shoe Tree*, the precise date and time of which are also unknown, Hammons tossed shoes over the top of *T.W.U.* It is generally agreed that Hammons threw twenty-five pairs over the course of several nights.[17] Tied together by the shoelaces, the shoes—apart from sneakers, there were high heels and galoshes—dangled over the edges of the industrial steel plates. The most widely circulated image of *Shoe Tree* reinforces *T.W.U.*'s spatial power, and relation to the body. Bey cuts off any context for the work, intimating frontality and fixity for a sculpture that was intended to be experienced as an unstable, constantly changing relation to the viewer. Shot from below, the sculpture fills the entire frame, extending the intensity and unintelligibility of its scale. The effect of the photograph is disorienting, seeming to align with Serra's intentions—he disdained aerial documentation, which for him implied a falsely autonomous distancing of the viewer, and inaccurately flattened the work into a gestalt form that would be immediately and uniformly received as optical, rather than bodily, knowledge.[18] However, *Shoe Tree* diverted attention away from the vertical force of *T.W.U.* and toward the flaccid, drooping shoes, softening its monumental upward stride through farcical diminishment.[19]

Hammons's two performances destabilized the threshold between unseen actions and their visible display, such that rumor and hearsay suffuse the content and the enactment of these actions and their photodocumentation. Rumor weakens "presence" or liveness as the constitutive factor of performance; as Frazer Ward has put it, "performance does not only happen when and where it happens."[20] Indeed, misremembering, invention, or alternative rendering were part of Hammons's intent. These tactics have important implications for artistic practice in the 1980s public sphere, positing guerilla, historically marginalized, hyperlocal, performative modes of inventive play as antidotes to what critic Thomas Lawson described as the "pious rectitude of postminimalism" that dominated public commissions and esteemed galleries alike[21] An earlier generation of artists associated with Fluxus, Happenings, and minimalism had declared photo-documentation reductive and unequal to the original action or event. Many either avoided or limited documentation, or staged images of performances specifically for publications or publicity materials. Yet photographs, among other forms of technological recording apparatuses such as tape recorders, would contribute to the indeterminate, contingent status of these artworks, rather than fix them into static, unchanging objects.[22] As performance art and its attendant discourses emerged in the 1970s, one of its constitutive factors was rumor. Aided by its entwinement with photography and video, performance thus acknowledged an intersubjective, mediated relationship with the viewer. As Anne Wagner has argued, artists such as Vito Acconci and Laurie Anderson questioned the validity of vision as primary mode of sensory information by disrupting or manipulating the "witness" function of documentation.[23] For Anderson in particular, rumor as a form of narration—in addition to pauses and lapses in memory—even helped shape performance's structure.[24]

In Hammons's case, reception and distribution are integral to how *Pissed Off* and *Shoe Tree* continue to unspool over time, refuting the notion of liveness as essential, while also recognizing the initial events as unique, if not discrete, components of the performances.[25] Images of *Pissed Off* appeared in the Spring 1982 issue of *The Flue*, an artist's magazine produced by the alternative space Franklin Furnace. *Shoe Tree* surfaced as both object and performance through its inclusion in the 1985 exhibition *After Tilted Arc*, at the Storefront for Art and Architecture.[26] Then, in 1990, photographs of both *Shoe Tree* and *Pissed Off* were shown in a reprise of Exit Art's *Illegal America* exhibition from March 3–April 7.[27] For this iteration of the show, Ingberman and Colo decided to add artists who they had not included originally, including Hammons. Also in 1990, images of *Pissed Off*, *Shoe Tree*, and the infamous performance *Bliz-aard Ball Sale* were featured in the retrospective *David Hammons: Rousing the Rubble* at P.S.1 Institute for Contemporary Art, where they had a wider reception.[28] The re-surfacing of these works thus coincides with the broader art establishment's explosive interest in the artist. In 1981, only the artist, Bey, and a handful of others knew that the actions had taken place at all.[29]

For Hammons, rumor both described and was drawn from a milieu of Black working-class social life. In an oft-quoted passage from his 1986 interview with Kellie Jones, he discussed the responses of those who watched him lug his circular sculptures made from empty bottles of the fortified wines Night Train and Thunderbird in Harlem:

> Sometimes I carry a whole arch of wine bottles around in the neighborhood. I walk from 125th up to 145th Street and people follow me, ask me questions, give me answers, tell me what I can do. They just give me tons of information and I don't give them any."[30]

In an interview with Steve Cannon, he elaborated further:

> In Harlem, I'll carry my wine bottles like I'm carrying a shopping bag, you know. And some woman will say, "Mister, excuse me, I been following you." (laughs) She'll say, "What are you doing with these?" I say, "Pardon me, what?" "You know," she'll say, "with these?" I say "Nothing. I'm just taking them for a walk." (laughs) [. . .] they'll say, "Is that Krazy Glue?" It's weighing like sixty, eighty pounds[. . . .] Krazy Glue is that glue that comes on late night television, and they think that's the glue to use for everything![31]

These reactions delimited the work: the viewers who happened to pass by were accomplices in these transgressions, their retelling or recounting of what happened only framed or presented after the fact. After throwing the shoes atop *T.W.U.* Hammons told Bey: "There's a piece that I made that you don't know about and probably nobody knows."[32] Such an admission undergirds Hammons's suppression of both *Pissed Off* and *Shoe Tree* for nearly a decade, and troubles the veracity of documentation by asking us to take the artist's word. Hammons's interest in the unofficial archive, the idea that "those who know don't tell," parallels Glissant's insistence on mystification as producing new forms of knowledge. Glissant writes:

> Western thought has led us to believe that a work must always put itself constantly at our disposal, and I know a number of our folktales

> . . . whose impact on their audience has nothing to do with the clarity of their meaning.[33]

The implication is that a populist or egalitarian approach to art-making does not necessarily equal a straightforwardness of access or legibility. As a form of communication, rumor deliberately mystifies or interferes with the visible order of procedures that produce and regulate statements. It makes itself entangled with, or indistinguishable from, the purported truth.[34] Rumor translates private gossip into the public sphere as "shared public knowledge"; it might be wielded in spheres of labor, family, and home to avoid repercussion and exposure, to shelter in a community of belief and protection, or to obtain access through deliberate misinformation.[35] However, whether or not Hammons is telling the truth, whether or not anyone "knows" of the work's existence, ceases to be important. Rather, it is the refusal of the idea that a lie directly opposes truth that conditions the social and aesthetic legibility of the work and, as Brian O'Doherty has put it, helps "efficiently keep history at bay."[36]

The Racial Politics of Public Space

Pissed Off might be read as a symbolic "pissing contest," an assertion of who gains the final authoritative use of the city, Hammons or Serra.[37] However, Hammons had bigger issues in mind, hence the title that he ultimately bestowed. For the 1990 *Illegal America* exhibition, Hammons wrote a statement that rarely, if ever, has accompanied the photographs since:

> "Pissed Off" is about the fact that in New York City a man doesn't have any public access to relieve himself in a decent manner. There is no way for a gentleman to relieve himself in a gentlemanly way without having to buy a drink. Keeps the rage going.[38]

The language of the statement is carefully worded, as in the genteel connotations of "decent" and "gentlemanly," which contrast sharply with the last sentence: like other artists living and working in downtown New York in the early–mid 1980s, Hammons could not but be enraged by the city's unequal allocation of spatial and economic resources.

The repetition of "relieve" as a pointedly masculinized euphemism invokes relief from bodily discomfort, but also connotes relief as a concrete and substantial form of aid withheld by government institutions. While nothing in the statement openly references homelessness, "man" and "gentlemanly" may allude to the single man as the persistent image of homelessness in the American cultural imaginary, despite the women and families who also sought relief.[39] The explosion of public sculpture at this time coincided with the forces of urban redevelopment that generated housing disinvestment, displacement, and eviction.[40] A result of economic restructuring, large-scale revoking of social services, and state and municipal decisions over rezoning efforts and redlining, the city's number of homeless in shelters numbered around fifteen thousand total in 1979, then jumped to fifteen thousand a month by late 1983. In the eighties, single men were not only the fastest growing and most *visible* of "unhoused" people on the New York streets, but the group pathologized most as a social problem by New York residents and the city alike.[41]

In tandem with these developments, neoliberal city politics and the mass media constructed hypervisible representations of the homeless as "vagrants." Yet this urban imaginary—whose anxieties were rooted in protecting an allegedly unified, bourgeois public sphere—invisibilized the human needs of the homeless, which justified the production of exclusionary spaces and policing of quality of life on the part of the city.[42] That Hammons was actively considering the spatial exclusion of homeless people throughout the decade is seen in a pen drawing from 1989, in which he loosely sketches a park bench surrounded by boxes and a grocery cart. Below, a caption reads "Homeless ain't home," perhaps implying the absence of a homeless person from a space that has been made home, or a biting critique of the notion that these environs could entail a home of any kind.

By pissing and throwing shoes, Hammons transgressed a site-specific sculpture that denaturalized and revealed space as a site of social conflict, but in doing so opened up a space for its own critical reckoning. *T.W.U.* made as good an alternative as any for "relief." Debuting April 24, 1980, the sculpture sat at the corner of West Broadway between Franklin and Leonard Streets outside the entrance to the Franklin Street IRT station. It was a recognizable landmark in the downtown neighborhood whose lofts provided homes and studios for many, predominantly white, artists—Serra himself had lived there for twelve years. He had named the sculpture for the Transport Workers' Union, because the work was completed on the day that the eleven-day transit strike ended in negotiations deadlock.[43]

Three equally sized steel plates, each two and three-quarters inches thick and twelve feet wide by thirty-six feet high, supported one another in an interdependent, counter-balanced "H" shape, which was anchored into a cement block in the ground.[44]

Yet *T.W.U.* also bore the marks of neighborhood customization: the sculpture was regularly adorned with graffiti, posters, fliers, trash, crumpled beer cans, and at one point, flung paint. Local reception also included posters with the phrase "Kill Richard Serra," pointing to the symbol of gentrification and institutional establishment that Serra's sculptures had rapidly become.[45] Neglecting the social histories of its immediate environment, *T.W.U.* had refused its own politics of place. Indeed, Serra diverted discussions of "place" toward "space," as in a conversation with Friedrich Teja Bach, who noted the "shift in the place quality" of Serra's sculptures as he increasingly made works for urban environments.[46] While *T.W.U.* attempted a model of site-specificity that actively intervened rather than assimilated to its surroundings, this same impulse marked it as a neutralizing, externalizing force of imposition, discounting public space as "an uncertain social realm where, in the absence of an absolute foundation, the meaning of the people is simultaneously constituted and put at risk."[47]

Considering the policed circumstances under which *Pissed Off* took place, the rage that Hammons alluded to nine years later confirms the fears stoked by the appearance of Black mobility in urban public space. By the turn of the 1980s, social and economic conditions had, on the surface, improved for the Black elite and middle class with wider opportunities for advancement in both public and private job sectors, and greater Black representation in municipal administration, popular culture, and mass media amid a new celebration of multiculturalism.[48] Yet, even as multiculturalist discourses encouraged liberal "tolerance" and openness, they resulted in diversity as an individualist, quota-based outcome, rather than an ongoing, collectivizing process. Cultural visibility itself was expected to serve as a corrective to history, yet the representation of Black people in the public sphere frequently elided or concealed the intersectional dynamics of power and economic status. As M. Nourbese Philip argues, in its anxiety to gloss and assimilate difference, multiculturalism failed to parse linguistically between words such as "poor," which connotes a passive, immobile state, and "theft," which describes the functioning process that renders the former. Writes Philip,

> The contradiction at the heart of the word "poor" is patent . . . for poor people have not only produced much, or laboured much, but they have had much taken away from them, and were then described as producing little. The word itself now encapsulates, reflects, perpetuates, and so magnifies the theft.[49]

Once theft and other acts of so-called violation, such as pissing in public, are understood within historical contexts of spatial dispossession and enclosure, we can begin to interrogate the dominant views of deviancy and criminal behavior, and understand "illegality"—for instance, the "relief" of oneself, as Hammons would have it—as a relative concept with differential consequences. *Pissed Off*, then, frames the relative nature of "illegality" when faced with structural inequity and limited mobility.

If *Pissed Off* might be read as allegorizing the city's lack of fundamental facilities, in doing so it exceeds the very sociological and ethnographic premises that characterized these situations for New York's publics, and translated "objective" observation into state surveillance.[50] In the late 1960s and throughout the 1970s, Conceptual artists critiqued, parodied and mimicked the statistics and photojournalistic formats that structured liberal reformist efforts to elicit sympathy for the disenfranchised, particularly in the New Deal era—what Martha Rosler called "the social conscience of liberal sensibility presented in visual imagery."[51] Rosler's famed *The Bowery in two inadequate descriptive systems*, 1974–75, paired twenty-one black-and-white photographs of empty alleys, stoops, and facades with twenty-four photographs of descriptive phrases meant to evoke drunkenness and impropriety. Whereas this work is often read to demystify systems of representation in its disjunctive montage tactics, it does not give up dominant photodocumentary forms entirely.[52] Rather, Rosler radically re-envisioned these "inadequate" systems of description, extending the veneer of information's neutrality toward something like poesis in order to outstrip sociological or ethnographic tools: "There is a poetics of drunkenness here," she wrote, "a poetry-out-of-prison."[53] Artists such as Rosler, Martha Wilson, Vito Acconci, Bruce Nauman, Pope.L, and Hammons employed "objective" measurements toward corporeal gestures and movements dependent on intersubjective exchange, in many cases undermining empirical observation as reliable. In this way, these artists beg an understanding that goes beyond the performance of self or "presentation of self" applied from sociology discourses.[54] In the 1978 performance *Times Square Crawl*, Pope.L crossed Times Square on hands and knees, dressed in a brown suit and yellow safety vest—in later iterations, he would drag himself on his elbows. This "downtrodden" horizontality exaggerates and surpasses the purported objective realism with which the overdetermined imagery of the "vagrant" or the bum, the stereotyped Black "underclass," irrationally saturated the public imaginary in the early 1980s. Unlike Hammons's more furtive entries into the street, Pope.L's intervention could not but be seen—the photographs reveal *Times Square Crawl* as a spectacle that forced viewers to acknowledge where empathy meets repulsion, where the shame of witnessing abjection becomes enjoyment.[55]

Hammons's actions around *T.W.U.*, however, moved more seamlessly into the street's already-existing streams of activity—its characters, histories, processes, and materiality—working within a lineage of conceptual and performance events predicated on refusing any separation between "art" and everyday action. Some of these events, like those of Fluxus artist George Brecht, isolated readymade events that were at once singular and repeatable toward "the details of everyday perceptual experience," though these occurrences could easily remain unnoticed or imperceptible, melting seamlessly back into the routine hustle.[56] Hammons's attraction to the street emphasized Black life within, and against racial capitalism as a form of redress, and posited the readymade codes of the street's inhabitants as productive of a legitimate mode of city existence. He isolated the ways in which anyone perceived outside the social order disrupted normative spatiality. As he put it: "That's where their power comes from. I saw a homeless [man] by himself in a subway car once during rush hour . . . Only he or a king could ride in a car alone at that hour."[57] This pre-generated power differential, rooted in late capitalism's restricted economic opportunity, became grounds for a new formal vocabulary that reformulated the material of conceptualism, challenging the concept of its long-vaunted dematerialization.

Indeed, conceptual efforts to remove the discrete "frame" of art contested the modernist idea that art must exist autonomously, referring only to itself. In 1970, Adrian Piper wrote of her desire to view an artwork along the same spatio-temporal planes as commonplace occurrences:

> unobtrusively insinuating art into a nonart situation really interests me; and doing this in such a way that people react to an obvious but

> uninterpreted (as art) presence, rather than such a well-defined artificial environment or theatrical action. I like the idea of doing away with all discrete forms and letting art lurk in the midst of things.[58]

Piper initially tested the boundaries of "art" through methodical experiments evaluating viewer perceptions against her own perception of herself as art object; Hammons's *Pissed Off* arguably slipped even more stealthily into the behaviors of daily life. Yet what both artists ultimately encountered was the prohibiting and curtailing of blackness as inherently part of daily life. In *Pissed Off*, unlike many performance art works informed by minimalism, the differential play of power across bodies that could not benefit from the privilege of neutrality became the work's objective.

Since at least 1979, Hammons had explored emptied bottles of the cheap, and abundant, fortified wines Thunderbird and Night Train as aesthetic material, perhaps best known in the form of his "bottle trees." After gathering the empty wine bottles from around Harlem, particularly near The Studio Museum in Harlem, Hammons adorned the branches of trees growing out of patches of dirt in the pavement of vacant lots with bottles, and nestled arcs of bottles strung together with glue and wire into facades of buildings. He even contemplated a Thunderbird redemption center: in a statement of plans prepared for his Rome Prize application, Hammons wrote:

> Frankly, during the period for which the Fellowship is requested I plan to continue walking, watching, taking mental notes and creating from the movement. While I plan to create a wine bottle redemption center (the bottles from which a sculpture installation will be created), many other works will be executed—based on the popular culture in which I exist.[59]

Pope.L used not the bottles, but the substance that filled them in his 1978 *Thunderbird Immolation*, in which he threatened to set himself on fire outside a complex of galleries, including those of Castelli and Sonnabend, at 420 West Broadway. Dressed in an ironed white shirt and black dress pants, Pope.L sat on a yellow fabric and encircled himself with matches while he mixed up a concoction that included Thunderbird, Wild Irish Rose whiskey, and Coca-Cola. As he began to douse himself in the liquid, gallery officials exited the building and ordered him to leave the premises.[60] In Hammons's use of the vacant bottles, these artifacts do not evidence the explicit trace of who drank from them, despite his oft-quoted declaration that "[a] Black person's lips have touched each one of those bottles."[61] Rather, in their very absence of human trace, the bottles index consumption to the systems of value by which they were produced, specific to the socioeconomic situation of cheap wine production in the 1980s which targeted low-income consumers. Pope.L and Hammons both sought to preserve the racialized and classed material forms of sociality that traditionally had no legitimacy as forms of social life, even or especially in Euro-American avant-garde lineages that sought an explicit closure of art and life.[62] In other words, both revealed the ways in which conceptualism's limits became apparent when art was shown to be inseparable from the same power relations—racial imaginaries, gender hierarchies, class entrenchment—that threaded in and through the real space of life.[63]

Rumor as a Politics of Audience

Hammons passed *T.W.U.* frequently as he traveled to Just Above Midtown/Downtown Gallery, or JAM, where he purportedly discussed Serra's work on occasion with gallery proprietor Linda Goode Bryant, as well as his need to react to it.[64] JAM had relocated to 178–80 Franklin Street in 1980, christening its new space with the exhibition *Outlaw Aesthetics*, the accompanying materials to which promised a "bedazzling, bewitching challenge to artistic convention."[65] Once a commercial gallery on 57th Street, JAM was in its sixth year of operation by the time it moved downtown as a nonprofit, defining itself as "an alternative space serving 'new' and 'emerging' artists specifically, yet not exclusively, Afro-American."[66] In this context, the publics associated with experimental art were automatically presumed by mainstream establishments to be white, and thus entitled to established institutional space that at best, was incognizant of, and at worst disregarded, a Black experimental artistic practice and its art-going publics in and around spaces such as JAM, The Studio Museum in Harlem, Cinque Gallery, Kenkeleba House, Franklin Furnace, The Kitchen, Fashion MODA, and Taller Boricua. That these publics could, and did, overlap, was rarely recognized. JAM's revised mission contested conceptual differentiations between "uptown," which typically referenced the practices of Black artists above 96th Street, and "downtown," shorthand for largely white experimental circles below 14th Street.

Shoe Tree was noticed by two downtown critics and artists, Thomas Lawson and Susan Morgan. In 1979, Lawson and Morgan founded *REALLIFE* Magazine, which became an unofficial, often spontaneous archive for aesthetic, theoretical, and intellectual practices of the 1980s. Morgan later recalled going up West Broadway from Chambers Street, and passing *T.W.U.* covered in shoes:

> . . . when I walked by in the mornings, there would be dozens of pairs of sneakers, each pair tied together by its shoestrings, tossed over the top of the sculpture. They'd be taken down and then, in the night, more shoes would appear. It was so smart and subversive, the best critique imaginable, and word was it was David Hammons doing this.[67]

Without confirmation of who had defiled *T.W.U.* with footwear, Morgan implied the enduring power of rumor ("word was . . .") to temporally extend a work beyond its immediate occurrence, directly impacting Hammons's later, canonical art institutional visibility. Her recollection of *Shoe Tree*, and her later chance meeting with the young curator Kellie Jones, led to Jones's interview with Hammons in *REALLIFE* in 1986, likely the most significant and enduring primary source with the artist on record.

Hammons began to engage more purposefully with the conversations about public art in 1985. He accepted an invitation to participate in *After Tilted Arc* at the Storefront for Art & Architecture, for which artists responded to one of the most contested public projects in United States history. Framing the invitation for submissions as a call to reimagine how *Tilted Arc* was produced, curators Tom Finkelpearl, Glenn Weiss, and Kyong Park asked artists to "explain, narrate, or invent the public mythology" of *Tilted Arc*; to redesign the sculpture, or Federal Plaza, in order to "provide a synthesis of the needs" of the public; or to propose a new public artwork for Federal Plaza entirely.[68] Storefront provided a packet of information and select articles for the participating artists, knowing how quickly criticism on the subject had already amassed.[69] Hammons submitted a small black-and-white photograph, now recognizable as Bey's image of *Shoe Tree*, pinned to a Xerox copy of "Letters to the Editor" from the October 14–20, 1981 issue of the *Village Voice*. Each short letter published in this section was a response to Peter Schjeldahl's initial, scathing, review of *Tilted Arc*—including a passionate defense of Serra from his gallerist, Leo Castelli.[70] With this gesture, Hammons revealed that he had gone so far as to intervene onto a currently standing Serra sculpture, albeit not *Tilted Arc*; further, he insinuated that direct action spoke more strongly than the voluminous ink spilled on the subject, symbolized by the simple, unceremonious juxtaposition of Bey's photograph on top of the "Letters to the Editor" page. While reacting as much to the unending Richard Serra Discourse as to Serra's body of sculpture at a moment in which no less than three Serras were on view downtown, Hammons also importantly framed Serra's inability to make work that was truly "public," despite situating it in open, freely accessible places.

In his own public art installations across Manhattan and Brooklyn in 1985 and 1986, Hammons mobilized unpretentious practices seen as craft or vernacular architecture, continuing his efforts to obscure singular authorship of the works. These folk practices, including what Hammons called "[t]hat Negritude architecture," had no claim on "place" in a geographic sense; rather, they tapped into the placelessness of art forms that migrate—like rumor—within and across Black diasporas through oral and embodied inheritance, materially resonant in ways that may not, at first, be legible to dominant white audiences.[71] This public practice began, arguably, with *Shoe Tree*. A "shoe tree" is quite literally a tree with discarded footwear tossed over the branches or occasionally nailed to the bark, commonly seen along highways and roads across North America and in international contexts. In some instances, the trees act as commemorative or celebratory markers where shoes from memorable occasions might be wielded as forms of adornment with personal significance for the thrower.[72]

In this regard, the shoe tree, while not specific to a Black diasporic tradition, might be understood as similar to what Zora Neale Hurston described as "lies," or Black folktales that are mythical, occasionally made up on the spot, and rerouted through the repetition and familiarity of hearing.[73] The elaborate narration of the lie provides a measure of control where no singular truth or story exists—for instance, uncorroborated rumors that reference violence toward African American individuals and communities are, nevertheless, consistent with past experiences and lived histories.[74] Writing of storytelling practices in the Caribbean, Lauren Derby argues that rumor, gossip, and hearsay are "unsanctioned speech act(s)" that formulate important communicative modes that can take on different uses in relation to dominant regimes of power—for instance, create climates of suspicion, incite violent repercussion, or enact political critique by way of spiritual explanation.[75] Whether rumor or folktale, such discursive models act as crucial vectors of dissemination amid intimate and familiar groups, and reject modes of knowledge that privilege, or confirm "truth" by way of rarified credentials or expertise. Each of these forms of speech evade codification, which would turn them into myth or legend.

Not only did the content of *Shoe Tree* rely on unstable significations of the tossed shoe lore, but its reception proved to be informal, happened upon, and whispered about, creating a diffuse, decentralized flow of information that contributed to the uncertainty surrounding *Shoe Tree* as an artistic action at all. The varied folkloric histories of the tossed shoes, dispersed among contexts and points of origin, and circulated by way of the "illegitimacy" of rumor, may well be why they appealed to Hammons as performative tactics. Further, the urban legend of shoe tossing might be understood, again, as an insurgent form of sociality—difficult to measure, having little to no correlation to the evidentiary, sociological truth claims of a physical site or the conventional facts of aesthetic display and comprehension. The inability to quantify sociality as "fact" per Frantz Fanon's mistranslated phrase "fact of blackness" gives new possibility to lived realities otherwise reduced to pat abjection, or the objectifying interpolative encounter Fanon described so famously.[76] Shoes dangling from power lines signify differently to different audiences, and very often, none of these meanings can be finally confirmed.

For some, the shoes may signify a game or sense of play, as in stealing someone's shoes and throwing them out of reach. For others, the furtive signal of tossed sneakers is a local and insular code of the street, legible in Black and Latinx communities where space is reclaimed to mark territory. Depending on the context, dangling shoes could signify a particular crew that runs a block, or mark the location of a drug deal. Therefore, more significant than their meaning is the collective function of the dangling shoes, like graffiti's tagging, of marking a "right to the city."[77] Understood through the necessary conflicts and exclusions by which social space is produced—for and by whiteness—graffiti writers and shoe tossers exercise authority by reimagining space. "Place" can be ascertained beyond empirical, geographic or quantitative, means—"the range of kinds of places—as intimate as the body, and as abstract, yet distinctive, as a productive region or a nation-state."[78] In other words, place does not refer to an already-existing neighborhood or geographically organized set of buildings, wherein space is frequently delineated through dispossession or displacement. Instead, it is brought into being through social interaction and its varying levels of registration on different bodies, including and especially through Black residents and their stakes in how space is produced.

As graffiti writing thickened around New York City's built environment, its audience was by default the unsuspecting inhabitants of a neighborhood. Tags got more elaborate and progressed beyond the signing of a name; with the inscriptions of the collective SAMO©, for example, viewers were addressed directly through aphoristic, lyrical tags that critiqued bourgeois complacency and punk stylization alike. Though the team behind SAMO© is now legendary, their inscriptions were initially understood precisely through neighborhood whisperings and rumors, which only heightened once the partnership of Al Diaz and Jean-Michel Basquiat was officially named.[79] Graffiti emerged specifically under the terms of concealment, both for the protection of the writers' anonymity, the tactic of surprise, and the perceived difficulty of its execution.[80] Like graffiti, the tossing of shoes occurred collectively and anonymously, mapping new means of indexical marking: I was here. Not coincidentally, the concealed terms of *Shoe Tree*'s execution rubbed against Serra's self-professed foregrounding of how *T.W.U.* was constructed. As he wrote in the text "Rigging" from 1980: "The work has evolved to where I can't physically manipulate it, due to its mass. I need to employ technology. I have to deal with cranes and whatever processes will get the work into place. . . . steel mills, ship yards, bridge companies, whatever. Nine-tenths of the work involves those extensions. There is nothing mysterious about it. All of it can be figured out with crews beforehand."[81]

In *Pissed Off* and *Shoe Tree*, performance and photograph do not necessarily have a cause-and-effect relation, pointing to Hammons's skepticism toward empirical fact. We can only "know" the performances by accessing them through the photographs, which is, of course, a way of never really knowing what happened in either performance. Anne Cheng reminds us:

> the rhetoric of "becoming visible" that has energized so much of progressive racial politics often elides the contradictions underpinning social visibility and remains inadequate to address the phenomenological, social, and psychical implications inhering in what it means to be visible (especially for a subject historically all-too-seen and not seen at all).[82]

If, for Hammons, telling and knowing are not equivalent to showing, neither is knowledge equivalent to documentation, the putative truth or transparency of which is continually called into question.

Critiques of the traditional protocols for discerning art historical evidence have abounded, in art history and visual studies.[83] Krista Thompson has challenged the truth-value of photography as documentation—in her argument, the inadvertent ahistorical usage of photography in scholarly research on enslavement in the British West Indies helps us imagine the real historical effects of slavery, which essentially extended into the tourism and sugar cane industries as though never abolished.[84] Drawing her method from James Baldwin's book *The Evidence of Things Not Seen*, Thompson argues that we must question our dependency on the photograph's allegedly transparent status and enforcement of historical evidence, and revalue absence in the photographic record as an intrinsic part of historical representation. Hammons similarly manipulates the efforts of close looking in producing actions that in some cases were never even recorded and exist solely through word of mouth. His play with the photograph's indexical function reveals the archive's mutability, given that his performances' historical details and processes of making continue to reveal themselves over time at varying junctures of individual and collective memory.[85] That archival evidence is rarely sufficient for institutional memory when it comes to racial violence is also a crucial underlying factor in Hammons's distrust of photography, and the kind of witnessing it engenders.[86]

Documentation of Hammons in the act of tossing the shoes continues to be intentionally suppressed—though one grainy, low-resolution video-still exists that captures him preparing the throw, and, somewhere, a video to which it corresponds. Significantly, the sequence of events in *Pissed Off* has circulated more widely in public display than that of *Shoe Tree*, coinciding with one more extant document: a Xeroxed poster bearing Hammons's signature, and dated "81." Here, again, the grainy, pixelated resolution of a copy opens up the context and timing of its creation to uncertainty and its production in consultation with Bey for *The Flue*, where it was positioned among an advertisement for a Franklin Furnace benefit and performance series, a text from the organization describing grants—playfully called "fuel"—to support working artists, and an article on the Russian avant-garde artist El Lissitzky. On the poster, Bey's photographs do not supplant or stand in for the actions, but rather call attention to their highly unstable, ambivalent, and mutable processes of reception and distribution. As such, this documentation refuses to provide any answers, instead opening up inquiry as its own populist correlative to "official" history. Hammons ensures that even if those who knew did in fact tell, the telling would inevitably complicate, rather than illuminate, history's linear, narrative structures.

Notes

1. Under the auspices of the nascent organization Exit Art, the show was planned for the alternative space Just Above Midtown Gallery, from September 1 to October 3, 1983 and then was pushed back to 1984. Despite JAM's commitment of $8,200 from the NEA, the exhibition did not take place in 1984 either, nor did it in 1985. Letters Linda Goode Bryant (1984) and Jeanette Ingberman's notes from Exit Art (1983) that she was still working on the exhibition in 1985 and 1986, ultimately never to have it come to fruition. Linda Goode Bryant Letter to Jeanette Ingberman 1984, Exit Art archive, Series III, Box 153, Folder 7, Fales Library & Special Collections, New York University; Exit Art NEA organization grant application form, 1983, Performances not to be seen, Exit Art archive, Series III, Box 153, Folder 7, Fales Library & Special Collections, New York University.

2. Jeanette Ingberman, Exit Art NEA organization grant application form, 1983; Performances not to be seen, Exit Art archive, Series III, Box 153, Folder 7, Fales Library & Special Collections, New York University.

3. Manthia Diawara, "Make It Funky: The Art of David Hammons," *Artforum* 36 (9) (1998): 120.

4. Lorraine O'Grady has preempted my concern: "I'm leery of the kind of discourse I recently read on David Hammons that foregrounds terms like 'magical' and 'reclusive'—rather than, say, making an analytical comparison to Damien Hirst's stage-managing of his career." Lorraine O'Grady, Email Q&A with *Artforum* editor, http://lorraineogrady.com/writing/emailq-a-w-artforum-editor-2009.

5. Édouard Glissant, *Caribbean Discourse: Selected Essays*, translated by J. Michael Dash (Charlottesville: University of Virginia Press, 1989).

6. Kellie Jones (2014) has touched on Hammons's tendency to perform absence and elusiveness, and Elvan Zabunyan (2005) has discussed Hammons as resisting "integration" into the mainstream, and seeking marginality as a site of resistance (following bell hooks). The latter point is also echoed by Elena Filipovic (2017). My analysis differs in that I see obscurity as aiming ultimately to trouble the conventional structures of "inside" and "outside" that have pervaded literature on art as institution, and especially African American artists' critiques of institutions. Kellie Jones, "'There Is a Word': Absence, Presence, and David Hammons," Paper presented at The Museum of Modern Art, New York, 2014; Elvan Zabunyan, "David Hammons: 'Outside Thoughts,'" in *Black Is a Color [A History of African-American Art]*, 135–167 (Paris: Editions Dis Voir, 2005); Elena Filipovic, *David Hammons: Bliz-aard Ball Sale* (Cambridge, MA: Afterall Books/MIT Press, 2017).

7. Sampada Aranke (2017) has also noted opacity in relation to Hammons. Additionally, Tobias Wofford (2011) points out, in his essay on Hammons's "Spade" series, a "productive opacity" that for him "result[s] from Hammons's play with language as well as those that

incorporate indexical signs" (2011, 132). Diverging slightly from these trains of thought, I argue that (willful) obscurity pertains more closely to intersubjective and interpersonal relations, given Hammons's concern with the immediate network of Black peers and artists who collaborated with him. Sampada Aranke, "Material Matters: Black Radical Aesthetics and the Limits of Visibility," *e-flux* 79, https://www.e-flux.com/journal/79/94433/material-matters-black-radical-aesthetics-andthe-limits-of-visibility; Tobias Wofford, "Can You Dig It? Signifying Race in David Hammons's 'Spade' Series," in *L.A. Object & David Hammons Body Prints*, edited by Connie Rogers Tilton and Lindsay Charlwood, 86–135 (New York: Tilton Gallery, 2011).

8. Édouard Glissant, *Caribbean Discourse: Selected Essays*, translated by J. Michael Dash (Charlottesville: University of Virginia Press, 1989), p. 59.

9. Fred Moten's (2008) and Lewis R. Gordon's (2017) respective readings of Frantz Fanon challenge Fanon's insistence on the impossibility of a Black person coming into being for another Black person, apparently prohibiting the existence of a Black sociality. As Gordon writes: "Why must the social world be premised on the attitudes and perspectives of antiblack racists? Why don't blacks among each other and other communities of color count as a social perspective?" (297). Lewis Gordon, "Phenomenology and Race," in *The Oxford Handbook on Philosophy and Race*, edited by Naomi Zack (New York: Oxford University Press, 2017), http://www.oxfordhandbooks.com.ezproxy.cul.columbia.edu/view/10.1093/oxfordhb/9780190236953.001.0001/oxfordhb-9780190236953-e-53; Fred Moten, "The Case of Blackness," *Criticism* 50 (2): 177–218.

10. Tina Campt, *Listening to Images* (Durham, NC and London: Duke University Press, 2017), p. 10.

11. Throughout, I use "performance," "street intervention," and/or "street performance" interchangeably. Though others have insisted on differentiation of the terms, I maintain that Hammons's notion of performance is coextensive with notions of intervention and "non-theatrical performance," as Allan Kaprow (1976) termed it, which are intermedial and defamiliarize the conventions of staging and theatrical framing in a lineage that stems from the visual arts. Allan Kaprow, "Non-theatrical Performance," *Artforum* 14 (9) (1976): 45–51.

12. According to Exit Art's notes for the 1990 *Illegal America* wall labels, Hammons talked the officer out of giving him a ticket. Exit Art statements and labels for *Illegal America*, Exit Art archive, Series I, Box 24, Folder 15, Fales Library & Special Collections, New York University.

13. Celia W. Duggar, "In New York, Few Public Toilets and Many Rules," *New York Times*, May 21, 1991.

14. I take this methodological approach, which in art history has been explored most recently by Krista Thompson and Richard J. Powell, from Saidiya V. Hartman's (2008) notion of "critical fabulation."

15. Simone Browne, *Dark Matters: On the Surveillance of Blackness*. Durham, NC and London: Duke University Press, 2015; and Khalil G. Muhammed, *The Condemnation of Blackness: Race, Crime, and the Making of Modern Urban America* (Cambridge, MA: Harvard University Press, 2010).

16. Leigh Raiford, *Imprisoned in a Luminous Glare: Photography and the African-American Freedom Struggle* (Chapel Hill: University of North Carolina Press. 2011).

17. Elena Filipovic, *David Hammons: Bliz-aard Ball Sale*. Cambridge, MA and London: Afterall Books and MIT Press, 2017; and Kellie Jones, "The Structure of Myth and the Potency of

Magic," in *David Hammons: Rousing the Rubble*, edited by David Hammons and Alanna Heiss, 15–38 (New York and Cambridge, MA: Institute for Contemporary Art and MIT Press).

18. Yve-Alain Bois, "A Picturesque Stroll around 'Clara-Clara,'" *October* 29 (Summer 1984): 34.

19. For a longer discussion of Serra's, postminimalists', and minimalists' associations with masculinist tropes of power, see Chave (1990) and Bryan-Wilson (2007). Anna Chave, "Minimalism and the Rhetoric of Power," *Arts* Magazine 64 (5) (1990): 44–63; Julia Bryan-Wilson, "Hard Hats and Art Strikes: Robert Morris in 1970," *Art Bulletin* 89 (2) (2007): 333–359.

20. Frazer Ward, *No Innocent Bystanders: Performance Art and Audience* (Hanover, NH: Dartmouth College Press, 2012), p. 7.

21. Kate Fowle, "Interview with Thomas Lawson and Susan Morgan," in *REALLIFE* Magazine 1979–1990, 4.03–4.15 (New York: Artists Space, 2007).

22. Liz Kotz, *Words to Be Looked At: Language in 1960s Art* (Cambridge, MA: MIT Press. 2007).

23. Anne Wagner, "Performance, Video, and the Rhetoric of Presence," *October* 91 (Winter 2000): 59–80.

24. Roselee Goldberg, "Public Performance: Private Memory," *Studio International* 192 (July/August 1976): 19–24.

25. While my project is sympathetic to the critique of visibility and marketability posed famously by Peggy Phelan (1993), I posit Hammons's work as exceeding both the ontology of performance as predicated on presence, yet resistant to the idea that the logic of performance is always already dictated by and through media as put forth by Philip Auslander (2006). My account also diverges from that of Amelia Jones (1997) and Mechtild Widrich (2014), who argue that the experience of a live situation should not be privileged over the knowledge gained in documentation and its witnessing after the fact. Rather, I maintain that the ambiguity of reception that emerges between an initial event and its documentation is precisely what must be preserved. Peggy Phelan, *Unmarked: The Politics of Performance* (New York: Routledge, 1993); Philip Auslander, "The Performativity of Performance Documentation," *PAJ: A Journal of Performance and Art* 84 (3) (2006): 1–10; Amelia Jones, "'Presence' in Absentia: Experiencing Performance as Documentation," *Art Journal* 56 (4) (1997): 11–18; Mechtild Widrich, *Performative Monuments: The Rematerialisation of Public Art* (Manchester, UK: Manchester University Press, 2014).

26. David Hammons, "Artist's Page, PISSED OFF," *The Flue* 2 (1) (Spring 1982): 28.

27. *Illegal America*, curated by Jeanette Ingberman and Papo Colo, initially went on view at Franklin Furnace from February 10 to March 6, 1982, before Exit Art secured its first permanent location on Broadway and Prince in Soho, from 1984 to 1992.

28. Both *Rousing the Rubble* and *After Tilted Arc* were curated by Tom Finkelpearl. The former traveled to the Institute for Contemporary Art, Philadelphia (March 15–April 28, 1991) and the San Diego Museum of Contemporary Art (August 17–November 10, 1991). The latter was on view at Storefront for Art & Architecture (November 7–December 1, 1985).

29. In the previously published version of this article, I wrote that Hammons chose not to display or discuss the actions until the 1990 *Illegal America* reprise exhibition at Exit Art.

30. Kellie Jones, "Interview with David Hammons," *REALLIFE* 16 (1986): 2–9.

31. Steve Cannon, Gail Shilke, Jemeel Monodic, David Henderson, and Keith Gilyard, "Interview with David Hammons," *A Gathering of the Tribes* 1 (1) (1991): 1–7.

32. Dawoud Bey, Conversation with the author, 2017.

33. Édouard Glissant, *Caribbean Discourse: Selected Essays*, translated by J. Michael Dash (Charlottesville: University of Virginia Press, 1989), p. 107.

34. Michel Foucault, "Truth and Power," in *Power/Knowledge: Selected Interviews & Other Writings*, 1972–1977, edited by Colin Gordon, 109–134 (New York: Pantheon Books, 1972).

35. Lauren Derby, "Beyond Fugitive Speech: Rumor and Affect in Caribbean History," *Small Axe* 18 (2) (2014): 125.

36. Brian O'Doherty, *Inside the White Cube: The Ideology of the Gallery Space* (Berkeley: University of California Press, 1999).

37. Copeland (2011) takes this idea up briefly. Huey Copeland, "Mal d'anthologie: Clifford Owens and the Crises of African American Performance Art," in *Clifford Owens: Anthology*, edited by Christopher Y. Lew, 15–31 (New York: MoMA PS1, 2011).

38. David Hammons, "Statement for Illegal America," David Hammons artist file, Illegal America, Exit Art archives, Series I, Box 24, Folder 24, Fales Library & Special Collections, New York University, 1990.

39. While homeless families with children are currently the fastest growing segment of the homeless population—and of these, 65% who have children are women—most studies show that single homeless adults are likely to be men, as they comprise 67.5% of the single homeless population nationally, and 76% of the homeless populations surveyed. See National Coalition for the Homeless, "Who Is Homeless?," Fact Sheet, July 2009, https://www.nationalhomeless.org/factsheets/Whois.pdf. See also Kim Hopper, *Reckoning with Homelessness* (Ithaca: Cornell University Press. 2002).

40. Rosalyn Deutsche, *Evictions: Art and Spatial Politics* (Cambridge, MA: MIT Press. 1996).

41. Ariel Eisenberg, "'A Shelter Can Tip the Scales Sometimes': Disinvestment, Gentrification, and the Neighbourhood Politics of Homelessness in 1980s New York City," *Journal of Urban History* 23 (6) (2017): 915–931.

42. Todd G. Shields, "Network News Construction of Homelessness 1980–1993," *The Communication Review* 4 (2) (2001): 193–218.

43. As reported in the *New York Times* (Stetson 1980), the citywide strike—the second in New York's history—ended with a split vote among the TWU executive board on the proposed agreement, and the decision to send ratification by mail ballot for the union's members to decide. Damon Stetson, "Mail Vote Is Planned," *New York Times*, April 12, 1980, A1.

44. Public Art Fund erected *T.W.U.* in concert with another commissioned sculpture by Serra. *Arc*, a one-hundred-and-ten-ton sculpture comprised of five twelve-by-forty-foot curved steel plates, was sited in St. John's Rotary outside the Manhattan exit of the Holland Tunnel. Both of these sculptures have been eclipsed by the infamy of a third downtown Manhattan sculpture: *Tilted Arc*, commissioned in 1979 by the Art-in-Architecture program of the General Services Administration of the United States, installed in 1981, and removed in 1989.

45. Barbara Rose, "Talking about Art," *Vogue* 171 (2) (1981): 320; and Calvin Tomkins, "Man of Steel," *The New Yorker*, August 5, 2002.

46. Richard Serra, 1975, "Interview with Teja Bach," in *Richard Serra: Interviews, etc. 1970–80*, edited by Clara Weyergraf-Serra (Yonkers, NY: Hudson River Museum. 1980), p. 55.

47. Rosalyn Deutsche, *Evictions: Art and Spatial Politics* (Cambridge, MA: MIT Press, 1996), p. 268.

48. Manning Marable, *Race, Reform, and Rebellion: The Second Reconstruction in Black America, 1945–1982* (London: Macmillan Press, 1984).

49. M. Nourbese Philip, "Women and Theft," in *Frontiers: Selected Essays and Writings on Racism and Culture, 1984–1992*, 72–78 (Stratford, ON: Mercury Press and Inland Book Co., 1992), p. 76.

50. Simone Browne, *Dark Matters: On the Surveillance of Blackness* (Durham, NC and London: Duke University Press, 2015).

51. Martha Rosler, "In, around, and Afterthoughts: On Documentary Photography," in *Decoys and Disruptions: Selected Writings, 1975–2001*, 151–207 (Cambridge, MA: MIT Press, 2004), p. 176. See also Allan Sekula, "Dismantling Modernism, Reinventing Documentary (Notes on the Politics of Representation)," *The Massachussetts Review* 19 (4) (1978): 859–883; and Jeff Wall, "'Marks of Indifference': Aspects of Photography in, or as, Conceptual Art," in *Reconsidering the Object of Art: 1965–1975*, edited by Ann Goldstein and Anne Rorimer, 247–267 (Los Angeles and Cambridge, MA: Museum of Contemporary Art Los Angeles and MIT Press, 1995).

52. Steve Edwards, *Martha Rosler: The Bowery in Two Inadequate Descriptive Systems* (London: Afterall Books, 2012).

53. Martha Rosler, "In, around, and Afterthoughts: On Documentary Photography," in *Decoys and Disruptions: Selected Writings, 1975–2001*, 151–207 (Cambridge, MA: MIT Press, 2004), p. 194.

54. I take this phrase from the title of Erving Goffman's (1959) well-known *The Presentation of Self in Everyday Life*, which has since been used to theorize a wide range of performance art, but especially that of Acconci. Erving Goffman, *The Presentation of Self in Everyday Life* (Garden City, NY: Doubleday, 1959).

55. Saidiya Hartman, *Scenes of Subjection: Terror, Slavery, and Self-Making in Nineteenth Century America* (New York: Oxford University Press, 1997).

56. Julia Robinson, "From Abstraction to Model: George Brecht's Events and the Conceptual Turn in Art of the 1960s," *October* 127 (Winter 2009): 77.

57. Louise Neri, "No Wonder: David Hammons and Louise Neri," in *David Hammons: Yardbird Suite*, edited by Deborah Menaker Rothschild, 63–69 (Williamstown: Williams College Museum of Art, 1994), p. 64.

58. Adrian Piper, "Talking to Myself: The Ongoing Autobiography of an Art Object (1970–1973)," in *Out of Order, out of Sight*, Volume 1: *Selected Writings in Meta-Art 1968–1992*, 29–55 (Cambridge, MA and London: MIT Press, 1996).

59. On June 15, 1982, the state of New York enacted the Returnable Container Act, also known as the "Bottle Bill." The bill went into effect a year later on June 1, 1983 as part of New York's Environmental Conservation Act, declaring that anyone who redeemed a bottled beverage would automatically earn five cents.

60. Kristine Stiles, "Thunderbird Immolation: Burning Racism," in *William Pope.L: The Friendliest Black Artist in America* (Cambridge, MA: MIT Press, 2002), pp. 36–44.

61. Kellie Jones, "Interview with David Hammons," *REALLIFE* 16 (1986): 2–9.

62. In taking up the notion of forms of social life historically deemed "illegitimate," I look to Saidiya Hartman's (1997) reading of performance under the terrorizing conditions of enslavement. Drawing on Michel de Certeau, Hartman posited small, everyday practices as tactics of resistance and refusal that constitute survival, for instance "work slowdowns, feigned illness, unlicensed travel, the destruction of property, theft, self-mutilation, dissimulation, physical confrontation with owners and overseers that document the resistance to slavery" (51). Per Hartman's larger arguments, made here and elsewhere, about the "afterlives of slavery," it should become clear how, in a neoliberal, late twentieth century context, Hammons's deployment of similar tactics tap into performative models of redress and movement within constraining circumstances. Saidiya Hartman, *Scenes of Subjection: Terror, Slavery, and Self-Making in Nineteenth Century America* (New York: Oxford University Press, 1997).

63. Hal Foster (1989) gestured to this at the end of the 1980s, in his critique of art historical approaches to 1970s art: "The very premises of the indexical model of seventies' art—that artistic signs can be 'empty,' that cultural messages can exist 'without a code'—are disproved by later artists involved in a critique of (art) institutions and representations: for these artists, no body or site, representation or event, is ever simply present or uncoded" (259). Hal Foster, "Wild Signs: The Breakup of the Sign in Seventies' Art," *Social Text* 21(1989): 251–68.

64. Elena Filipovic, *David Hammons: Bliz-aard Ball Sale* (Cambridge, MA and London: Afterall Books and MIT Press, 2017), p. 148 n98.

65. Outlaw Aesthetics exhibition brochure, Just Above Midtown gallery, 1980, Lorraine O'Grady papers, 1952–2012, Series III.B, Box 10, Wellesley College Archives.

66. Janet Henry, 1980, Letter to Lorraine O'Grady, Lorraine O'Grady papers, 1952–2012, Series III.B, Box 10, Wellesley College archives, Wellesley, MA.

67. Kate Fowle, "Interview with Thomas Lawson and Susan Morgan," in *REALLIFE* Magazine 1979–1990, 4.03–4.15, New York: Artists Space, 2007. I am grateful to Leah Pires for sharing this material with me.

68. "Exhibition Information," *After Tilted Arc*, September 1, 1985, Storefront for Art and Architecture Archives, accessed February 3, 2021, https://archive.org/details/198511_aftertilt00thom.

69. In addition to Hammons, participating artists included Bill and Mary Buchen, Dina Bursztyn, Rosemary Cellini, Dan Coma, Green Market CENYC, Sandy Gellis, HERA, Kristin Jones & Andrew Ginzel, Tadashi Kawamata, Kazuko, Jeffrey Kipness, Sandford Kwinter & Francoise Schein, Ed McGowin, Deborah Ossoff, Robert Parker, Scott Pfaffman, Toshio Sasaki, Carolee Schneemann, Vernon Shetley, Leonid Sokov, Michael Sorkin, Nancy Spero, Mierle Laderman Ukeles, Alan Wexler, Hannah Wilke, Steven Woodward, and anonymous contributors.

70. See Peter Schjeldahl, "Artistic Control," *Village Voice*, Oct. 14–29, 1981, 100.

71. Kellie Jones, "Interview with David Hammons," *REALLIFE* 16 (1986): 2–9.

72. Shoe trees are still very much in practice, as seen in the wide variety of recent newspaper articles detailing their mysterious meanings and, in some cases, removal. See Maggie McNeary, "Shoe Tree in Central Arkansas to Be Cut Down," *Arkansas Online*, June 2017, 9, http://www.arkansasonline.com/news/2017/jun/09/arkansas-shoe-tree-be-cut-down; and Ashley Powers, "End of the Road for the Shoe Tree," *Los Angeles Times*, February 16, 2011, http://articles.latimes.com/2011/feb/16/nation/la-na-shoe-tree-20110217.

73. Zora Neale Hurston, *Dust Tracks on a Road* (New York: Harper Perennial, 1996).

74. Patricia A. Turner, *I Heard It through the Grapevine: Rumor in African-American Culture* (Berkeley and Los Angeles: University of California Press, 1993); and Coco Fusco, "The Bodies That Were Not Ours: Black Performers, Black Performance," *Nka: Journal of Contemporary African Art* 5 (1) (1996): 28–33.

75. Lauren Derby, "Beyond Fugitive Speech: Rumor and Affect in Caribbean History," *Small Axe* 18 (2) (2014): 131.

76. Fred Moten, "The Case of Blackness," *Criticism* 50 (2) (2008): 177–218.

77. Henri Lefebvre, "The Right to the City," in *Writings on Cities*, edited by Eleanore Kofman and Elizabeth Lebas, 147–160 (Malden, MA and Oxford, UK: Blackwell Publishers, 1996).

78. Ruth Wilson Gilmore, "Fatal Couplings of Power and Difference: Notes on Racism and Geography," *The Professional Geographer* 54 (1) (2002): 15.

79. Philip Faflick, "SAMO© Graffiti: Boosh-wah or CIA?," *Village Voice*, December 11, 1978.

80. Jeff Chang, *Can't Stop, Won't Stop: A History of the Hip-Hop Generation* (New York: St. Martin's Press, 2005); and Ivor Miller, *Aerosol Kingdoms: Subway Painters around New York City* (Jackson, MS: University Press of Mississippi, 2002).

81. Richard Serra, 1975, "Interview with Teja Bach," in *Richard Serra: Interviews, etc. 1970–80*, edited by Clara Weyergraf-Serra (Yonkers, NY: Hudson River Museum, 1980), p. 123.

82. Anne Anlin Cheng, "Skin Deep: Josephine Baker and the Colonial Fetish," *Camera Obscura* 23 (3) (2008): 63.

83. See, for example, Preziosi (1992) and Berger (2015). Donald Preziosi, "The Question of Art History," *Critical Inquiry* 18 (2) (1992): 363–386; and Martin A. Berger, "The Problem with Close Looking," in *A Companion to American Art*, edited by John Davis, Jennifer A. Greenhill, and Jason D. LaFountain, 113–127 (Hoboken, NJ: Wiley and Blackwell, 2015).

84. Krista Thompson, "The Evidence of Things Not Photographed: Slavery and Historical Memory in the British West Indies," *Representations* 113 (1) (2011): 39–71.

85. Brent Hayes Edwards, "The Politics of Scraps: Archives and Counter-Archives," W.E.B. Du Bois Lecture Series, Hutchins Center for African & African-American Research, Harvard University, 2015, http://hutchinscenter.fas.harvard.edu/brent-h-edwards-w-e-b-du-bois-lecture-series-1-3.

86. Elizabeth Alexander, "Can You Be BLACK and Look at This? Reading the Rodney King Video(s)," *Public Culture* 7 (1994): 77–94.

How to See Like Hammons

Sampada Aranke

“HAS ANYONE ELSE SEEN THESE.” Scribed on a wall in pencil, this fragment served as crude wall text for a vitrine in David Hammons’s 2019 exhibition at Hauser & Wirth in Los Angeles. The vitrine, filled with memorabilia, photocopies, and rare primary documents, was but one of many locations where Hammons displayed Hammons. This was not the first time Hammons wrote directly on the wall. In his 2016 Mnuchin career survey, he also employed this strategy. In that show, the wall texts also served as captions and commentary. This tactic within a broader strategy of exhibition-based intervention creates a space where the artist’s hand and the artist’s voice are not divorced from each other. Commentary accompanies objects and gives rise to a kind of analysis of the present—with each iteration of penciled wall text, we are brought into the present tense of the work, the place where historical relevance meets the artist’s opinion about its current iteration, a mobilization of graphite as an invocation of contingency, temporariness, the possibility of erasure. . . .

While many have suggested that penciled wall text like this reflects art-world commentary by curators and collectors who attempt to ascertain the uniqueness or rarity of the work at hand,[1] I maintain that these written scripts are actually broader engagements with questions of what subjects and objects are even on display in the first place.[2] To ask, or to state, “Has anyone else seen these?” in the context of an exhibition is to slyly pose a question that already has an answer: yes, or maybe, or no. Any answer to that question proves Hammons’s point: that he himself is both the seeing subject and object to see. To extend the stakes of this declarative call and

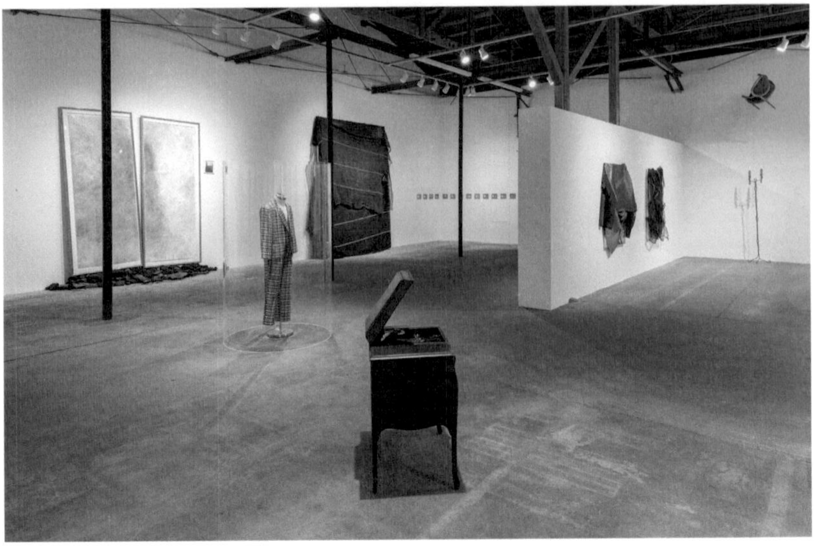

Installation view, *David Hammons*, Hauser & Wirth, Los Angeles, 2019.

its cheeky response, Hammons's question and answer is also, and actually, a question about history itself. To have seen, to have been seen, approximates a relationship to art history and its conceit—that to gain some kind of archival longevity, one must have their work seen and one must have been seen, a feat for an artist characterized as prickly and antisocial in his sociability.[3] It must sound a bit curious to suggest that a Black artist methodologically pivots ocularcentrism even while engaging sight. By both leaning into and troubling vision as a sense, Hammons offers a critique of sight as it is otherwise operationalized in everyday life as a form of surveillance that is a part of a totalizing violence against Black life. Instead he moves that same concern around vision toward another kind of maneuver entirely. To be invited to see, and even more precisely to see like Hammons, is a methodology driven by a Black radical aesthetic critique and one I have provisionally named the Hammons effect.

Glamor and allure of mystery aside, Hammons's approach to his own persona as an artist has generated frenzied whisper networks around his infamous reputation, unabashed no bullshit lack of filter, and commitment to messing with the protocols of propriety perpetuated by and within the art world. In fact, my own Hammons obsession peaked in 2016 when I realized that every single time I mentioned wanting to write on him to artists, curators, or collectors, I was presented with immediate tales about the artist of repute. These interactions made it clear that I needed to write not about Hammons himself, though that would be crucial to the project, but rather about the stories, rumors, and states of aesthetic influence presented by him. It's as if there's a whole world made by, about, and for Hammons, activated by the way he does art in the first place. The impact of the Hammons effect will be taken up in a research project in which I track how curators, collectors, and artists have been aesthetically, conceptually, and financially impacted by Hammons's artistic strategies.

This essay, however, focuses on the iterative gestures that give rise to a methodology that swerves, misuses, and deforms normative racial protocols of contemporary art.[4] I will turn to modes through which Hammons approaches his work's exhibition, the artist's own interviews in which he comments upon his priorities and aesthetic strategies, and varieties of criticism and writing on Hammons by popular and art-world coverage. This methodological maneuver is part and parcel of Hammons's decades-long practice and serves to enact a Black aesthetic determination already sleeved in its own method. This essay works to unpack how Hammons throws into methodological disarray the question of art's histories with his relentless invocation of Black aesthetic practices that deform, if not refuse, their own making.

Straining Credibility

"Some of what he told us strained credibility," writes Calvin Tomkins in a 2019 *New Yorker* profile of Hammons.[5] Having already described the artist as an elusive and private, stubborn yet charming, curious yet assured figure, Tomkins ends his profile with a surprised realization that the artist "was still nourishing the Hammons myth—making himself appear more reclusive and otherworldly than he is."[6] In one fell swoop, Hammons is suddenly a generator of his storied reputation through white lies, fibs, exaggerations, withholdings, and any other kind of offerings that strain credibility. Tomkins is not exceptional in his presentation of Hammons. For decades critics, curators, and scholars have found him to be particularly slippery, obstinate, and downright mysterious.[7] At stake in these presentations are not only racially charged subtexts on an artist's reputation but also the question of how one imagines Hammons to bear the burden of

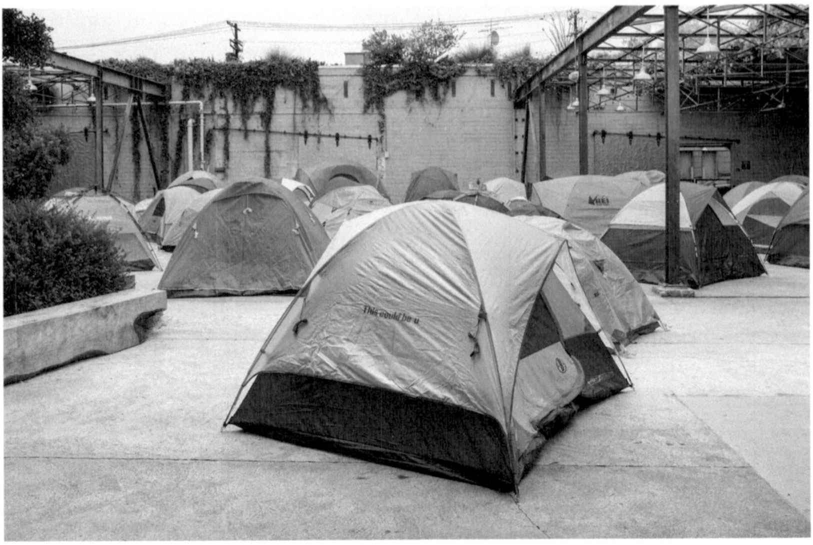

Installation view, *David Hammons*, Hauser & Wirth, Los Angeles, 2019.

authenticity, journalistic accuracy, and some kind of plausible refutation of how he has been figured throughout his career. This says nothing of how these demands are incongruent with how his art work is praised, specifically for its heightened referentiality to Black life through the imaginative gesture, willful refutation, and humorous critique. No demands for credibility are pressed upon the work, as the artist is given full license to run away from demands for factual accuracy.

What strikes me as an undercurrent in these depictions of Hammons is how they can't even see how his embodiment of conceptualism is particularly *Black*, which is to say that his approach to the artistic genre is a misdirection and deformation of the notion of accuracy itself.[8] As Hammons has noted, "I don't trust the word. I trust the eye."[9] A general distrust in a discursive apparatus in many ways explains Hammons's misuse of discourse as material itself. Hammons often turns language on its head, bends the assumed normative principles of words and their meanings, and sometimes outright breaks the rules in order to create a dissonance between the object and its discursive association.[10] I take up Houston Baker's notion of deformation as part of a Black radical aesthetic. In Baker's formulation Black American aesthetic practices are disinterested in achieving white canonical status by repeating formal traits within these works, and instead these practices turn to a deformation of mastery.[11] A deformation of mastery strives toward a wink at the canonical and yet ultimately bends or breaks such forms through an uptake that essentially accounts for how Blackness has always already transformed and impacted the form in the first instance. This concept is much akin to Greg Tate's poetic insistence that "what has always struck Black observers of this phenomenon isn't just the irony of white America fiending for Blackness when it once debated whether Africans even had souls. It's also the way They have always tried to erase the Black presence from whatever Black thing They took a shine to."[12] While Tate is speaking to the violent inclinations of white supremacist appropriation (cultural and otherwise), I find the attention to Black presence and an accompanying viewership that sees that presence to be particularly helpful when we think of the historical contingency of canons and their formations. As such, the forms that reach canonical significance also calcify into historical truths and become policed through the language of accuracy itself. By pointing to the instability of truths, Hammons instead redirects us toward the material conditions that open up new forms of looking—at both the artist and the object. Credibility is strained through the method of deformation and redirection, compelling us to look toward something else entirely.

Material Redirection

While the artist is highly aware of the centrality of sight in one's "making it" in art history, he or she has little to no use for the kinds of weighted associations a given artwork has to maintain in order to gain entry into disciplinary textbooks. Hammons cares little for questions of aura, originality, singularity, or even sustained market value driving his practice. Elena Filipovic has brilliantly accounted for this in her 2017 study of Hammons's *Bliz-aard Ball Sale*, noting how "Hammons has regularly changed (sometimes several times) the composition, presentation, and constituent elements and title of any number of his pieces once they left his studio thus rejecting the fixity, stability, and finality of the conventional work of art, not to mention entirely challenging its role as a product to be easily consumed."[13] Filipovic goes on to share how when asked by collectors to repair an element of a work that has broken, "Hammons has been known to further break or simply dispose of the original artwork, replacing it with a new version, so little is he preoccupied with the aura of originality and the value accrued by a piece in the process of its becoming 'historical.'"[14] The artist even stopped making his famous body prints in part because they were doing so well in both exhibition and financial circuits.[15] These detailed insights into Hammons's recurrent devaluation of the material and capital value imbued in the singular art object is also a recurrent apathy toward a general condition of art history. What might be seen as temperamental or impulsive acts are instead depicted as embodiments of refusal and ways the artist implements an emphasis on the processual qualities of his work. History, in these acts, is not evidenced by fixity but rather by the present-tense relevance of the work, deconstruction and reconstruction, and the multiplicity inherent in a given work's potential.

This activation of the present is seemingly incompatible with or at least in direct contradiction to Hammons's simultaneous deployment of aesthetic strategies to be considered within or intervene upon art history and its market imperative. Pushing against a notion of conceptualism grounded mostly in the discursive apparatus, Hammons's impact on this artistic approach lies in large part in the way he sees and composes material. Reflecting on his first meeting with Hammons, poet Ben Okri notes that "to walk with David is a lesson in seeing, and not just ordinary seeing. He's a supernatural noticer. He'd draw my attention to people working and the materials they used, and to trash and discarded things, and the relationships between them. You realize how little you see."[16] This attention to materials and their uses allows Hammons to shift away from a question of the originality of a given mark or composition and instead opens up a means of material citation and construction. Objects are given license to use their weight—historical and material—in order to redetermine their conceptual associations.

Take, for example, Hammons's large crate works, in which paintings peak out of their ruptured wooden shipping crates. When viewers look at these paintings, they are met with gestural brush marks in hues that span purples, blues, blacks, and whites. One is left to wonder about the nature of these works: Are they some of the wondrous Ed Clark paintings owned by Hammons?[17] Are they Hammons's early or recent experiments in abstraction? Is there even a painting in there? Can this whole object be called a painting? Here the crate, an object of protection for transport, a crude readymade container for precious commodities, and a ubiquitous and even damageable object itself, takes on an expanded set of associations.

The displayed crate throws into crisis the question of what it means to see art works—what counts, what mediates, what filters, what obscures our experiences of loaded traditional mediums. Even further, we could also ascertain how the crate itself offers a hard sleeve of security, protecting the contents from damage, harm, or panoptic modes of surveillance. The crate makes it hard to see, hard to access, hard to damage the art object and forces the viewer to reflect upon the nature of seeing itself. Could the demand to see in entirety be a form of consumption harmful to the object that is seen? What of the protocols of sight that are aimed toward securing the seer's cultural capital?[18] Could we, instead, see another way?

In many ways the Hammons effect is an activation of a way of seeing as facilitated by the artist himself. Fully motivated by the principles of trust more than even the stability of the eye, Hammons has frequently activated his own line of sight as one that could contain the collective. Perhaps our greatest takeaway from a Hammons work is not to ask "Has anyone seen these?" but instead "How can we see like Hammons?"

Notes

1. Jonathan Griffin, "Is David Hammons Trolling His Gallery?," *Frieze*, July 12, 2019, www.frieze.com/article/david-hammons-trolling-his-gallery; Colony Little, "David Hammons Returns to LA with Wicked Tricks and Subtle Jabs," *Hyperallergic*, July 29, 2019, hyperallergic.com/511276/david-hammons-hauser-wirth-los-angeles; Catherine Taft, "Catherine Taft on David Hammons," *Artforum International*, September 1, 2019, www.artforum.com/print/reviews/201907/david-hammons-80636; Calvin Tomkins, "David Hammons Follows His Own Rules," *New Yorker*, December 2019, www.newyorker.com/magazine/2019/12/09/david-hammons-follows-his-own-rules; Rachel Wezler, "David Hammons Taunts the Art World in Los Angeles," *Art in America*, August 16, 2019, www.artnews.com/art-in-america/aia-reviews/david-hammons-hauser-wirth-62704; Janelle Zara, "A Few Blocks from Skid Row, David Hammons's New Show at Hauser & Wirth Asks Angelenos to Imagine Themselves as Homeless," *Artnet News*, May 20, 2019, news.artnet.com/exhibitions/david-hammons-in-los-angeles-1551100.

2. As this essay transforms into a long-form project, I plan to spend a considerable amount of time on the relationship between objecthood, subjecthood, and presence in Hammons's work. Key elements of this project will require an attention to the ways that in the stories that surround Hammons's persona are effects of the artist's own prioritization of presentness throughout his practice. This will enable a consideration of Hammons's impact on processes of valuation, canonization, and institutionalization and how these processes are vexed in relation to Black artistic production. Ultimately I hope to demonstrate how Hammons creates avenues for art historical imaginations that prioritize Black radical presence.

3. This project is both indebted to and in conversation with key writings on and about Hammons, including Huey Copeland, "A Seat at the Table: Notes of an Institutional Creature," *October*, no. 168 (2019): 63–78; Elena Filipovic, *David Hammons: Bliz-aard Ball Sale*

(Cambridge, MA: Afterall Books/MIT Press, 2017); Tom Finkelpearl, "Ideology of Dirt," in *David Hammons: Rousing the Rubble*, edited by Alana Heiss, 61–89 (Cambridge, MA: MIT Press, 1991); Kellie Jones, "Good Mirrors Ain't Cheap," in *David Hammons: Five Decades*, 15–28 (New York: Mnuchin Gallery, 2016); Kellie Jones, "In the Thick of It: David Hammons and Hair Culture in the 1970s," *Third Text* 12, no. 44 (1998): 17–24; Kellie Jones, "Interview with David Hammons, *REALLIFE Magazine* (1986); Abbe Schriber, "'Those Who Know Don't Tell': David Hammons, c. 1981," *Women & Performance* 29, no. 1 (2019): 41–61; Robert Farris Thompson, "David Hammons: 'Knowing Their Past,'" in *An Aesthetic of Cool: Afro-Atlantic Art and Music*, 92–105 (New York: Periscope, 2011); Tobias Wofford, "Can You Dig It? Signifying Race in David Hammons's 'Spade' Series," in *L.A. Object & David Hammons Body Prints*, edited by Connie Rogers Tilton and Lindsay Charlwood, 86–135 (New York: Tilton Gallery, 2011).

4. While too much to go into in this essay, the normative racial protocols I refer to include a circumscription of whiteness as the default racial category of the presumed universal subject of contemporary art. This subjectivity is reinforced in terms of market-based, institutional, and even formal traits of valued works. It is not enough to say this as a totalizing fact, and there are of course moments of interruption in this default prioritization of whiteness. Much has been written about the whiteness of the contemporary art world. Select texts have been influential in my analysis: Berger, *White*; D'Souza, *Whitewalling*; Fernandez-Sacco, "Check Your Baggage"; Nochlin, *Women Artists*; Pinder, *Race-ing Art History*.

5. Tomkins, "David Hammons."

6. Tomkins, "David Hammons."

7. Copeland, "Seat at the Table"; Mark Godfrey, *David Hammons: Give Me a Moment*, Athens: George Economou Collection, 2016; Filiopovic, *David Hammons*; Finkelpearl, "Ideology of Dirt"; Jones, "In the Thick of It"; Jones, "Interview with David Hammons"; Schriber, "'Those Who Know Don't Tell'"; Thompson, "David Hammons"; Wofford, "Can You Dig It?"

8. The Blackness of Hammons's conceptualism is a topic that will be explored with further consideration and detail in the book-length project.

9. Tomkins, "David Hammons."

10. I'm grateful to my peer reviewer for the insightful connection to Hammons's use of language as material. Scholarship on Hammons has attended to the artist's punning and wordplay as a deployment of his status as art-world trickster. Dawoud Bey, "In the Spirit of *Minkisi*: The Art of David Hammons," *Third Text: Third World Perspectives on Contemporary Art and Culture* 8, no. 27 (1994): 45–54.

11. Houston Baker, *Modernism and the Harlem Renaissance*, Chicago: University of Chicago Press, 1987.

12. Greg Tate, "Introduction: Nigs R Us, or How Blackfolk Became Fetish Objects," in *Everything but the Burden: What White People Are Taking from Black Culture*, edited by Greg Tate, 1–14 (New York: Harlem Moon, 2003).

13. Filopovic, *David Hammons*, 94.

14. Filopovic, *David Hammons*, 94.

15. Filopovic, *David Hammons*, 43.

16. Quoted in Tomkins, "David Hammons."

17. Brian Boucher, "David Hammons Curates Edward Clark," *Art in America*, January 28, 2014, www.artnews.com/art-in-america/features/david-hammons-curates-edward-clark-59674/.

18. I by no means want to reinforce the very mythological and celebrity status of Hammons that the project aims to deconstruct. I specifically speak here of capital as a way to point to Hammons's place in the art world. As he is an artist who has accrued financial and cultural capital, his deformation of and maneuvers within the art world can be seen by some as acts that can only be done because of his prominence among a particular art world elite. This is, of course, true, and part of the Hammons effect includes maintaining a critical position toward the artist.

In Conversation

Linda Goode Bryant and Senga Nengudi

LINDA GOODE BRYANT: Where do we start? Do you want to start at the beginning?

SENGA NENGUDI: Well, I know the story well, but maybe we should start at the beginning—beginning when you met David, and you became aware of his body prints. Was he doing body prints before you met?

LGB: Yes, I met his body prints before I met him. And that happened at Spelman College in Atlanta. I was an art major with a focus on painting, and there was a professor—Barry Gaither, who eventually went to Boston, but was down at Spelman for a year or two—who taught a class on African American art. It was the first history class that I recall focusing on African American artists. Many of the older artists I already knew because my work-study project was cataloging works in what is now the Clark Atlanta University collection. Much of that collection came out of the Atlanta University Annual competition for African American artists [1942–1970]. When I was there, the works had not yet been cataloged so I made a proposal to do it and they said OK. So I knew all those folks. I knew their work, I saw it and touched it. I was very much into Jacob Lawrence. But I didn't have awareness of more contemporary artists. In that class, Barry showed slides of David's work, and when I saw his body prints, I was bowled over.

SN: What year was this?

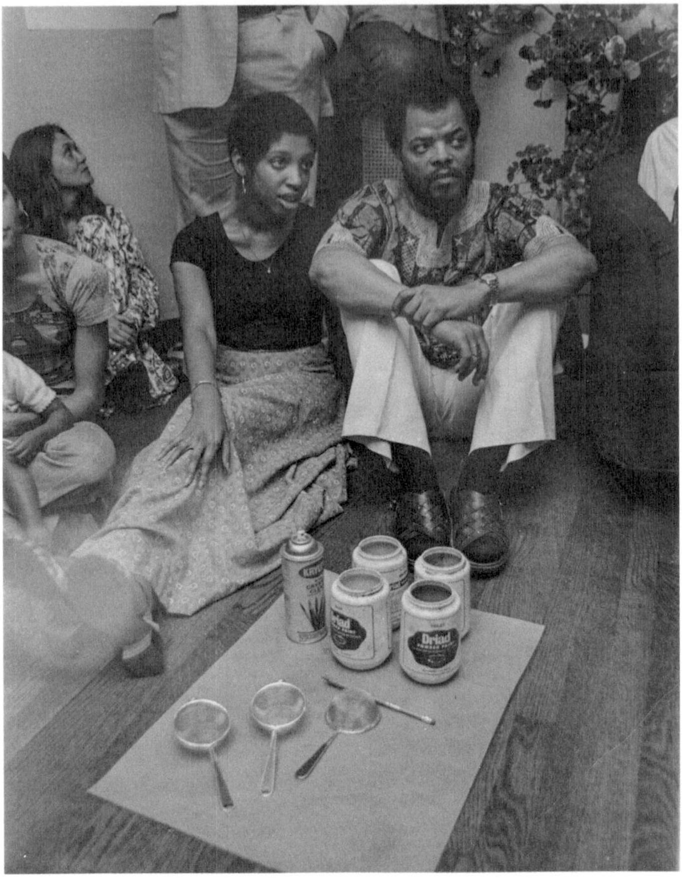

Seated man and woman at a body print-in held in conjunction with David Hammons's exhibition *Greasy Bags and Barbeque Bones*, Philip Yenawine's house, 1975. Photograph by Jeff Morgan.

LGB: Sometime between '68 and '69. I was a sophomore or junior. The body prints were something to me. I tried to track down what I could about how he made them, but that was during the period when David wasn't telling people how he made them. As an artist, I thought there was something really special there.

SN: Had you always been interested in art?

LGB: Yes, I was five or six when I told my parents I wanted to go to art school. I don't know where they found the money, but they managed to send me to a Saturday class at what was then called the Columbus Gallery of Fine Art, but later became the Columbus Museum of Art. Every Sunday we ate dinner with our whole extended family and friends of the family at my maternal grandmother's house. We called her Big Mom. The house was the size of a shoebox so we were eating all over—the tables were extended, card tables put out. I remember at one Sunday dinner when I was twelve a family friend asked what I wanted to do when I grew up, and I said, "I want to be Picasso's first Black mistress." They asked, "Why is that?" And I said, "Because that's the only way the world will look at my artwork." I was pretty conscious about the world I lived in, and thought, "This is how I'm going to make it happen." Even at that age, I was completely captivated by Picasso's work.

SN: My first situation was also with Picasso. It wasn't the mistress thing so much—although that could have been a fantasy at some point—but I was so excited about the fact that he was constantly changing his style. He never rested on one style and was constantly exploring. And I went through a blue period too. In high school, I made a lot of blue paintings in that style. The important thing to me is that he didn't dwell or spend his entire career doing one style. He was ever growing.

LGB: He was also obsessive about his work, and I connected to that obsessiveness. I have a bit of that. It was inspiring to know that someone could be that focused, dedicated, committed, and obsessive, as part of his creative genius.

SN: I related that a bit to David as well. As I began to know him further down the line, obviously.

LGB: David's work stayed with me after I graduated, and I always hoped that I'd meet him so I could ask him how he made the body prints. There was an organization back in the day called the National Conference of Artists, and ultimately we met through that in 1974, but it took two years. The conference happened annually, typically during spring break on a Black college campus because many of the artists at that time were professors at Black universities. I was at Spelman during the time when Nikki Giovanni and Ida Lewis were there. I somehow connected with them, so when Ida went to New York to start *Encore* magazine she told me that when I came to New York, I should get in touch with her if I wanted to write. I knew that the artist Elizabeth Catlett was going to be at the NCA that year, which was at Howard University in Washington DC. I loved Catlett's work so I pitched a story idea to Ida and she said sure.

When I was interviewing Elizabeth Catlett—who was just wonderful—Connie Harold, an artist I knew from New York, came bursting into the room and said, "Linda! I'm sorry, but Linda, David Hammons is here. Come!" Everybody in New York that I hung out with—and I hung out with artists—everybody knew I had this thing about David Hammons body prints. I said to Connie, "I'm doing this interview." But she kept rattling on about all these California artists that were there—Betye Saar, and I think Alonzo [Davis] and Dale [Brockman Davis].[1] Elizabeth Catlett was wonderful and insisted that I go and that we would continue our conversation later. I was so silly, saying, "There's no way I can meet him now. What would I say?" It was such a little girl thing. Catlett looked at me and shook her head. Connie left and I continued my interview. Later, Connie told me they were going to come to New York following the conference and there was going to be a party that I should attend. But I didn't. The following year the NCA conference was held in Chicago. I know Alonzo was there again because they had the watermelon pins that people bought at the DC conference and other items from Brockman Gallery. They were selling them at a table in the conference center lobby. We finally met there. I was in the lobby talking with folks when Helen Ramsaran, a New York–based sculptor who is also from Columbus, rushed over to me and, though she's quite petite, pushed and pulled me over to the table. The next thing I knew I was standing in front of him and I said, "Mr. Hammons, are you telling people how to make your body prints? Will you tell me how you make your body prints?" And he said, "Yeah. No big deal." He told me how he did it and I thanked him. At some point he looked up and said, "You got another question?" And that's how I started talking with David.

How about you? How did you meet him?

SN: I met him through my cousin Eileen Abdulrashid who came from Chicago—that's where I was born—and stayed with my mother for a little bit when she first moved to LA. My mother was always the connecting link. Eileen was an artist, and I loved her work. She was a sculptor and a painter, and much more gregarious than myself—I'm the wallflower. She would always say, "Come on. Let's go to this party. Let's go to this situation." Often it was a kind of artist party. David was usually there, and Dan Concholar, LaMonte Westmoreland, and probably Alonzo [Davis]. There was a whole group of Black artists that lived in Altadena. David would always show up in a snazzy car, usually very special classic cars. And he was always dapper. He had the most interesting clothes, as did Dan—that's why we called him Dapper Dan. This was long before the other person who is now in the limelight, the designer Dapper Dan on 125th Street. We all hung out together, and even at that point, David had a reputation for being all that. I saw his body prints at Brockman Gallery, which was owned by Alonzo Davis and Dale Davis. Actually I went to Dorsey High School with them. I knew Alonzo but Dale was much younger than we were. And Bob Kardashian was our class president. He was a very nice guy, and I think . . . Well, I'm not going there!

LGB: Did you and Alonzo know each other because you were both artists and in an art class together? Did you have art classes?

SN: Oh yes, I lived in the art room. There wasn't a particular relationship with Alonzo, but I know that after I graduated, Dale had the same art teacher that I had. She was a lovely person. Later he came back and became the art teacher at Dorsey himself.

Me and my friends from art class thought we were bohemians. We would frequent jazz venues like the Lighthouse in Hermosa Beach and places on the Sunset Strip, but because we were too young we couldn't get inside. We would stand outside and listen.

LGB: Were you also interested in dance at that time? Did one hit you before the other?

SN: I took dance classes—ballet and that kind of stuff at the recreation centers, but art class was mostly in elementary school. I was always taken with it.

LGB: When did you know that was what you wanted to do?

SN: It almost wasn't a decision. It was a triangle. I wanted to teach, I wanted to dance, I wanted to do art. In elementary school, I was such a freak for the art supply closet. Oftentimes I would be the supply closet monitor, and I would get a genuine charge and a thrill when I went in there and saw all the different colors, the crayons, the notebooks, the pencils, the brushes. I'd get my little freak on just looking at these wonderful things, and seeing how they were lined up compositionally.

Eventually I was an art major and a dance minor because I felt that I didn't have "the dancer's body" nor a ponytail, and at that point the idea of a dancer was really limited. I felt as though I could do art forever because dance is about the body and that limits you. It's always been back and forth, back and forth. I was really happy with the onset of Happenings and things like that where I could incorporate everything about myself in my work.

LGB: What type of work were you making when you first started out, beyond high school, let's say?

SN: In college I was experimenting with sculpture, stone, and fabric, and printmaking. I didn't see myself as focused on something in particular. I was simply taking it in, developing skills. In '68, just before I moved to New York, which was in '71, I started making forms, and stuffing them with cotton or whatever. I was always into stuffing things. But when I started to do the water sculptures, I decided to use this plastic and then put water in it. I put water in because of this whole interest in the essential and the body. With the water in the plastic forms, just touching it was, to my mind, very essential. It also created a lot of its own energy in the plastic. If you touch it, then it responds to you.

LGB: *R.S.V.P.*[2]

SN: Yes. I was doing that before I moved to New York, and probably when I first met David in the late '60s because that's when Eileen came to LA. We did a show together—myself, Eileen, and my partner at the time, Roger Summers, in a really interesting space. John Manno was one of my teachers at Cal State LA. He was a true New Yorker and he brought a concept that was absolutely new to us in LA, which was to go to one of the worst neighborhoods, down on Main Street, and get a studio for a very reasonable price. He created it as a studio and a gallery space, and that's where I had my first exhibit of my water sculptures. I don't know if David came or not. Then I moved to New York, and I lived in Spanish Harlem, and that conference called . . . ?

LGB: . . . NCA. National Conference of Artists. It was the Black artist organization.

SN: Eileen called and said she was going to be in town for the NCA and needed a place to stay. I agreed right away but I had no idea she was going to bring the band, so to speak. They all came in—Dan Concholar, David, Eileen, and another woman artist that was a close friend of David's. And then Betye Saar. Betye was there for one night and the next morning she said, "This is too bohemian for me." There were no extra beds and everybody was camped out all over the place on the floor. It was great fun. Everyone did little drawings while they were there. Our real friendship began then, when David stayed with me in New York. When I returned to LA to live, I think he felt as though he should return the favor, and he was very open to me using his studio when I needed it. He was trying to decide whether he wanted to live in LA or New York, and he would go back and forth, back and forth. It took him forever to make that decision, and when he was out of town, I was able to use his space.

LGB: Is that when you were first up close to the body prints? What work was there at that time?

SN: Yes, it was. I feel as though I recall David doing a whole session of celebrities, printing their bodies and I thought it was a fundraiser for JAM [Just Above Midtown], but I know you said we didn't meet then. I recall that the show—or the event—happened at his studio on Slauson. I was the assistant, and I had to grease the bodies.

LGB: Right. So this is how I remember it: One of the questions I asked David that first day we met was about when he was going to come to New York so that we could see the body prints up close and personal. I had only seen them in books. Samella Lewis and Ruth Waddy wrote several books focused on African American artists and I think I saw them there.[3] But

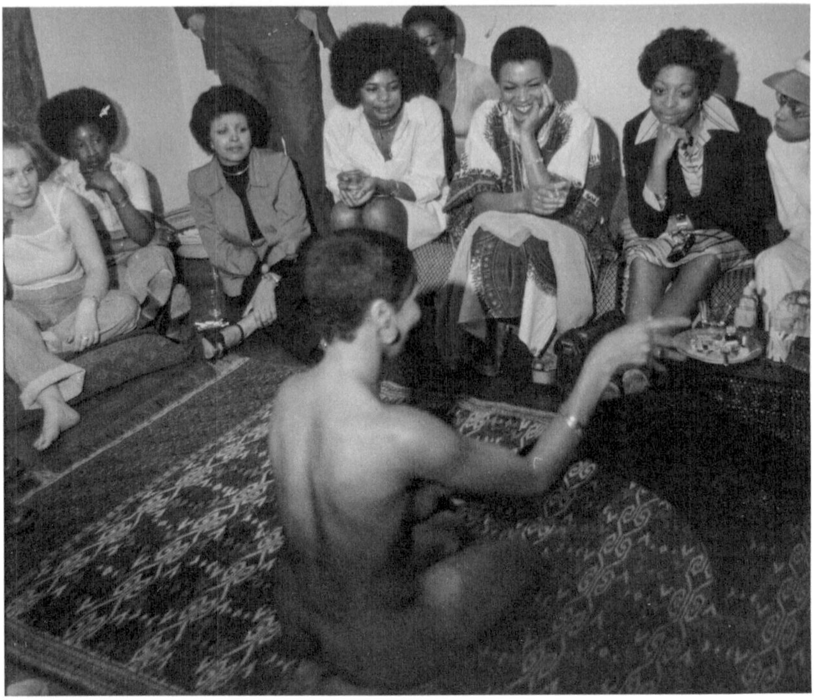

Seated woman pointing at women at a body print-in held in conjunction with David Hammons's exhibition *Greasy Bags and Barbeque Bones*, Philip Yenawine's house, 1975. Photograph by Jeff Morgan.

David's response was, "I don't show in white galleries." I said, "I guess I'm going to have to start a gallery." Prior to that I was working at The Studio Museum as the Director of Education, and I also oversaw the artist residency program. Artists were always hanging out at the museum—visiting artists who were in that program and who were older than I was. They would always talk about how, "They won't let us, they won't let us . . ." I reached a point of frustration with that conversation and said, "Fuck them. We'll do it ourselves." And these older artists were going, "Oh, you're so naïve. We don't have any money. Blah, blah, blah." All the things that make sense, but that's just not me.

SN: Thank goodness that's the case.

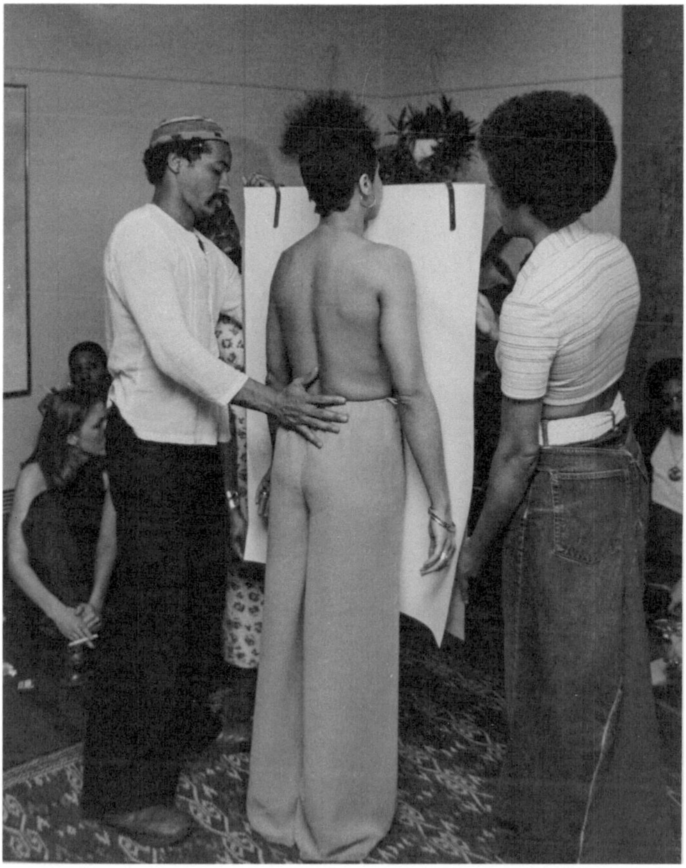

Standing woman pressing herself against paper at a body print-in held in conjunction with David Hammons's exhibition *Greasy Bags and Barbeque Bones*, Philip Yenawine's house, 1975. Photograph by Jeff Morgan.

LGB: When David said that, it sealed the deal. I came back to New York to start the gallery and everybody said, "You're crazy, and you can't do it." Now we're going to jump forward: I opened JAM in November of '74, and I came to LA in the summer of '75 because I was trying to raise money to keep the gallery open. We did a body print evening in New York City that made *Jet* magazine because Charlie Mingus came, along with some other celebrities. I helped that night with rubbing down. The thing that was really wild was that my son was five years old at the time, and his preschool teacher, Suzette Wright, and I had become friends. When I said, "I've got to find somebody who's willing to get naked for the body printing," Suzette said, "I'll do it. Why not?" Suzette is wonderfully insane.

SN: Oh my god.

LGB: Here we are, in this snazzy penthouse off Central Park that belonged to Phil Yenawine, who I knew because I had been a fellow and an intern at the Metropolitan Museum when he was head of the education department. He and his wife also took care of all the food and the alcohol as I recall. Lots of people came and I had to oil down Suzette. And Kenneth, my son, was like, "Oh my. What's happening here?"

SN: Oh my god!

LGB: Oh my! Then we did a second event in LA. Celebrities were invited, and the actress Denise Nichols was one of the celebrities that got printed. But we did do a press conference at David's studio, and there was a female there, but I think David would have introduced me to you unless he was too consumed by doing the body print . . .

SN: As you're speaking, I remember that it was a press conference and I bet that was me. I oiled Denise Nichols. I think she was married to Bill Withers.

LGB: I can't believe it! We didn't get introduced. That was so wild because David's daughter Carmen was there; she was just a little girl.

SN: I think some of the sweetest moments with the body print situation was when he did it with Carmen. He did little projects with the kids.

I might say that David has always had the knack of drawing celebrities. He's always had that knack because everybody can sense his genius, and they see it. They don't even have to sense it. His energy is so attracting that he's always had that celebrity vibe.

And so yes, I was there and I did Denise. I said, "Hey, wait a minute. I have to do a girl? I have to grease down a lady?" I thought I was going to grease down muscular men.

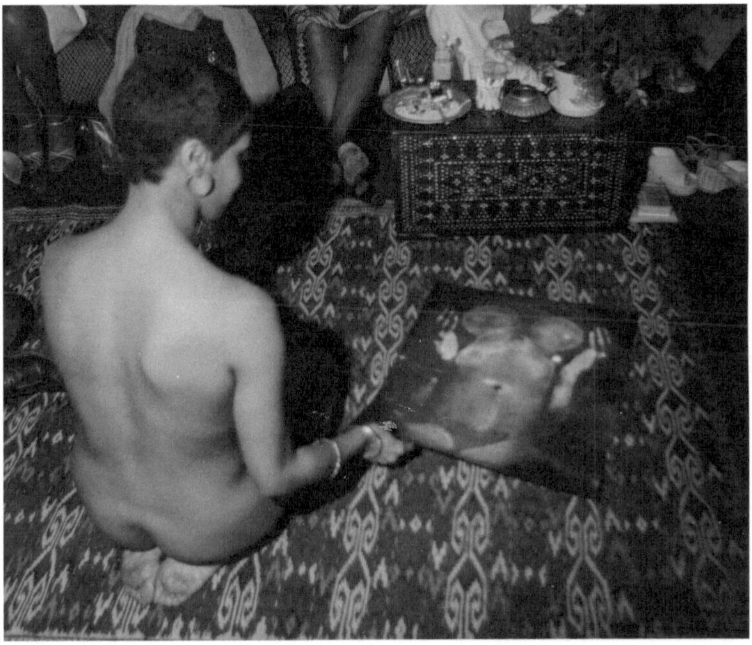

Kneeling woman looking at a painting at a body print-in held in conjunction with David Hammons's exhibition *Greasy Bags and Barbeque Bones*, Philip Yenawine's house, 1975. Photograph by Jeff Morgan.

LINDA: I didn't stay in LA at that time but later I was there for about six weeks, maybe more. I declared freedom as a single mom. I was living in New York with my brother Paul, his friend Ikey, and my two children in a living room, a bedroom, and one bathroom, and I said, "I'm getting out of here."

I took the kids, packed them up, and dropped them at my ex's. He opened the door and I said, "Meet your children." I went home to get my bag and said to my brother, who is six years younger than me, "I'm going to LA. MoMA is hiring guards. You have an interview for a job on Monday morning. Make sure you get it." He did. And I left. I was out there for a while, staying at the studio on West Slauson—a huge Fred Astaire dance studio.

SN: I don't know if it was Fred Astaire, but it was used during the war. You know how they had those 1940 movies where they have a dance hall that everybody would go to? It was more like that. I think its history could have been that it was a dance hall during wartime.

LGB: There were a lot of rooms. I remember that. And I would read a book or two or three. It was the first time I ever had time by myself. David was there when he was making his work. And it was like theater—the way he'd look at the empty page and decide how he was going to lay what part where, and then how that emerged when he sifted the powder on top of it and it became visual. There was something theatrical about it. There was something magical, which theater can be. As you know, dance movement can also be magical. That was another phase of my relationship to the body prints.

SN: Recently I have been hearing a phrase—usually related to fashion—that I've really picked up on. It's, "And then you create the reveal." What you're talking about is once the powder goes on, there's the reveal.

LINDA: Yes! I think it was in those weeks that I was there that David and I fought. David and I have notoriously fought from the beginning. We're Cancer Leos. I'm not an astrology buff, but maybe that's it. We can be oil and water, and at the same time be so in unison and so deep. David has a way of wanting to shut it down, and I felt like he was not listening to my point. Somehow or another, I connected with Dan Concholar and went and stayed with him for a few days. Dan was an angel.

SN: So cool. You could not ruffle his feathers for anything. He was always so chill and so loving.

LGB: I had not seen David create before, and being in the studio, I connected to the thought and deliberation that he goes through when he has a vision in his head. There is so much mental work that goes into what David does to the point that I'm sure it must be painful. You get to the place where you're trying to noodle something out and you're going, "Where is it?" Gosh, you feel like you can almost touch it, but you can't. You're trying to make sense of it, and you have to because you have to make it.

There is a lot of agony in that process, and observing him certainly provided an example for understanding that it is just the process, and you'll survive it even though you feel like you can't push beyond. He doesn't seem to experience angst over it because he's not expressive in that way. But at the same time, he is so deep in it—in his thought.

I have a high regard for people who go to that place as part of the process of moving a vision to something tangible that can be seen, experienced, and shared with others, because it's agonizing. We all do it in our own way.

SN: It's like climbing a mountain. You always have the risk of falling off and dying. But there's a drive that keeps you going. And you have to do it. And it's so exciting. It's such a charge. In this case, you could say the falling would be maybe a failure. But you still have to do it. You still have to take the risk. And there's no way I can explain it except to say that I know his body posture. I know what it looks like when there's an idea brewing in him, and it's undeniable. It's very distinct when you see it. You feel that something is happening.

LGB: The other thing that fascinates me is that he is *always* making things. It can be anything. I'm looking at things on his desk, and all of a sudden he'll wonder, "How can I deal with this?" And it's quiet. He's not saying anything out loud. He's with people, but he is in this as well.

SN: If he could not do art each day, he would die.

LGB: I think so too. Even if that art is silent. Like I said, that process where he's trying to distill down, "What is this idea? What is this vision?" He can be very quiet in his body. He's not verbalizing. He's very quiet, but he is constantly working.

SN: And he sees it in everything. He sees whatever concept he's dealing with. It could be a spider web or a line of crackers with a little toy fighter. You know that piece. But anyway, he takes something as simple as crackers, and then all of a sudden it has this social, political meaning.

LGB: Yes. I'm so glad you said that. There was a bodega down in SoHo where water was running out of a hole in a trash can and making an indentation in the sidewalk. He would examine and explore it. Everything he saw became part of his library, his archive, his tools, his supplies.

As I have experienced David's work, the body prints really were the last work he did that required materials he purchased from art supply stores. Quite frankly, he was like, "I'm not making those anymore." His whole thing was, "I should not have to *buy* to *make*." He was doing the shovels, the spades, when I was out there, along with body prints. That was when he was shifting from the body prints to the spades. His first show at JAM was hair, and wire, barbecue bones, and brown paper bags. When I opened JAM, that was at a time when the debate among Black artists about who is a Black artist, and what defines you in terms of being a Black artist, was still raging.

You had those folks who worked figuratively, and those who were increasingly working more abstractly—that was a huge debate. Everybody was going crazy. You're not a Black artist if you're not doing red, green, and black flags and mothers nursing. And that translated to, you're not a Black artist if you're doing European art, which is abstract. The body prints somehow bridged that. The body prints were figurative, and at the same time abstract and conceptual in many ways. But in New York, those debates were constant as artists came through JAM, which was an artist's place, but also, Black folks from all walks of life would come to see what was at JAM.

SN: You were on front line with that one.

LGB: I was totally in the front line, and the objection by Black artists in New York City, whether they were working figuratively or in an abstract continuum, was, "You cannot show LA artists. This is our real estate." Those two camps were fighting too. And when I first opened up, I showed both camps. I showed artists that were working figuratively, and I showed artists that weren't. I stood my ground and said, "No one can tell me who I'm going to show. I'm going to show LA artists because I think they're doing experimental shit, and y'all ain't doing it here." I wanted to do that. I wanted to bring that energy to New York.

SN: Incredibly brave.

LGB: It was unbelievable. People were really not happy with me. But like I said, I think the body prints, once they were here and in the gallery—

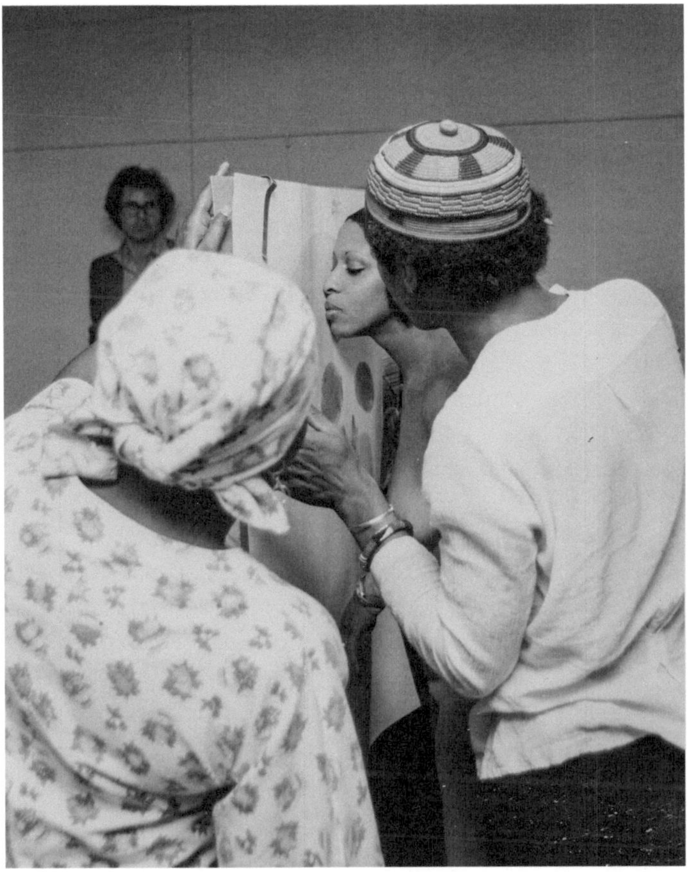

Standing woman pressing her face against paper at a body print-in held in conjunction with David Hammons's exhibition *Greasy Bags and Barbeque Bones*, Philip Yenawine's house, 1975. Photograph by Jeff Morgan.

though I never did a body print show because David said, "I ain't doing that anymore. I'm doing this."

SN: Wow. And so he allowed you to have those to sell to sort of support the gallery?

LGB: Yes, we worked together to come up with the body print evening events to raise money for JAM in New York and LA. They were hosted by celebrities in each city and guests came to see him make body prints. They could also have their bodies printed and purchase those prints. Prior to David's initial solo show at JAM, I showed and sold the body prints along with other work that wasn't on exhibit. When his show was scheduled I assumed it would be a body print exhibit and prepared collectors who wanted body prints. When I contacted David to get the title of the show and an image for the invitation, he let me know he wasn't doing body prints anymore.

For a new collector or a seasoned collector who always bought figurative work, the body prints were not a stretch. They were such a tremendous bridge. They had political content, and then at times they weren't political. The body prints were always Black bodies, to my knowledge—that was concrete. The image wasn't conceptual or abstract. The images were Black figures. At the same time, the composition, proportions, and image of the figures were abstract. Lips weren't lips. Eyes weren't eyes. They were abstractions of lips and eyes—marks he made with a bent finger or an object to suggest rather than realistically represent lips and eyes. The body prints were a bridge from figurative to a kind of abstraction that people connected to and didn't associate with or reject as being European.

I think the most significant night was in 1975 when he opened his first solo show at JAM [*Greasy Bags and Barbecue Bones*] with the hair, wire, bags, grease, and barbecue bones, and everybody came—artists from Camille Billops and Vivian Browne to Joe Overstreet. Steve Cannon and that whole crowd.[4] It was a large swath and everybody was angry. David was the first LA artist that showed at JAM.

SN: Oh my goodness.

LGB: Oftentimes the arguments about me showing LA artists descended on David. It might have been okay if I'd done Raymond Saunders, who was already showing with Terry Dintenfass. His work might have been more palatable. David's position was always, "I can't be bothered with all the stuff you're bothered with like selling," and, "I can only be bothered with making what I want to make. I won't be confined by art supplies." He brought an edge to everything he did. So everybody wanted to come and see what he was going to do for his JAM show. If I've ever had a regret about technology it is that we didn't have video at that time at JAM.

SN: You weren't able to photograph or film it?

LGB: Yeah. It should have been filmed. People were angry. Furious. And that night, they all got into it. Everybody was talking. It was crowded; you couldn't get in or out of the door. At some point I tapped a wine bottle with a knife and I turned off the music. I said, "Instead of everybody talking at once, why don't we talk with each other in our little corners?"

David's charm is manifested in different ways, but what's consistent is his way of observing, listening and taking in everything that's going on around him. In those moments he doesn't speak. So he didn't speak. A couple of times male artists in the room got very aggressive with him: "Say something. Say something, motherfucker." It got so heated. I was nervous. There was an exchange between Janet Henry, and Joe Overstreet. I thought Joe was going to let loose on Janet, and I wondered how I would throw myself between them. Still, David would not speak. In that way, he diffused the anger. It took a while, but he diffused it by not talking. People had to talk it out for themselves. For David, the work speaks for itself.

SN: The thing about David is—and I've seen him in all settings—that he can charm an alcoholic that's been sitting on the same corner for three weeks, and he has equal charm with the head of a corporation. There is no difference to him. It's a kind of kindness. I've seen him with all sorts of people, and they all gravitate to him and feel comfortable with him.

LGB: One of the arguments people were making was, "How can you call this art? These are dirty brown paper bags." Everybody was already angry because he was from LA, and also because of whatever extra energy David just causes people to have. But then all of a sudden other people in the room were wondering, "Well why do we have to buy art supplies to make things? What are you trying to say? Are you saying it's not art because it's a brown paper bag instead of a white piece of paper from Pearl Paint? What's your point?"

He became this catalyst—or that show became a catalyst for people questioning and then resolving that it was okay to make work with whatever you need and want to make work with. That was the last time I heard any debates about abstract versus figurative and using any material you want to use.

SN: It was an exciting time to have this exchange of ideas.

LGB: Let me ask you, when did you and David discover you both had a fascination with Japan and Japanese culture?

SN: That's a really good question. I would tell David about my adventures in Japan, and somehow it just clicked and he fell in love with it as much as I did.[5] I would tell him about my adventures, and my feelings about Japanese culture. I shared artwork with him, classical as well as conceptual stuff.

LGB: What was it about the culture that drew you to Japan?

SN: It started with a book of the contemporary art of Japan. The beginning of the book was just warmed over New York kind of painting, but in the back was the Gutai group, and I was instantly taken with them. I was validated by the way they did stuff. That was my driving force, though I never met any of them while I was in Japan.

And David, he has such grace with what he does. He has such a special touch. So there's always a cultural aspect of it, and humor. There are a lot of layers to what he does, and you have to kind of search for it and be a part of it when you're looking at the work. You have to be actively involved. He has that kind of grace, and it's usually relatively simple. It's not weighed down. There is also that aspect of Japanese culture. I hate to use the word simple because it usually means simple-minded, but there is a simplicity, grace, and elegance in the Japanese culture.

LGB: We meet people who are very covered and cloaked, and then you've got people who are confident in their essence, and you're drawn to that. I can't imagine anyone not being drawn to or hypnotized by the essence of something.

It's the same with David's work. His gallery, his museum was the streets of Harlem. The wine bottles, the basketball hoop, everyday life in the world itself was where the work existed, and that drew people. It wasn't self-conscious work. It was essence. But it forced you to go to it, and to explore it, and not need anybody to mediate or shape your relationship with it.

Your relationship with his work was dependent on what you brought to it, and what it said to you. That conversation was very personal and intimate.

SN: I'm thinking of two body prints of his. One is the man who is wrapped in the American flag and the other was the admissions door. Those were amazing and they speak to social issues. Even now, the Black Lives Matter movement has taken on his Black flag [*African American Flag*, 1990]. They've taken it on as a symbol, and it is so exciting. He's given so many gifts to us.

LGB: I'm also reminded of David's Jesse Jackson piece—*How Ya Like Me Now?*[6]

SN: I loved that.

LGB: In terms of the initial response to it, I love it too. It's an amazing piece, and it was amazing when everybody was raising hell and trying to tear it down. He was like, "Motherfuckers, just hold up a second. Look at what that is. Use your eyes, take it in, think about it."

SN: But then what happened? He took the sledgehammer that they had used for a destructive act, and put it into the concept of the piece. Genuinely genius.

LGB: How egoless that was in terms of the primacy of the work! It wasn't about his ego in that moment. This is the reaction; it should be in the work. It wasn't, "I don't believe they didn't understand it," which is my line.

SN: A lot of it has to do with David telling you to think. Just simply think. See what's around you, and understand how it can be transformed into something so much higher than what you're seeing. It's the crackers again. You never can look at a stack of Saltine crackers again without thinking about that piece. Think not only about what I'm saying here, but about what I'm using, and what you too can use.

LGB: His resourcefulness is the best. Can I add another word to your "think"—which is "feel"? A lot of his work makes me emotional, hits me emotionally, and that runs the gamut of what I've known him to make from body prints to the paintings.

SN: I think my adjective would be "graceful." I'm constantly taken by how gracefully he does things. They are exquisite, like a violin concerto. Graceful and elegant. Elegant. That's what I would say.

LGB: You know what's wonderful about life? When we're fortunate enough to wake up the next day, wake up into tomorrow, and it's another day to learn and discover. I've discovered a lot about us in this conversation.

SN: Yes. Me too. Me too.

LGB: I didn't expect that, so thank you.

SN: Thank you. It was so much more fun doing it together.

Notes

1. The artists and brothers Alonzo Davis and Dale Brockman Davis founded Brockman Gallery—one of the first major galleries run for and by Black artists—in 1967 in Los Angeles's Leimert Park neighborhood. Brockman showed the work of artists such as Dan Concholar, Maren Hassinger, Ulysses Jenkins, Senga Nengudi, John Outterbridge, and Noah Purifoy. David Hammons had his first solo exhibition there in 1971.

2. *R.S.V.P.* is a series of sculptural installation works by Nengudi that was first shown in the artist's solo exhibition at Bryant's gallery Just Above Midtown (JAM) in 1977. The works, which consist of pantyhose that are knotted, stretched, filled with sand, and tacked to the wall in various formations, initially grew out of Nengudi's reflections upon the changes her body underwent during her first pregnancy. Nengudi also stages movement-based performances in which she and others directly interact with and, as the title suggests, "respond to" the installations.

3. The artist, author, educator, and art historian Samella S. Lewis (b. 1924) was the first African American woman to receive a doctorate in art history. Together with the artist and activist Ruth G. Waddy (1909–2003), Lewis authored the publication *Black Artists on Art*, Vols. I and II (Los Angeles: Contemporary Crafts Publishers, 1969 and 1971), which features David Hammons and images of his body prints.

4. Poet, playwright, and novelist Steve Cannon (1935–2019) was the founder of *A Gathering of the Tribes*, a literary magazine and gallery, performance space, and salon that he ran from his home in New York City's East Village. Cannon met Hammons on a park bench in the late 1970s and the two became close friends and collaborators.

5. In 1966, Nengudi traveled to Japan to attend a year-long postgraduate program at Waseda University in Tokyo.

6. Hammons's 1988 work *How Ya Like Me Now?*—which takes its title from the song by Kool Mo Dee—was commissioned by the Washington Project for the Arts for the 1989 exhibition *The Blues Esthetic: Black Culture and Modernism*, organized by Rick Powell. The large-scale painting portrays the African American civil rights leader and two-time presidential candidate (1984 and 1988) Reverend Jesse Jackson with pale skin, blonde hair, and blue eyes. During its installation on 7th Street facing the National Portrait Gallery in Washington, DC, the work was attacked by several young Black men who used sledgehammers to knock it down. Hammons subsequently repaired and installed the work inside the WPA gallery with a row of sledgehammers placed between the painting and the viewer.

Index of Names

Publisher contact:
The MIT Press
Massachusetts Institute of Technology
77 Massachusetts Avenue, Cambridge, MA 02139
mitpress.mit.edu

EU Authorised Representative:
Easy Access System Europe, Mustamäe tee 50,
10621 Tallinn, Estonia
gpsr.requests@easproject.com

Printed by Integrated Books International,
United States of America